PENGUIN BOOKS

THE DEAD ROAM THE EARTH

Shortly after his parents died, Alasdair Wickham went to live in his grandparents' house, which was haunted. He has taken the supernatural for granted ever since and has been researching the field for the last thirty-five years. The author of several novels, he lives in the United Kingdom.

The Dead Roam the Earth

True Stories of the Paranormal from Around the World

Alasdair Wickham

PENGUIN BOOKS

PENGUIN BOOKS
Published by the Penguin Group
Penguin Group (USA) Inc., 375 Hudson Street, New York, New York 10014, U.S.A.
Penguin Group (Canada), 90 Eglinton Avenue East, Suite 700, Toronto, Ontario, Canada M4P 2Y3 (a division of Pearson Penguin Canada Inc.)
Penguin Books Ltd, 80 Strand, London WC2R 0RL, England
Penguin Ireland, 25 St Stephen's Green, Dublin 2, Ireland (a division of Penguin Books Ltd)
Penguin Group (Australia), 250 Camberwell Road, Camberwell, Victoria 3124, Australia (a division of Pearson Australia Group Pty Ltd)
Penguin Books India Pvt Ltd, 11 Community Centre, Panchsheel Park, New Delhi – 110 017, India
Penguin Group (NZ), 67 Apollo Drive, Rosedale, Auckland 0632, New Zealand (a division of Pearson New Zealand Ltd)
Penguin Books (South Africa) (Pty) Ltd, 24 Sturdee Avenue, Rosebank, Johannesburg 2196, South Africa

Penguin Books Ltd, Registered Offices:
80 Strand, London WC2R 0RL, England

First published in Great Britain as *The Black Book of Modern Myths* by Century 2011
Published in Penguin Books 2012

1 3 5 7 9 10 8 6 4 2

Copyright © James Buxton, 2011
All rights reserved

LIBRARY OF CONGRESS CATALOGING IN PUBLICATION DATA
Wickham, Alasdair.
[Black book of modern myths]
The dead roam the earth : true stories of the paranormal from around the world / Alasdair Wickham.
p. cm.
Originally published: The black book of modern myths. Great Britain : Century, 2011.
Includes index.
ISBN 978-0-14-312226-5
1. Supernatural. 2. Parapsychology. 3. Occultism. I. Title.
BF1040.W53 2012
130—dc23 2012020983

Printed in the United States of America

Except in the United States of America, this book is sold subject to the condition that it shall not, by way of trade or otherwise, be lent, resold, hired out, or otherwise circulated without the publisher's prior consent in any form of binding or cover other than that in which it is published and without a similar condition including this condition being imposed on the subsequent purchaser.

The scanning, uploading, and distribution of this book via the Internet or via any other means without the permission of the publisher is illegal and punishable by law. Please purchase only authorized electronic editions and do not participate in or encourage electronic piracy of copyrighted materials. Your support of the author's rights is appreciated.

Contents

The Dead Roam the Earth

INTRODUCTION

If magic is an attempt to influence events through non-physical and nonreligious means, then this is an age of magic. Whenever you hear a contestant on a TV quiz show say they totally believe they are going to win, they are saying that belief will help them achieve their goals. Whenever an athlete or sporting hero touches a talisman before a match, or says that they have 110 per cent faith in their ability, they are saying that a force that has nothing to do with the physical or the intellectual is behind them. Fifty years ago, the gap between desire and achievement would have been bridged by effort. Increasingly today we bridge that gap with belief, and although it is not called magic, in truth it is nothing else.

The Dead Roam the Earth does not set out to investigate whether or not supernatural forces exist. Instead, it looks at how we respond to them in the twentieth and twenty-first centuries. More specifically, it takes advantage of the Internet and shows how a web of discussion is throwing new light on the supernatural as people from all over the world pool experiences and post footage. We can read about incubi from Sumatra and watch exorcisms in Sudan. We can enter chatrooms where some people believe that yoga leads to demonic possession and damnation, while others argue that human/demon relationships are the last great taboo, comparable to the worst forms of racism.

All this shows one thing: there is no contradiction between the modern world and the supernatural world. In Japan, priests routinely exorcise office blocks while besuited office workers watch respectfully, then go back to their computers. Modernity, far from marginalizing supernatural phenomena, is providing increasing numbers of channels for it to move into the natural world – thus film sets become the new haunted abbeys, shopping centres the new haunted inns, digital recorders the new mediums. And the more we know, the more we want to know. In the past, rumours that a house was haunted might put off buyers; today, estate agents use it as a selling point. A hundred years ago, decent folk might have scurried past a haunted graveyard when darkness fell. Today, they wait until midnight then descend by the coachload for guided tours.

This book takes a global view and this too is fascinating. It shows the richness and diversity of the supernatural and how different cultures accommodate it. Take demons. Belief in demons has been growing since the 1970s and with it has come a hardening of attitudes towards them. For some this might seem a no-brainer. Demons are bad and so, by definition, the risk of possession is so great that extremes of exorcism must be tolerated. However, by looking at demons from an international perspective, this book calls attitudes of this sort into question. If fundamentalists saw how possession is treated in other cultures and adapted their practices, lives could be saved. Innocent lives would be saved.

But *The Dead Roam the Earth* is not just a compendium of stories from around the world. It examines how electronic recording equipment has revolutionised spiritual communion as much as human communication, and reveals why films can and do become cursed. It looks at possession, both from the point of view of people trying to expel demons and those trying their hardest to become possessed. It looks at warfare where soldiers, inventors and strategists are always looking for the edge, and – surprise, surprise – finds the devil in the details. It looks at some famous murders, and, for the first time, exposes the supernatural workings behind them. It looks at liminal creatures – owlmen, mothmen, and giant, muscle-bound women of the mountains – and finds out where they come from and what they do. It listens to things going bump in the night in sleepy suburban backwaters – and then chucking the bed across the room.

In short, it explores the richness and diversity of the supernatural ecosystem around the world and looks at the latest attempts of science to measure the power of the supernatural on a global scale.

All of this begs the question: Why do people believe in ghosts? My own experience is typical: an anomalous, intense experience that's impossible to deny and impossible to prove. My parents died when I was a child and my sisters and I went to live in a wing of my grandparents' house – a rambling old rectory in the heart of the Lincolnshire countryside. The wing had been converted for us: prior to that it had been a line of outhouses that ended in a stable and above the stable had been a room where my grandfather's reclusive sister had lived. I never saw my great aunt – she died long before I and my sisters moved to the Old Rectory – but the old stable was turned into the sitting room and the room she had lived in became the wing's main bedroom, where I slept.

It was in the middle of the summer holidays when I was woken up by a sound on the stairs. The wing was full of noises – starlings scratched and scrabbled in the eaves – and I never forgot the night when I was woken up by huge, slow monstrous breathing outside my window. It took all my courage to force myself out of bed and peer through the gap in the curtains – to see a cow in the next door field peacefully chewing the cud.

But this was different. The stairs were squeaking softly, as if someone were walking up them, getting as far as the half landing in the middle where they turned a corner, then turning round and going down before starting the process all over again.

I was terrified. To get out of the house would involve going down the stairs and my grandparents slept in main part of the house, way of out earshot. What was more, the stairs had history. I'd rescued a stray kitten the year before and found it one day, standing at the top of the stairs, ears flattened, hissing – and staring down at the landing. I hadn't sensed anything then and the kitten had run out of the house and never come back.

Creak, creak, pause . . . coming closer. Creak, creak, pause . . . going away. Creak, creak, pause . . . coming closer. What if the thing made its mind up and carried on up the stairs and into my room? Fear became terror and my terror rose and rose. Everything in the room became imbued with horror: the shadows on the wall, the way my clothes lay on a chair, the darkness under the bed, the darkness on the stairs.

I literally thought that I might die of fear so what I did next was not an act of bravery; it was an act of survival. I knew that putting on the lights would not solve the problem; whatever was out there would simply retreat into the outer shadows made even darker by the light. No, to solve this, my instinct told me, to make the fear go away, I had to enter the world of the disturbance itself and meet it on its own terms.

So in the darkness I got up out of bed, left my room, went to the stairs and looked down into the half landing where the darkness seemed to pool. The creaks were at the bottom of the stairs, out of sight round the corner. I heard them pause before beginning their relentless creep upwards towards me and I did the only thing I could think of. I sat down in the darkness and tried to understand it.

There was no blinding flash of realisation; no cold fingers touching my feet; nothing running gibbering away. Except, as I forced myself to relax, to become one with darkness, I seemed to feel it relax around me. The creaking on the stairs paused. Started. Stopped. And I leant my head against the wall and went to sleep. I have never been afraid of the dark since then and if I ever do feel terror creeping after me, I turn and pause and wait for it. Then the change happens and an odd feeling of peace descends that seems to spread from me into the darkness, and from the darkness into me.

Perhaps my approach was cavalier. Perhaps I should have called in a ghostbuster or priests and asked for the house to be purged and blessed, but in all honesty I don't see how it would have achieved anything I did not achieve myself. Moreover I would not have had an experience that was important, enriching and empowering. Like everything in this world and beyond, there are dangers in the supernatural world and explorers should tread carefully. But then there are dangers in *this* world – people are run over by ambulances on their way to save a life; nature lovers die in the wilderness, killed by the very place they love. The supernatural world is no different. Here is a taste of what you can find out there, today.

CHAPTER ONE

THERE'S SOMETHING THERE

Ghosts and Visitations

Metheringham Airfield is a quiet strip of land in rural Lincolnshire. Once the home of the RAF's 106 squadron, it now houses a small museum that opens for a few days a week on certain months in the year. On summer evenings, you're likely to pass by without noticing it. If you're driving on that road in winter, however, you'd better take care, especially if you draw level with the airfield at about 9 p.m. – because that's when motorists are sometimes startled by a young girl who comes running out of the darkness, distraught, her long coat and chestnut hair flapping. She begs for help with her boyfriend, who has crashed his motorbike; sometimes she bangs in desperation at the car windows. But when you get out of the car to investigate, she is no longer there.

Some people have reported the girl as wearing a green coat; others say her coat is brown, with an RAF badge, and that she wears a green scarf. Almost everyone says that, after she vanishes, the air carries a strong scent of lavender. She's thought to be Catherine Bystock, a young woman from Horncastle, who was in the RAF and who died one night in World War II after a crash involving her boyfriend's motorbike. He survived.

What are ghosts? Such phantoms/presences/visitations – whatever you want to call them – are a universal phenomenon. You can track them across continents, cultures and political systems. And for all that they have the expected cultural differences, they are remarkably consistent in the essentials.

They are fragmentary and elusive. They are strongly tied to place, usually haunting a location that was important to them in life. They generally manifest in ways that are perceptible to just one or two senses – the Metheringham Lass can be seen and heard but not touched, for instance; or they might register only as a smell, or a disembodied voice. Often when people feel a ghostly presence, they are registering it with their nerve endings – a ripple of air against their face; the pressure of an unseen hand on the shoulder.

Many feel that the ghosts are trying to communicate with them. They pick up a sense of need, or of being trapped. And indeed lots of ghosts do seem to be caught in a loop, manifesting in the same way over and over again.

It's as if some part of their living selves has become imprinted on the surroundings, endlessly repeating actions that have a significance we can only guess at. Sometimes, the actions are connected to the circumstances of their death, especially if it was sudden or violent. But not always: there are other ghosts at Metheringham, inside the airfield perimeter, and they make themselves felt quite differently.

Danny, whose father worked for the RAF during the Cold War, remembers him coming home in the 1960s with a curious story. In those days the RAF would regularly make secret trial flights from the UK into Soviet airspace, to establish times and fuel requirements for a hypothetical nuclear bombing raid. To conceal the location of the actual UK nuclear airbases, the missions would return to old RAF airfields scattered around the country. One day, Danny's father was sent to Metheringham to be ground crew for an incoming mission. After the bomber had been safely landed and evacuated, he was walking away when he felt a fist thump him hard between his shoulder blades. He swung round, expecting to see an overenthusiastic colleague, but there was no one. Of course there wasn't, he realised; he'd been the last man to leave the plane. He reported it, as any anomaly near a plane had to be reported, in case he'd been feeling some form of energy surge or explosion, but a technical investigation found the equipment to be in perfect order. He wasn't surprised: he'd very definitely felt a fist thudding into his back. When he confided in the other staff, they nodded and swapped similar stories. They'd grown to accept these 'anomalies'. The airfield had been highly active during World War II, with hundreds of young men training and flying from it. They'd gone to work every day knowing they might not come back; scores of them had died. It seemed that the intensity of their last weeks had left its mark – incidents like the ghostly slap on the back would occur every now and then, almost always in the same low-key way, as if the young men's camaraderie were reverberating across time.

Sometimes these imprints are more distressing. As a young mother, novelist Fay Weldon lived in the pretty Cambridgeshire village of Saffron Walden. It was a peaceful setting from the outside, but the house she shared with her mother and sister was disturbed by a powerful grieving presence. At times, the atmosphere would become tight with distress and the cat would stare and hiss at nothing. And one night, when Fay and her baby were alone, the feeling of a presence became overpowering and she heard sobbing from the next room. Her baby began to cry inconsolably; Fay tried to make herself go into the room next door for his dummy but she was too afraid to move. She stayed, rocking her baby and listening to the weeping, until it finally died away. Afterwards she told her mother, who said that she too felt there was a bitterly unhappy presence in the house; within days, they left for good.

Denmark

Dragsholm Castle in Denmark, built in the twelfth century and now a flourishing hotel, harbours several ghosts. Guests enjoy its haunted reputation, but staff are not always so sure, especially on a lonely night. There's the Grey Lady, reputedly a housekeeper from the eighteenth century, who haunts the second floor, being most often seen or sensed in a room facing the moat. Though the owners consider her a benevolent presence, watching over the castle, many employees are unnerved by the sense of being observed. And if you talk about the Grey Lady in the rooms where she's believed to have lived, furniture rattles and sharp noises sound out of nowhere, to signal her displeasure.

The sound of horses' hooves and carriage wheels on the cobbled courtyard signals the ghost of the Earl of Bothwell, James Hepburn, trying to effect a spectral escape. In the sixteenth century, the earl, third husband of Mary Queen of Scots, was imprisoned in the castle dungeons for murder. Chained to a pillar, he went slowly mad before dying here.

The most upsetting ghost is known as the White Lady, though really she's believed to be only a girl. She haunts the fourth-floor corridors, sometimes briefly visible as a white wraith, freezing witnesses with the faint sounds of sobbing, intense chills and a palpable sense of despair. A terrible clue to this ghost's identity was uncovered in the 1920s, when workmen doing renovations found a small skeleton, in the remains of a white gown, walled up inside the castle. She seemed to prove the long-standing legend that one of the former owners of the castle had ordered his daughter to be drugged and walled up alive after she had become pregnant by the castle's stable-boy.

Some places seem more receptive to ghosts than others. It's as if, by virtue of their history or location, they are more apt to store fragments of past lives – or perhaps are less able to let them go. Inveraray Jail in Scotland is one such. The building dates back to Victorian times, when the law was so harsh that children who stole food or clothes could be locked up, whipped, forced to do hard labour and transported. The jail is now a historical monument, open to the public, and scores of visitors have experienced strange and distressing sensations there. Cell number 10 seems to harbour a particularly unhappy presence while, in the old kitchen, where convicts, then as now, were put to work, many people have felt there's someone hiding, terrified, behind the door. Photos taken inside the jail occasionally show misty figures or blurred silhouettes where the photographer remembers seeing only empty space. So many people have had these experiences that the jail has become famous and is a favourite destination for paranormal investigators and commercial ghost tours. As ghost-hunting grows in popularity, Inveraray Jail is likely to become familiar from TV, but in among the dry ice and the atmospheric lighting, it's worth remembering the bleak origins of what we're witnessing: year upon year of human suffering. It's as if the ghosts, or – to put it another way – the fragments of human consciousness that still inhabit this place from long ago, crowd around the visitors, trying to draw comfort from them.

In 2005, one team of paranormal investigators found evidence that led them to a similar conclusion. Spectre is one of a growing number of parascience organisations that seek to record the physical manifestations of hauntings. Certain physical phenomena have long been associated with reports of ghosts – notably cold temperatures, alterations in light and shadow, and unexplained sounds; parascientists aim to record and measure these. Various theories have developed about these phenomena, one of the most robust being that cold spots might be a side effect of unusual activity in the electromagnetic fields.

On that occasion, the Spectre researchers had permission to spend the whole night in the jail. They toured cells, corridors and the courtroom, monitoring conditions with digital thermometers, cameras (including infrared cameras), and sensitive audio recorders which they set up in different locations to catch any EVP activity.[1] In cell 9, they measured a steep drop in temperature: from 16.8 to 9.0 degrees in ten minutes. After checking that it could not have been caused by a draught or air current, they set up an EVP recorder and moved on. In another part of the jail, they heard a slamming sound from the direction of cell 9, as if something had fallen over; they returned, but everything was as they'd left it. At 2.30 a.m. they went into the courtroom. The temperature was reasonably mild, registering 16 as they sat down in one of the upper rows of seats. Soon, however, one of the researchers felt the air around his arm growing colder, so they began measuring the temperature at five-minute intervals. It dropped steadily: within half an hour it was 10 degrees. (Again, there were no draughts to explain it.) At 3.05 another loud bang from elsewhere in the jail drew them off to investigate; returning at 3.25, they found that the place where they'd been sitting had warmed up again, and was back to its previous 16 degrees. Almost immediately, however, they felt the chill set in again, and this time the temperature dropped so fast that by 3.45 it was just 6.4 degrees. The researchers had a strong sense that the cold had come in response to them; to test it, they began moving round the courtroom, recording the temperature as they went. They found that the cold would follow them; it appeared to be clinging to them.

1 Electronic Voice Phenomenon – ghostly or unexplained voices or sounds that appear when a tape is played back, though they were usually unheard by those present at the time.

And it was not a simple matter of cold diffusing from its source, because when they'd gone full circle and reached their original seats again, they found that the spot had gone back up to its original temperature. The team's cautious comment was that this was 'difficult to explain through natural effects' and that they could not rule out that it might have been due to 'a spiritual presence' keeping close to them.

And in cell 9, where the temperature had also plummeted? When they replayed the EVP tapes, two loud reports were heard, about ten minutes apart. Nothing had fallen over and there was no indication of what could have made the sounds. They had both happened at times when the researchers were in other parts of the jail, almost as if something in the cell were trying to attract their attention.

A classic case of haunting: Inveraray Jail offers cold spots, groans and a chilling atmosphere. (Photo courtesy of Inveraray Jail)

Hauntings often occur in places where people have been crammed together, and where they have shared hardship or intense emotions. So prisons and hospitals, places of work such as factories, mines, quarries, and sites like barracks and battlefields nurture ghosts. They populate overcrowded housing districts, and the sites of former slums – sometimes lingering after the old buildings have been pulled down and replaced.

In the 1980s, a network of old vaults was rediscovered under Edinburgh's South Bridge. Created back in the 1780s as storage and workshop space, during the Industrial Revolution the vaults became home to brothels, pubs and any people in need of shelter, including hundreds of Irish immigrants fleeing the potato famine. Families of ten or more would live in a single room. Sanitation was nonexistent, so disease was rife, as was crime. Burke and Hare, the infamous duo who robbed graves and murdered people in order to sell their bodies to the medical schools, used to hunt for victims there.

When the vaults were being excavated in the 1990s, workers were often puzzled by hearing footsteps and voices, or seeing shadows move, and then discovering that there was no one there. And, once the vaults reopened as a tourist attraction, their reputation as an eerie place, with an uncanny atmosphere, spread fast. Visitors have repeatedly encountered cold spots – the sudden, bone-gripping cold that seems separate from the surrounding air. In the light of lamps and torches, the shadows play tricks, of course, but it's surprising how often people's cameras capture patches of darkness that seem to hover in the air, human-shaped. Stones have been thrown from directions that turn out to be deserted. People have felt breathing on the backs of their necks and their clothes being tugged. And then there are the sounds – a chuckling, accompanying a scampering of feet, is thought by vault employees to be Jack, a young boy who lived here until he was murdered by a fellow vault-dweller, a violent man nicknamed Mr Boots. Jack can most often be heard in the area around the wine vault, where several people have felt a confiding presence close by, and the sensation of a small hand slipped into theirs. The ghost of Mr Boots, meanwhile, is most often encountered in the back rows of the vaults, where people often stumble and complain of feeling shoved or crushed, both physically and by a sense of malevolence.

Are Jack and Mr Boots actual human spirits, haunting the tunnels? Or have these historical identities simply been assigned to forces and presences that we sense but don't know how to interpret? Certainly, there seem to be personalities attached to the phenomena. Investigations using psychics, mediums and electronic monitoring equipment have come up with a range of identities. There's a five-year-old girl who was murdered by a fat man; a mother struggling to bring up a baby and an older child after her husband became mentally ill and abandoned her; a young man who thinks he's just passing through the vaults temporarily while he's down on his luck.

In a public session run by paranormal investigators Ghost Finders Scotland, a whispering voice was picked up on a tape recording, which, when enhanced on computer (again publicly), was heard to identify itself as Jackson and the year as 1867. And a number of people swear they have encountered the ghost of Maggie Dickson, who lived before the vaults ever existed but who was hanged in 1728 on the ground above them for the crime of concealing a pregnancy and leaving her dead baby's body by the river. Maggie's story outlasts her hanging – after watching her being put in her coffin, onlookers heard noises from inside. When it was opened, she was found to be still alive. Had the execution taken place in England, she would have been hanged again, but under Scottish law once was enough – she was considered legally dead and beyond the reach of the law, so went free. Maggie – or 'half-hangit Maggie' as the tourist trade has dubbed her – went on to live a long life, having more children and earning her living by running an inn – which must have seemed a sweet triumph considering she'd originally been made pregnant by an innkeeper. In fact, it's tempting to think that for a survivor like Maggie, haunting the vaults might be an active choice – the ultimate way of refusing to quit.

Perhaps, also, the vaults act as something of a magnet for spirits. As already suggested, this might be due to the sheer intensity of human life they have held. Neuroscientists now know that thoughts and impulses travel through our brains as electrical charges, leaping from synapse to synapse, and that these synaptic pathways are strengthened by use. The more an area of the brain is stimulated, the more receptive it becomes. It could be that the same is true of places, so that locations that have already collected strong psychic energy, via intense experiences, will act as receptors to any new, questing or seeking energy on the loose.

In the case of the vaults, this process might be aided by the fabric of the buildings – granite. Granite is a volcanic rock that often registers high electromagnetism. Occult guru Colin Wilson (who lives near the ghost-ridden granite uplands of Bodmin and Dartmoor) has a theory that these magnetised rocks act like magnetic tape, capturing psychic vibrations, both human and spirit in origin.

Electromagnetic fields are a natural occurrence but they are also amplified and manipulated by industrial processes. Could they be a factor in why certain industrial sites such as shipyards seem so prone to haunting?

Cammell Laird shipyard used to form the heart of the Liverpool docks. Occupying a vast 140-acre site, for around 170 years it was one of the biggest and most innovative shipyards in the world. The first steel ship, the *Ma Roberts* was built there, as was the second, RMS *Mauretania* and the first all-welded ship, the *Fullagar*. Iconic ships the HMS *Ark Royal* and HMS *Prince of Wales* came from there, as did submarines, merchant ships, passenger lines and oil tankers. But by the second half of the twentieth century, the shipyard, like the city of Liverpool, was in decline, and at the turn of the millennium only a few offices were still occupied in a wasteland of disused wharves, jetties and warehouses. One of these was housed on a single floor of a dilapidated 1960s block, originally built for designers of nuclear submarines. Here, in the late 1990s, employees saw dark figures moving slowly in the shadows at the end of a corridor. People going into the nearby kitchen felt an uncanny sense of being watched. The temperature would drop inexplicably and the shape of a man was seen to walk across the corridor and disappear through a wall into the old boardroom. Upstairs, footsteps could be heard crossing rooms that were known to be empty, while distant doors slammed when there was no one near.

Antarctica

Pristine and unspoiled, bleak and pitiless, Antarctica presents unusual challenges to the people investigating the paranormal. How can you identify a cold spot in sub-zero conditions? How can you listen for unusual sounds when the wind is howling like a banshee? How can you spot a spectral being against a white glare or driving blizzard?

And yet, wherever humans endure the limits of experience, others are likely to experience their suffering, even after they're dead.

An American scientist, who blogged about her time on McMurdo Station near Scott Base, reported a terrifying encounter in a securely locked storeroom. Stores are not heated, and anyone left in one would freeze to death, which is why people visiting them make sure they are empty before they leave them and can be completely certain that they are empty when they open them – if they find them secured.

The blogger unlocked the door, opened the store, and went in – and that's when she heard the footsteps pacing back and forth on the floor above. Her skin prickled and she was frozen with fear for a while, then managed to call out to a colleague. A colleague confirmed what she had experienced and said she had heard the footsteps too, a few weeks earlier. The blogger listened to the footsteps for ten minutes before being called away.

But her experience is by no means unique. The explorer and mountaineer Sir Edmund Hillary was greeted by the ghost of Ernest Shackleton when he went on a pilgrimage to the great man's hut. In 1979 a New Zealand airliner crashed into Mount Erebus and the bodies of the 257 victims were stored, frozen, in the gym at Scott Base. They haunt the place, and sightings are not rare, though seldom talked about. At the South Pole, no one can hear you scream.

Some employees felt they were being watched, and several, at different times, felt a strong impulse to whistle or sing, as if the urge had been implanted into them.

The site owners called in Para.Science, a team of investigators that takes an informed sceptics' approach, and they set about trying to find conventional scientific explanations for the phenomena. After identifying some possible causes, such as reflected car headlights creating shadow anomalies, and draughts causing doors to slam, they were left with certain phenomena that defied rational explanation. These included a pattern of lights coming on in a locked part of the building, footsteps being heard overhead and figures appearing – sometimes to the Para.Science researchers themselves. These figures were often quite matter of fact, and would be taken for employees until a headcount showed otherwise; one Para.Science researcher was so convinced she had someone in the room with her that she made him a cup of coffee.

From the BAE Systems shipyard in Cumbria, where military shipbuilding continues, come rumours of similarly strange happenings. A crane driver, sitting in his cab, his hand well away from the controls, was shocked when the crane began to move of its own accord. Another worker saw a ghost brush past him as he was changing overalls. Many employees have reported hearing bangs and seeing shadowy figures come and go. An experienced foreman, not known for his vivid imagination, refused to go into certain rooms at night simply because he was too frightened. BAE management were not prepared to let psychic investigators in – too disruptive, presumably, and you don't need that kind of publicity when you're specialising in military contracts for submarines and surface ships. It's said, however, that they did yield to Union demands and allowed a local vicar to perform an exorcism, which has restored quiet, so far . . .

These contemporary hauntings arise out of a long association between shipyards and the dead. Ships have always exacted a human cost in the making. The tradition of breaking a bottle of champagne over the bows of a newly launched ship has its origins in a Viking ceremony, when the wooden slipway was lubricated with the blood of a captive to ease the launching and honour the gods. In more recent times, the sacrifice of lives has more often been accidental, a by-product of the sheer danger of the work. Under the gleaming towers of London's new office district in the Isle of Dogs, you can still glimpse, emerging from the mud, the slipways used by the SS *Great Eastern*. The ship was the largest in the world at the time, and huge hydraulic rams were built to push it into the river. One exploded, killing its operators, whose bodies are still sometimes seen staggering across the Thames mud. The ship itself was haunted by the ghost of a riveter's mate who got lost inside the double-skinned steel hull, was sealed in and never escaped.

The *Queen Mary* is now moored in Long Beach, California, USA. Once the largest and fastest cruise ship in the world, it is now an extraordinarily haunted location. An engineer in overalls appears at the heavy, watertight door 13 to the engine room. A little girl is sometimes seen by the swimming pool and, after she vanishes, wet footprints remain on the deck. People have experienced a kind of psychic vortex, akin to a blackout, in the changing rooms where a woman was once raped. A smell of cigar smoke sometimes floats through the suite where Winston Churchill stayed while planning D-Day. Another, more harrowing haunting also dates back to World War II, when the *Queen Mary*'s Cunard colours of black, white and red were painted over in wartime camouflage. So successful was this that she was dubbed the Grey Ghost, and it was in this guise that she loomed out of the waters over another much smaller British naval ship, HMS *Curacao*, and crushed it beneath her 80,774 tons. Wartime orders forbade the crew to stop and pick up survivors, so the Grey Ghost ploughed on remorselessly. All 300 seamen on the *Curacao* drowned, and some people have reported hearing scrabbling and beating sounds from the outside of the hull.

A different kind of haunting afflicts the USS *Hornet*. This huge aircraft carrier has a distinguished history that includes action in the Pacific Ocean during World War II and the safe collections of astronauts from *Apollo 11* and *12* after their rockets re-entered earth's atmosphere and touched down in the sea. The ship, however, has been plagued by accidents, many of which have killed or maimed crew, often in grisly fashion. Sailors have been smashed by the propellers, sucked into air vents, or been blasted off the decks by the backwash of jets as they take off. At least three have been decapitated by snapping cables. To date, an estimated 300 servicemen have been killed carrying out peace-time duties, and many who have served and are still serving on board believe the USS *Hornet* is in the grip of ghosts. Crew members have reported hatches opening and closing in empty rooms and voices talking on decks that turn out to be deserted. Some have seen officers walking ahead of them down corridors, only to disappear. Cold spots come and go in different areas of the ship, often bringing an atmosphere of sick dread. The *Hornet* has, incidentally, the highest number of recorded suicides in the US Navy.

So what's going on here? Is the ship haunted by harmful ghosts, intent on disturbing the crew and destroying life? Has it become cursed, perhaps as a consequence of actions committed by its crew in the past? Are the sceptics right to dismiss the high rate of accidents as simple bad luck, and the ghostly sights and sounds as the crew's imagination? Or could it be that known and unknown science are combining here, with the ship's powerful electromagnetic fields (all that cabling and weaponry) capturing the turbulent psychic energy that has been produced by a series of tragic and violent events? Could the ghostly presences be not so much deliberately haunting, as trapped?

The next question is – has anyone tried to do anything about them? And here we run into a wall of silence. America is a country of strong Christian belief, where blessings and religious ceremonies are widely performed. It wouldn't be surprising to hear that exorcisms had been carried out on the *Hornet*. But while religious services regularly take place on board, the US Navy is saying nothing publicly to confirm or deny suspicions of hauntings, and of possible steps taken to tackle them. You can see their dilemma – it wouldn't fit with the image of the world's most powerful and sophisticated armed forces to be struggling internally with a force of another kind.

Laos

In the second half of the twentieth century, Laos was unwillingly sucked into the conflict that threatened to tear neighbouring Vietnam to pieces. Communist fighters from Vietnam took refuge over the border in Laos and the Americans duly bombed them, without too much thought of the effects on the population. But at least the Laotians had the supernatural on their side. A man and his son were trying to get back to their village when they were caught up in a firefight between Vietcong and American special forces. They dived into a bomb crater that was being used by buffalo as a mud bath and sheltered there as the bullets whined past their heads.

As night fell, the fighting grew less intense and finally stopped altogether. The man led his son out of the crater, but which way to go? He thought it more likely that the Vietcong would have retreated into paddy fields nearby and so decided to head home through the forest that covered the high ground. But as they were setting off they met two peasants, a mother and daughter dressed in traditional clothes, on the road.

'I wouldn't head for the high ground,' the woman said. 'There are Vietcong and Laotion rebels hiding out there. They'll shoot first and ask questions later.'

The man thanked her and turned around but then noticed his son staring after the women. He told him not to be so rude but then noticed that his son's lower lip was trembling and even in the twilight he could see he was shaking.

'What's the matter? Have you seen guerrillas?' he asked.

'No. It was those women. They were floating,' the boy said.

The man realised he had been talking to a ghost but his instincts told him to trust her. Later, he heard that guerrillas, hiding out in the hills, had shot and killed two travellers who had passed that way.

Other cultures are much more pragmatic in their attitude to hauntings. In the Philippines, it's widely accepted that ghosts exist and that while most people see them only fleetingly, some people have what they call an 'opened third eye'. This is common enough for them not to make a career out of it – most people with an opened third eye live ordinary lives and do ordinary jobs; but when hauntings happen, their friends will turn to them for more information.

In the early 2000s, a little girl began appearing to employees in a call centre in Cebu City. The firm had just moved into a converted warehouse. It was a large space and, as in all call centres, people worked in close physical proximity, gathered in large open-plan offices, but separated into individual units by their phones and computer. It was when individuals were alone with their thoughts that the little girl came. First she appeared as a reflection in a female employee's computer monitor, wearing the kind of smart dress Filipino girls put on for Sundays. A few days later a male employee was standing in the men's toilets when in the mirror he saw the cubicle door behind him swing slowly open, to show a little girl sitting on the toilet, looking at him. He closed his eyes and started praying; when he looked again, the girl was right in front of him, chanting the prayer along with him. He had a horrifying impression that her skin was starting to fall away from her flesh before he fled in terror.

More peculiar experiences followed, introducing new characters and sensations. The woman who had seen the little girl in her computer screen fell asleep in the office one day and dreamed that hands were round her throat, choking her. A colleague known for having an open third eye looked across the office to see a friend hard at work in the corner, oblivious to the fact that a man was hanging from the air-conditioning unit above her. He dangled with a rope round his neck, his foot almost nudging the employee's head.

Someone taking an illicit nap in an empty room was half roused by a noise. Thinking it was a friend checking on him, he asked to be woken later. 'All right,' said a clear, light, girl's voice.

A woman manifested next. Her face appeared as a reflection on computer screens, just like the girl's, though never with it. In the women's toilets, employees could hear her voice crying, or sometimes singing softly.

One of the call-centre managers complained that she kept finding ashes on her desk. She suspected a practical joke, but her co-worker on the management team (another with the gift of the open third eye) told her quite calmly that her desk was being regularly visited by the ghost of a man, disfigured by burning.

It's as if the haunting was trying to tell a story piecemeal. When the employees investigated the history of the building, they discovered that while it had been a warehouse, a young family – father, mother and daughter – had lived there. The father had killed his wife and child and, later, overwhelmed by remorse, had killed himself.

In that case, the employees took no dramatic steps to deal with the haunting. Some said prayers for the unquiet spirits, once they discovered what had happened, but the emphasis was on living with the haunting rather than banishing it. Indeed, it was the company rather than the ghosts that moved on, relocating a few years later to new, purpose-built offices. Since then, members of staff haven't been disturbed by any adult ghosts, but every now and then someone catches a glimpse of an unexplained reflection in their screen that looks like a young girl, wistful and rather lost.

A more decisive approach was taken by another Philippines company. A factory manager was worried that a number of his employees had died suddenly, without obvious cause. The first death was unremarked, except as a personal tragedy. The second was seen as a strange coincidence. But when a third person died from the same department, people started to talk. The manager talked the matter over with a friend, who immediately asked him if anything had changed at the business. Nothing sprang to mind – certainly nothing that could cause the deaths of three people. All that had happened was that an old storage warehouse had been demolished to make space for executives to park in. The friend smiled and told him that this could be the cause of his trouble. The reason was simple: empty buildings could become the home of *engkantos*, spirits that need a calm, empty space in which to settle. If their home had been demolished, disturbances would ensue.

Engkantos are both revered and feared in the Philippines. Thought to originate from rebel angels, they have traditionally inhabited forests, and in particular the baleta tree. They are beautiful, tall, and prone to falling in love with humans, especially good-looking young ones, whom they sometimes abduct. Love them in return, however, and you will lose your soul. Some *engkantos* are helpful, others are malign; all are protective of the natural world, and if you harm, or even disturb, a river, tree or flower that is dear to an *engkanto*, you can expect to fall ill, perhaps even die. As the forests have increasingly fallen to make way for towns and cities, *engkantos* have taken to colonising deserted buildings.

With some scepticism, the manager followed his friend's advice and called in an expert team, which consisted of a medium and a cleanser. The medium stood in the new car park, where the warehouse used to be, and went into a trance; on emerging, he looked shaken. The place was infested with *engkantos*, he said, hundreds of them, all of whom had taken up residence in the warehouse and were now without a home. They were still gathering in the car park, resenting every intrusion; in particular, their fury had been roused by three employees who regularly stayed behind to do overtime and disturbed them by playing loud music. The *engkantos* had therefore afflicted them with sicknesses that had eventually killed them.

The usual procedure for quietening *engkanto* activity combines placating them (by leaving gifts, restoring the environment) with cleansing the area – throwing salt – to drive the *engkantos* away. On this occasion, however, the cleansing took priority, and something very close to an exorcism was performed. It seems to have worked – there have been no more mysterious deaths at the factory.

This haunting was quite different from the call-centre one, because of course *engkantos* are not ghosts. They haven't died and have never been human – they belong instead to the world of sprites, elementals and shape-shifters, which exist with different names but remarkably similar qualities in almost all cultures. Think of Muslim djinni, Celtic faeries, Chinese and Japanese fox spirits. All frequent lonely places, jealously guard their privacy and have a fiery, volatile relationship with humans. They also seem to have a close relationship with ghosts – at least, in so far as their chosen locations go. You'll often hear rumours of pixies, faeries, djinni, etc., in the same abandoned or ruined sites that are thought to harbour ghosts. One explanation could be that these sites are naturally occurring 'thin places', where the membrane that surrounds our rational reality becomes porous. That may well be the case for ruined abbeys, graveyards or sacred sites like Stonehenge. But factories and apartment blocks? Here we may be seeing another process at work – a building becomes abandoned and these inhuman entities move in. They create an eerie atmosphere; people entering the building have a sense of being watched, of not being alone, of a presence that is hostile to intruders. Which of course it is. Soon, the building has a reputation for being haunted, which grows as people report peculiar experiences – loose stones falling dangerously close to them, stairs giving way, illusions that either lead them into danger or save them from it at the last minute (or both).

In the past, these occurrences would have been enough for people to identify what kind of supernatural being they were disturbing. In Devon, until well into the twentieth century, people would have no trouble in blaming 'pisgies' – aka pixies – for such supernatural acts of malice, as well as for the occasional uncanny helping hand. Now, as the knowledge has been lost, we tend to lump all such things together as 'ghosts'. However, the evidence suggests that true ghosts do not have the power to inflict harm or play tricks. In fact, the key characteristic of ghosts is that they can do very little, if anything. They can seldom even communicate directly, though they often give the impression that they are seeking help, or have something they very much want the living person to know.

Take a haunting that happened recently in daylight, in the most mundane circumstances. In Yuma, Arizona, a man we'll call 'Mr L' stopped at a McDonald's for a quick cup of coffee. The restaurant was almost empty, so he noticed when a middle-aged couple walked in. The man was wearing a grey suit, the woman a floral print dress. Although he was immaculately turned out, it was clear the man was ill – he was grey-skinned and sweating and the woman kept wiping his face with a damp cloth as if to cool him down. After a while, she went to the cloakroom; once the door had closed behind her, the man walked up to Mr L and asked if he'd give him money to buy a drink. Mr L was nonplussed – how could someone so well dressed not have the price of a drink in McDonald's? Though he frequently gave small change to beggars, this time he found himself recoiling, and refused. The stranger just looked at him and turned away; a moment later, the woman came out of the cloakroom and the two of them left. Mr L watched them go through the glass doors, then inexplicably lost sight of them. He stood up for a better view, but still couldn't spot them, so he went to the window from where he could see the whole car park, but they were no longer there. If they ever had truly been there in the first place. He was left wondering what the man had really wanted. Could it really have been that small amount of money? And what would have happened if he'd given it to him?

New Zealand

Like Australia, New Zealand is cut off from the rest of the world and, until the Europeans arrived, culture, flora and fauna alike developed in their own way. Ghosts, however, are universal. In 2007 a boy at holiday camp woke up in the middle of the night, bursting for the toilet. He climbed out of bed, left the dormitory building and rushed to the lavatory block. Once in the cubicle, he was relieved to see that the one next to him was occupied so he would have some company.

Then, to his dismay, his neighbour started to bang on the walls. He asked it to stop, but then, to his horror, he heard a scrabbling and a scratching as if his neighbour was trying to climb the cubicle wall. As he heard the neighbour climb higher and higher, concern turned to fear and by the time 'it' had crawled to the top of the wall and filthy black hair was showing above the partition, the hair was standing up on the back of the boy's neck.

He ran screaming back to his dormitory, waking everyone up, including the supervisors. When he told his story, they went very quiet, then told him the story.

Three years ago, a girl had died in that toilet and lain, undiscovered, for four days, before the stink of her rotting body told people that something was wrong. Since then, they had always kept that cubicle locked, but she still got in and was still trying to attract the attention of anyone who visited the toilet next door.

When ghosts make a determined attempt to communicate, it usually takes the form of fragmented appeals that those on the receiving end have to try and decipher. In March 2009, five Chinese

Malaysian men found themselves in just that position. They were on a trip to Cambodia and checked into a hotel where they were sharing a room. It wasn't very welcoming, and two of the men cracked jokes about it being haunted. As they laughed, a third, 36-year-old Teow Hsium Choon, felt the atmosphere in the room grow live with tension. He waited for it to pass but it grew stronger; soon he felt as if he were surrounded by angry presences, pressing in on him.

The men went out, but Teow's distress intensified and, while they were in a bar, he passed out. His friends watched horrified as he had a seizure and then began sobbing. They were relieved when he started speaking but it was short-lived: in a woman's voice, and using not his usual dialect but the Hokkien language, Teow begged for forgiveness.

A few hours later he lapsed into a second trance; this time the voice that came out of his mouth belonged to an unknown man. It began bargaining with his friends. It would leave them alone if they would help track down his son, 38-year-old Chew Kon Lai, and his wife Chong Sim Choon.

Both manifestations had been shocking but also bewildering. Was the woman begging forgiveness for abandoning her husband? Or had they heard her voice from the past, pleading with the husband because she was afraid of him, and was that why she had run away? Or had she not run away of her own volition at all, but been taken?

And where did the husband want them to look for his wife and son? Were they here in Cambodia? Or had he picked the visitors because they came from Malaysia, and that was where his wife had gone?

Baffled, they have done their best. The five clubbed together to place advertisements in three Chinese-language newspapers, seeking the wife and son. And when that drew no response, they turned to Datuk Michael Chong, the respected head of the Public Services and Complaints department of the Consumer Affairs Bureau. Chong is famous for his success in investigating loan sharks, abductions and missing spouses. So far, he has had no luck, but the case is still open. So if you have any information on the whereabouts of Chew Kon Lai or Chong Sim Choon, or if you can shed any light on what has happened to them, please get in touch.

* * *

Another ghost recently began accosting people indirectly on a stretch of road in Herefordshire, England. In an eighteen-month period, more than twenty motorists found their steering suddenly unresponsive as they drove along the A465. Some felt as though someone was tugging the steering wheel; others manoeuvred the wheel with growing horror as they realised the car was not obeying them. In almost every case, they were unable to control the car, which swerved off the road and into a fence. The farmer who owned the fence asked the County Council to check the road for hazards but, after investigating the camber, carrying out speed checks and renewing the road markings, there was no logical explanation, and still the accidents continued. They always happened in the same spot and never left skid marks.

One night, a councillor involved in the investigations was having a drink in the Crown and Sceptre pub near the accident spot. Richard James knew many of the pub's regulars; however, the man who now approached him was a complete stranger. He told the councillor not to worry about the spate of accidents: no one would die there. They were caused, he said, by a haunting – a woman had died there in the 1920s or 1930s, after a struggle over the steering wheel. It was a strange conversation and it disturbed the councillor. The man couldn't or wouldn't give him much more detail, beyond saying he was a psychic – which suggests that perhaps he himself had seen something, at once vivid and incomplete, which would account for the confusion over the 1920s and 1930s.

Not surprisingly, after that encounter, rumours of the ghostly passenger took hold. Competing versions of the story circulated and there was much speculation as to why the phenomenon had suddenly started now, so many decades later. The last comment from local officialdom was that the parish council had asked the vicar to look into the matter, presumably with a view to performing a discreet blessing.

Roads are popular venues for hauntings. The most obvious explanation is that so many people die in road accidents, and moreover die suddenly and violently. But there may be another reason too, connected with the nature of roads themselves.

Roads are recognised as routes of spirit power in many cultures. For instance, the Anglo-Saxons believed that the dead travelled along human-made roads as part of their wanderings in the underworld, and that crossroads were thresholds where the two worlds touched – a belief echoed in the story, from America's South, that back in the 1930s Blues legend Robert Johnson met the devil at the crossroads and promised him his soul in exchange for preternaturally brilliant guitar-playing skills. The Chinese believe that energy flows down roads, and that houses and doorways should be sited with care, to avoid becoming sumps for negative energy. For traditional Australian aborigines, spirituality, culture and heritage are indissolubly linked to paths across the wilderness known as songlines, which adolescents must walk as part of their initiation into the adult world.

These days we might be cut off from our ancestors' mystical beliefs, but we still feel the uncanny, volatile power of certain roads. On a country road in Wales, there have been two recent incidents of drivers and their passengers being startled by a great white horse jumping out of a field and crossing directly in front of the car. White horses have a profound significance in Welsh myth, which continually links everyday life with the underworld.

Zorya Vechernaya, the personification of the Evening Star in Slavic myth, haunts a number of roads in Eastern Russia, where she can sometimes be glimpsed at dusk, driving a white chariot.

Where Hawaii's Highway 1 tunnels through a mountain, the shouts and cries of ancient warriors can be heard. Their ghosts regularly appeared to construction workers excavating the tunnel, and bones were found inside the mountain, suggesting that a sacred burial site has been disturbed.

And so on . . . earth spirits, ancestor ghosts and gods of place haunt roads, motorways and beaten tracks all over the world. No wonder human ghosts are drawn to join them. These can be divided into two main categories.

The first seem to be imprints of people who once frequented the roads. They manifest as fleeting sightings of carriages, cars, and people that stamp themselves vividly on the consciousness, then vanish. People who see them often feel as if they've been caught up in a pleat of time, as if the ghosts are just as real as they are, only belonging in another dimension.

A teenager on a coach trip in Brisbane, Australia, was amused to see a man wearing a white shirt and dusty-looking fawn trousers walking by the roadside with a little brown dog, which he was talking to. The dog was scampering round him, giving little jumps, as if in answer to whatever he was saying. The girl had the impression that they'd walked a long way and had further to go. She also noticed that the man was carrying a bundle wrapped in cloth under one arm and had some kind of drinking flask hanging from his belt. The coach overtook the pair and she twisted round to carry on watching them, but they were no longer there.

One British man, known in his neighbourhood for his keen interest in the paranormal, recently explained that it stemmed from an incident that had happened to him as a young man in the 1960s. He'd been driving along a deserted road in Cornwall when an old-fashioned open-top car had driven towards him. It was full of young men in high spirits and clothes that looked as if they dated from the 1940s. The three passengers were standing up in the car, their long coats and scarves streaming in the wind as they sang a song together. He was still trying to recognise the song when they disappeared, completely, leaving him alone in the landscape.

People who have had these experiences tend to remember them all their lives. Their impact is far out of proportion with how long they lasted, or any immediate effect – indeed, they usually have no practical effect because they are phantoms and intent on their own activities. They are literally 'in their own world'.

Then there is the other kind of road haunting, where the ghost is definitely connected with death and loss, and strong emotions of fear, panic or anger are present. Not surprisingly, many road ghosts turn out either to have died at the spot or to have been involved in an accident where someone else died, and to be caught in a cycle of repeating the event. It's not always a straightforward matter, however: one ghostly incident that took place recently happened just once, and appeared to be designed as a clue.

It was on a winter's evening that motorists on the A3 in Surrey watched with horror as a car skidded, lost control and swerved off the road. The police, acting on the public's reports, went to the scene and had to hunt some way into the bushes before they found the grim wreckage of a Vauxhall Astra, with a man inside. On looking closer, they were shocked to see that not only was the driver dead, but his body was in an advanced state of decomposition. He couldn't possibly have died in the crash they'd been called to investigate, so they went to look for a second car. Exhaustive hunting failed to turn up any other vehicle, though, or indeed any skid marks or signs of a fresh accident. Eventually police identified the driver as a young London man whom they'd been looking for in connection with an alleged robbery, and who had gone missing in July. Forensics concluded he had probably died back then, in a car crash identical to the one reported on that December evening – of which, incidentally, no physical evidence was ever found.

What was the haunting for? Given that it happened just once (most road hauntings are persistent), it's tempting to conclude that the ghost wanted his death to be discovered, and that discovery laid him to rest.

Rest doesn't come so easily to the young woman who haunts Route 20 outside Tokyo. Just as cars are about to enter a tunnel, she appears on the road ahead, holding a baby. Drivers swerve to avoid the pair, and there have been several accidents. As the drivers sit dazed in their cars (luckily none of the accidents has proved fatal), she sometimes approaches the windows to look in, at other times stays further off, hugging her baby. One man whose car she approached sat transfixed as she gazed hungrily into his face; then her expression changed and he thought he heard her groan, 'Wrong man', as she turned and vanished. Some people say this is the ghost of a woman who was killed in a hit-and-run accident and who is searching for the driver who killed her; others believe she didn't die on the road but is haunting it to seek out the father of her baby, who abandoned them. She definitely seems to be looking for someone.

Such ghosts, who are seeking someone or something, are often particularly disturbing. There's a doggedness about them, a despairing need, that is hard to bear. Paradoxically, though, they might not cause as much physical harm as other ghosts. Sometimes, ghosts who aren't in themselves very frightening cause death and destruction simply by virtue of where they appear: Hong Kong's Tuen Mun Highway, for instance, has a gruesome record of crashes caused by ghostly figures emerging from the middle of the road. Where crashes prove fatal, they seem to create more ghosts, with new figures appearing at spots where hapless drivers and passengers have recently died.

Serbia

As a car full of young Serb men drives down a dark country road to a party, a bloodstained face suddenly appears in one of the windows. Terrified, they drive on and make sure they take another road home. The next morning, however, pricked by conscience, they retrace their route they took. At the spot they saw the bloody face are a pile of flowers, wilted and withered, and a card mourning the death of a girl, killed at night, one month earlier.

By contrast, a ghost compulsively searching for company, or comfort, or someone they loved when alive, is likely to leave you physically intact. But the sense of their still-human need means that few who have encountered them ever forget the experience.

From Trueghosttales.com comes a story of an Oklahoma man who was haunted by a young girl who seemed to want something from him. When she first appeared in his family home one night, he was unaware of her – it was his girlfriend who stared, transfixed, and then told him that a girl of about 10 was standing at his side of the bed, staring at him. Next, his stepdaughter saw the ghost: this time she was standing just outside the bathroom door, watching the man as he sat on the sofa. She then moved closer to him, frightening the stepdaughter so much that she ran to him and asked to be hugged. The man's first direct experience of her came in the daytime, when he had come home early from work and was putting the rubbish out; he suddenly had a powerful sensation of being watched from the front door. Still, though, he saw nothing. It wasn't until he was standing in the kitchen making himself a snack one evening that he had the same feeling again and, this time, turning his head slowly, he saw a young girl with fair, shoulder-length hair and in a nightgown with embroidery round the hem, standing in the corridor, watching him through the doorway. He ran to where she was, but she vanished. After that, he tried several times to talk to her, but he asked his questions, 'Who are you?', 'Tell me about yourself,' in vain. He was never able to see the girl again and, soon afterwards, the family moved house. He still carries the memory of her, though, along with the regret that he wasn't able to find out more about her, or discover what it was she wanted of him.

Tunisia

Belvedere Park is a pleasant public garden in Tunis, much used by city residents and visitors. Occasionally, young men walking or driving there, usually at night, come across an attractive young woman wearing no jacket and clearly feeling the cold. Keen to get into conversation with her, they lend her their jacket and offer to take her home. Sometimes they walk her, sometimes they drive her, sometimes they get on so well that they detour into a café or restaurant along the way. In each case, when they eventually take her home, the girl takes the jacket inside with her. And in each case, when the young man returns to collect it, he finds that he is unable to see the girl again because, as the grim-faced parent at the door tells him, she has been dead for several years now.

In the Ukraine, the ghost of an older girl, on the cusp of adulthood, has been seen by many motorists as they approach a railway crossing. She is an insubstantial figure, most often seen in winter dusk or early darkness, incongruously wearing something long and white; she appears to be struggling desperately to push something over the tracks. To some people, she is grappling with empty air; others think they can make out the vague shape of a car in front of her. In October 2006, an 18-year-old girl and her 23-year-old boyfriend were killed at this spot, when their Lada got stuck on the tracks and a train hit them. They had been on their way to visit the girl's parents to tell them they had decided to get married. The girl's ghost always appears alone, presumably trying to defy the death that took away her future. There is another, troubling side to this haunting, though: the girl has also been seen materialising behind cars that are waiting to cross the line, pushing at them as if trying to force them on to the tracks and into the path of the oncoming train. Does she think that if someone else takes her place, she'll be free? Is she trying to win company in her loneliness? Or is she a blind wraith, not truly seeing her earthly whereabouts, just caught in endless repetition of one act? In any event, she can make no physical impression on the cars, for all her effort.

All the ghosts in this chapter were once attached, in life, to the place in which they appear. This is a pattern that holds good for all ghost manifestations worldwide. You'll also notice that very few of the ghosts could be described as being on any kind of mission. They are bearing witness to their lives, true, and in many cases to the circumstances of their death, but are seldom bent on revenge or reconciliation or, indeed, action of any kind. The fact that books, films and TV interpret ghosts as restless creatures wanting the help of the living to achieve closure says more about our need for a satisfying story than it does about the real nature of ghosts. The truth is, ghosts are not human, only the remnants of human lives.

All the same, they can have a devastating effect on the lives of the living, which is why every culture that has ever existed has invented death rituals. There is bodily disposal – burial, burning, or removal to some place away from the community, to preserve hygiene. There is also the ritual to ensure that the spirit takes its leave too. Very often a haunting can be brought to an end, or at least relieved of its distressing aspects, by performing a ceremony that commemorates the person in life and also firmly signals that this earthly life is at an end. Such rituals usually mark the place where a person lived and/or died and involve a request to leave in peace the people who have been witnessing the haunting.

The emphasis on place/people will be different according to culture. While most Western societies concentrate on cleansing the place, in Eastern societies there is often an equal concern with the living witnesses. For instance, in Japan, the belief is that while ghosts usually manifest in a place significant to them, they may attach themselves to people passing through that place and travel around with them – sometimes scores of them clinging to the same person at a time. The cleansing is therefore done directly on that person (see Tying Down the Demon, Chapter 9 for a fuller account.) There is also a connection with the place of burial: in Japan, graves are extremely important and the failure of the living to maintain the graves of the dead, and place the correct observances on them on holy days, is thought to be one of the key reasons that spirits become unquiet in the first place.

In Romania, a complex relationship exists between ghosts, land and people. Ghosts who rise from the grave are known as *strigoi* and they haunt their family, preying on them by stealing food and sucking blood from the cattle. The *strigoi* are initially invisible, visiting their family for short periods and returning to the grave in between. They then grow stronger, become visible, looking just like they did in life, and start to feed on family members as well as cattle, sucking out life force as well as blood. Eventually they feed on people outside the family too – by this time they return to the grave infrequently and have usually brought disease to cattle and humans in the neighbourhood. *Strigoi* can be destroyed if their bodies are dug up and burned or impaled on spikes, but only for the first seven years. After that, their tie with the grave is severed and they can live anywhere they like above ground; it's said that they often travel to new towns and begin lives as ordinary people, recognisable only by other *strigoi*, with whom they hold secret gatherings.

When changes are made to the places where ghosts lived, or died, or are buried, it often seems to spark new activity. All societies are wary of disturbing burial sites, and when it's clear that this is going to happen (in construction projects, for instance), some form of reinterment is usually provided, along with a ceremony. Where this isn't done, you often find reports of ghosts, as with Hawaii's Highway 1. But a site doesn't need to contain human remains to harbour imprints of former lives.

In 2009, staff at the newly built Royal Derby Hospital became afraid to go down certain corridors after the appearance of a shadowy figure, apparently wearing a long dark cloak, darting across their paths. It moved restlessly and seemed sometimes to appear out of one wall and vanish through another. It roamed wards and corridors alike, and was most often seen in departments around the morgue. Management asked the hospital chaplain to investigate and if necessary conduct a service. After that, news was hard to come by, as is usually the case where an institution is anxious to carry on with its daily routine. However, it's interesting to note that the hospital is built over the site of a Roman road, and that in the nineteenth century, part of it was occupied by a workhouse. A cloaked ghost might originate from either period, and locals with an interest in the paranormal (who are numerous, given that Derby is reputedly the most haunted town in Britain) believe that it's most likely to be either a Roman soldier who was garrisoned here or a workhouse inmate, disturbed by the ground being broken yet again and a new pattern of existence being imposed on the place he or she once inhabited.

Could it be that there are many, many more ghosts around us than we are ever aware of? We know that some people see them more readily than others, and those who are 'sensitive' often speak of having certain periods of their lives when they see many ghosts. Childhood seems to be a receptive time: there are many people who remember incidents from their childhood when they saw figures and even spoke to them, only to be told by adults that there was no one there. A girl has recently posted a typical plea for advice on a paranormal website: her sister, not quite 2 years old, has taken to running sobbing out of rooms in the house, clearly afraid. 'Guy! Guy! Guy!' she insists, pointing at something – or someone – no one else can see.

Our experience of ghosts is likely to remain partial and mystifying. But it is not likely to decrease. Consider this: we are living at a time of unprecedented population growth. There are as many people alive on the planet now as have ever lived in the whole history of the world before. Which means that in eighty years' time, the number of people who have died – the potential population of ghosts – will have doubled, within the span of one modern lifetime. We can only speculate what that will mean for our great-grandchildren. Unless, of course, some little part of us remains behind, to be a part of the continuing story.

CHAPTER TWO

CREATURES OF THE THRESHOLD

Monsters and Angels

It was on 16 January 2004 that a young police officer was patrolling alone in his car in the early hours of the morning, 3.15 a.m. to be exact, in Colonia Valles de la Silla, a small town in Mexico.

Leonardo Samaniego had had a quiet night so far – it was cold and people were only too glad to be indoors, so when he turned into Alamo Street, he expected it to be deserted. Instead, he was just in time to see something enormous fall from the bare branches of a tree. It dropped rapidly, but made no impact on the ground, seeming to hover just above it. Samaniego put his lights on full beam and saw what he took to be a woman in a black cloak, with dark brown skin and round, black, lidless eyes, floating a few feet above ground. She looked straight into the headlights for a second before flinching violently. Then she landed on the ground, writhing and struggling to cover her eyes, apparently in agony from the brightness.

The officer had a clear instant of recognising what seemed to be impossible – the word *bruja*, the Mexican term for witch, flashed into his mind – and then the creature was flying through the air, incredibly fast, and had fastened on his car. Samaniego saw dark brown arms and large hands with claws scrabbling against the windscreen; the black eyes, much larger close up, seemed to fill half the glass. Powered by terror, he jolted the car into reverse and accelerated backwards, shouting into his radio for backup. He managed to guide the car all the way up the street, with the creature clawing at the glass, and then he passed out. A few minutes later another patrol car reached him, followed by an ambulance. They found him unconscious but unharmed and quite alone.

In a state of shock, Samaniego gave his story to his fellow officers. He also gave it to doctors at the hospital where he was taken for examination – and, incidentally, tested for drugs, alcohol and mental instability, on all of which he came up clean. The precision of his story struck many people and an interview with him was broadcast on TV news. During the next few days, hundreds of reports of similar sightings came in.

Many of these were vague, suggesting optical illusions or copycat sightings. Some, however, shared telling details with Samaniego's account. These included two police officers from a neighbouring town who admitted that three days before Samaniego they had seen a large flying creature, like a cross between a bird and a human, but at the time had decided to say nothing, for fear of ridicule. And a brother and sister in nearby Colonia La Playa reported having seen it together, in the daytime, the encounter disturbing the brother so much that he felt sick for days. All four witnesses had seen the creature clearly, and all four insisted on a fact that both supported Samaniego's story and put an interesting spin on it – they said that the being wore no human clothes but was covered in feathers, and that the outspread arms that Samaniego had taken to be wrapped in a cloak were wings.

Two years later, on the afternoon of 17 May 2006, the well-organised and scientifically minded members of the Nuevo Leon UFO Club were outside their clubhouse, preparing equipment for their regular monthly meeting. Two of them had video cameras, so when an unidentified object was duly spotted flying steadily above the treetops, they both caught the evidence. The result baffled them: whatever it was appeared dark, with an irregular outline (unsuitable for an aerodynamic machine), and it flew without flexing or flapping. Because it was a long way off, it was impossible to tell its exact angle to the ground. Some people believed the entity was flying at an angle and they were looking at a pair of huge outspread wings, with the body stretched out beneath. Others pointed out that if the image was of an upright silhouette, it looked like the traditional image of a Mexican *bruja*, or witch. *Brujas* belong to a different tradition from the European spell-casting, cauldron-stirring witches, being more like hags or ghouls. They are closely associated with Santa Muerte, the death saint, who is often portrayed as a grinning skeleton in a wedding dress and who is venerated on the Day of the Dead as the link between the living and the underworld.

The footage was run on TV, spliced together with Samaniego's interview and a new interview with another police officer, Gerardo Garza, who had been horrified to encounter two not-quite human females, hovering several feet above ground in a cemetery. Like Samaniego, he had seen darkly wrinkled faces and talons, but he was also convinced their bodies were covered with feathers.

So what were people seeing? Beings that combined human and animal features; that could fly; that struck fear into them with a sense of otherness even when they did nothing more than pass by.

The words 'angel' and 'monster' have been whispered, but they aren't quite right. Nor is 'cryptid' – the scientific definition for an animal that has not yet been proven to exist. Those who've seen these creatures feel they are supernatural.

Encounters like this have taken place repeatedly over the past few decades. The Internet buzzes with theories about what they mean and why they're happening. The apparitions are always different – each has its own very distinct combination of animal and human characteristics, and yet fascinating similarities link them.

Let's start with what happened in West Virginia, USA.

Mothman

On 14 November 1966, Newell Partridge, resident of Point Pleasant, West Virginia, had settled down for an evening's TV. So when the picture broke up and the sound turned to a whine, his first reaction was exasperation. Then he realised that his dog, which was out on the porch, had started howling. There was no way he connected the two events; the Partridge's house was surrounded by fields so he suspected some wild animal had come close. Sure enough, when he went to investigate, his torch picked out two large red eyes about 150 yards away. The dog ran towards them, growling and snarling, but Partridge didn't follow. There was something odd about the eyes: they were too high to belong to a racoon or fox, and too large for a bird. Though he was a countryman and well used to wild animals, he felt uneasy, almost afraid. He went back indoors, leaving the dog to sniff around, and loaded his gun before he went to bed.

The next day, his dog had vanished.

There was no sign of a fight, only a series of paw-prints where the eyes had been, overlying each other in a ring, as if the dog had been chasing its tail.

The following evening, 15 November, four young people were driving round a disused explosives base near the town of Point Pleasant. This place had a curious history: a wildlife sanctuary before the war, it had been converted into a large complex of factories and storage domes and was now largely abandoned, the wildlife once again roaming round the derelict buildings and over the concrete storage domes. It was popular with teenagers, and the two couples in the car were on the lookout for friends. The figure they saw by the old power plant, however, was shockingly unfamiliar.

It stood upright, its body human-shaped but too tall, about seven feet, and with huge folded wings. It seemed to be dark grey all over, and in the dimness they couldn't make out the shape of its head, but they could see two large eyes, glowing red in the car headlights. For long seconds they were frozen; it was only when the creature turned and moved clumsily into the shadows that they could react. The driver spun the car round and accelerated off, but as they sped back towards the main road, they saw the creature again, standing on a hillock. Spreading its wings, it rose straight upwards and then flew through the air alongside them. It kept pace with them effortlessly, flying without flapping its wings, and they could all hear its high, constant squeal. And then it was gone – suddenly vanished as they reached the outskirts of town.

The teenagers were so shaken they went straight to the sheriff's office and reported the incident. They couldn't identify what they'd seen but thought it must have been some monstrous bird. A patrol car went back with them to the base, but there was nothing to be seen – only trees, empty buildings and shadows. One thing was odd, though: although police radios normally worked perfectly well on the base, tonight there was no signal, only a loud shriek.

The authorities are usually quick to suspect hoaxes, especially from teenagers, but they could see these four were genuinely frightened. The next day, the sheriff called a press conference to announce that something unidentifiable and possibly dangerous had been sighted in the area. Newspapers and radio stations were quick to pick up on the story and, inspired by the details of the wings, grey colour and huge eyes, dubbed the creature 'Mothman'.

There were repeated sightings over the next week as, night after night, curious members of the public thronged to the explosives base, along with journalists, scientists and paranormal investigation teams with varying degrees of expertise. Mostly, though, it was local people who had the encounters, and usually when they were not looking for them – like the Walmsley family, who were just leaving a friend's house when a dark figure rose up from behind their parked car. To them, the tall figure appeared headless, its red eyes set on the very top of its torso as it unfolded its huge wings.

A 17-year-old boy was chased in his car by a man-size winged creature. Two firemen saw what they described as a giant bird with red eyes. Five teenagers driving past a rock quarry caught an upright winged figure in their headlights – it was standing, not perching, and it stumbled off into the trees.

People most often described what they'd seen as a manlike winged creature or a bird with human limbs. Although the press had labelled it Mothman, it didn't strike those who encountered it as particularly mothlike. It didn't flutter its wings and there was nothing fragile about it. In fact, there was a brute power about the way it rose straight into the air and its rapid gliding flight. The most common reaction people had was terror – an overwhelming, unreasoning fear that they found hard to explain afterwards.

However, there was one interesting departure from this pattern. Just before 5 a.m. on 17 November, a music teacher was woken by her dog barking. She went downstairs and looked out of the window, where she saw a very large round object hovering about twenty feet up in the air, above the trees near the main road. It was glowing part red, part green, as if the colours were trying to resolve into a particular part of the spectrum. As she watched, the object moved in a sharp zigzag and vanished. The music teacher didn't know what to make of the experience and didn't tell anyone about it for several weeks, so it wasn't until later that she heard it had been on that same road, above which she'd seen the glowing orb, and just a few hours afterwards, that a boy had been chased in his car by something huge with wings.

A coincidence, or were the two phenomena related? Very much the latter, in the opinion of a man named John Keel, who now turned up in Point Pleasant. John Keel was a ufologist, who spent his time investigating UFOs – unidentified flying objects – suspected spacecraft, living creatures, lights, orbs; any strange activity in the skies. There was a large community of sky-watchers in the 1960s and hundreds of them converged on Point Pleasant that winter. Week after week people would be camping out at the explosives base, hoping to see Mothman. There were many theories about the true nature of Mothman, the most popular being that he was an extraterrestrial visiting earth.

Keel was well versed in ufology but experience had taught him to be sceptical. He arrived in Point Pleasant expecting to find nothing more unearthly than a giant bird. However, as he investigated, he quickly came across two other phenomena that were familiar to him – the glowing orb, and the dark-clad strangers.

Argentina

If the USA has Bigfoot, Argentina has downsized, or at least the little town of General Guemez has. Teenagers mucking around with their mobile phones caught the tiny creature crossing the road. It is small – people say knee high but it looks smaller – seems to be wearing a pointed hat and moves with a strange, stiff-legged motion, as if it does not have jointed knees. Many of the townspeople have seen it and over 90 per cent believe the sightings to be real.

Gnomes are nature spirits common to all cultures – Brazil, for example, records multiple sightings of Saci, a one-legged, pipe-smoking gnome with a red cap. Closely linked to the earth and minerals (which is why they are often represented as stone or concrete figurines), gnomes can move at will through the earth but are strangely clumsy in open air.

Mass sightings are rare, usually due to disturbance in the gnomes' earthbound habitat. In this case it may be down to increased mining for sulphur in the Las Casualidad mine, and uranium at Iruya, La Poma and San Carlos.

It was towards the end of winter, as the sightings of Mothman grew fewer, that the people of Point Pleasant began to report seeing the strangers. They were men wearing black cloaks, suits or coats. To some people, they appeared to have reddish-brown skin and slanting eyes. They often had questions to ask – directions, or the whereabouts of a local person – or something to sell, which also seemed to necessitate asking questions.

Keel immediately identified them as 'Men in Black'. These figures were the stuff of legend in ufology circles, as they had popped up after several UFO sightings, and were thought to be either government agents researching the sightings, or agents of the extraterrestrials themselves.

Once Keel put this together with the music teacher's orb, and with the appearance of another orb in March 1967, it seemed to him that Mothman must indeed be some kind of manifestation of nonhuman, non-earthly power. Especially when he heard the details of the second orb.

It appeared to a courting couple in their car one night, out on the explosives base. Tucked away in a discreet spot and happily absorbed in their activities, the couple were startled by a large ball of blue-white light that was suddenly hovering alongside the car. After a few seconds it vanished and the couple, dazzled and unnerved, straightened themselves up and drove as fast as they could into town. Arriving under the reassuringly mundane streetlamps, they were puzzled to discover that, though the whole episode seemed to have lasted just a few minutes, two hours had passed. Keel had come across this element of 'lost time' before, and it further suggested the involvement of metahuman forces.

Mothman disappeared from Point Pleasant around the end of March 1967 and Keel returned to his home in New York, making only occasional visits back to West Virginia. He was a busy man: the Mothman encounters had sparked interest all over the USA and 1967 was a bumper year for UFO sightings. Along with sightings came messages; Keel began to get letters and phone calls from people in widely scattered locations, all reporting that they had been visited by darkly dressed strangers and were now receiving regular communications from them. The strangers would usually reveal that they came from another planet and their messages were warnings or predictions, which often filled the humans with dread.

Keel gathered their information, treating the space-travel element with acute scepticism. Ironically, although he had become celebrated as a ufologist, he was less and less inclined to believe in visitors from other planets. He didn't doubt that something odd was happening – for all of that year his electronic equipment was going haywire, as if the electromagnetic fields were being continually disrupted – but he was coming to feel that the extraterrestrial explanation was wrong. It struck him as too glib; he suspected that in the rapidly modernising, space-infatuated 1960s, people were seizing on space travel and extraterrestrials as a convenient way of explaining the inexplicable.

Mothman: perhaps the best known liminal creature of the 20th century. Note the staring eyes and lack of neck. (Richard Svensson/Fortean Picture Library)

But what, then, was Mothman? And how seriously should he take the predictions? He was now being bombarded with reports of these. Sometimes he'd hear them 'directly' – people would call him and deliver prophecies in strange voices, as if they had become mediums. They ranged from the trivial – telling him where to look to find his watch – to the global, and, disturbingly, many of them ended up being at least partly fulfilled. For instance, several of the voices gave different versions of a warning about the pope. During early summer, the predictions began to correspond more closely, finally agreeing that the pope would go to the Middle East, where he would be assassinated, and that his death would be heralded by an earthquake. On 20 July the pope did announce an unexpected visit to Turkey; two days later, on 22 July, a terrible earthquake struck the country, killing more than 1,000. The pope's visit went ahead a few days later without incident, but the coincidence (if that's what it was) was profoundly shocking. Predictions continued to come in, often giving differing accounts of what was going to happen. Keel began to feel weighed down by a sense of dread and responsibility. He was being told things he felt he should pass on to the authorities, yet if he did, no one would be likely to believe him.

As the season turned from autumn to winter, two prophecies began to dominate. One was that there would be a nationwide power blackout in December, the other that a factory on the Ohio River would explode. Though the second prediction snagged Keel's attention because of its location – the Ohio River ran through West Virginia, near Point Pleasant – he was more concerned with the first, because he was hearing it more often, and because the consequences of a countrywide power failure would be catastrophic: cities would be plunged into darkness, air traffic control would fail; there would be fatal crashes, patients dying in hospitals, looting and murder.

Therefore he did not see it as especially significant when he heard that on 2 November, after months of quiet, a woman living near the explosives base in Point Pleasant had heard a loud squeal and looked out of her window to see a huge shadow on the grass. As she struggled to work out what was wrong with the shadow (it was midday, when shadows are at most a few inches), it seemed to solidify into the figure of a man, much bigger than an ordinary man, and all grey. It moved rapidly away, with an astonishingly fast gliding motion, into the trees. In the weeks since this incident, the woman had been having bad dreams about strange figures converging on the district near the river bridge.

The power-cut prophecies became more specific: several of them identified 15 December as the date, and warned that the blackout would come when President Johnson switched on the White House Christmas tree lights. That evening, John Keel followed the ceremony on TV. He sat tense as the switch was thrown, waiting for blackout, but the tree illuminated without a hitch. Just outside Point Pleasant, however, a tragedy was unfolding. In the rush hour, the 700-foot suspension bridge known as the Silver Bridge was crowded with cars. The traffic was heavier than usual because, besides the usual home-going rush, it included families who had been Christmas shopping. As more cars queued to file on to the bridge, those travelling across it were forced to slow. Suspended high above the water, drivers and their passengers felt the bridge judder and sway; then, horrifyingly, the main span buckled and split, and fifty vehicles went plummeting into the Ohio River. Bystanders rushed to help and rescue services were quick on the scene, but forty-six people died in the icy water.

The small town was shattered by the tragedy. For weeks, divers and rescue teams carried out the grim work of retrieving bodies. Some people who had gone missing that night were never found, and their relatives were told they must have been trapped underwater or swept away.

And Mothman? Immediately after the bridge collapsed, one family a few miles north saw a succession of large glowing lights rise into the sky above the old explosives base, hover, bobbing, just above the trees, and then move off towards the river. They didn't follow the movements attentively – they were too busy trying to find out what had happened. When they eventually looked to the skies again, the lights were gone. And so was Mothman. After the bridge disaster (which took place thirteen months to the day from Mothman's first appearance), the grey winged creature would not be seen in Point Pleasant again.

So what was the connection between Mothman and the disaster? John Keel was sure the two were entwined. Had the manifestations been intended as some kind of sign? Keel felt haunted by the bridge disaster, and by the fact that he'd been receiving garbled warnings about it. He was especially frustrated by that semi-true, obscure prediction of the explosion on the river. Putting that together with the false predictions of a power cut, he began to suspect he'd been given hoax warnings as a decoy, to distract his attention from where the tragedy was really going to happen.

In the 1970s, Keel wrote a book about it all, called *The Mothman Prophecies*.[2] Packed with witness accounts and digressions from other parts of Keel's paranormal career, it was a bestseller, and in 2002 was turned into a movie with Richard Gere. Which was pretty ironic, given that by then John Keel had more or less turned his back on investigating the paranormal, concluding that most paranormal happenings are a sort of spiritual white noise, a random teasing of us by nonhuman intelligences.

2 John A. Keel, *The Mothman Prophecies* (Tor Books, 2002; first published 1975)

You can sympathise with John Keel's disillusionment. But perhaps he was looking in the wrong direction for answers. In my opinion, he was led astray by the whole mid-twentieth-century UFO-hunting mindset. He might have been sceptical about green creatures whizzing round in flying saucers, but he was still thinking in terms of superhuman intelligences with something to teach us. And he tended to think they came from 'elsewhere'.

However, there is another way of looking at these events, one that requires you to set aside all ideas of space travel, aliens and assorted paraphernalia. And once you do this, another pattern emerges – one that connects the winged hybrids and the dark strangers, and even the orbs of light, with forces of the earth itself.

Consider the evidence. Mothman never tried to speak to the people who saw it, or interact with them in any way. All the encounters have the same flavour – the winged creature seemed intent simply on being. When observed, it would remove itself from human sight, quite often by flying. Sometimes it showed curiosity, as when it flew alongside the car, but it was a limited curiosity and always ended without contact.

Then add the fact that all the witnesses who saw Mothman experienced a particular kind of fear. This wasn't a physical fear for their own safety. It wasn't even panic. It was a profound, awestruck fear that they couldn't explain afterwards, but that Wordsworth and Kant would have recognised. It is the fear that awakes in people when they gaze at a mountain or stand on the shore of a deep lake – the terror humans experience when their imagination is overwhelmed by the power and mystery of existence itself. The philosophers and artists of the nineteenth century called it 'the sublime'.

And this is where the trail leads back into history, and much further back than the nineteenth century. Because Mothman and the winged/cloaked *brujas* of Mexico have much in common with other human–animal hybrids that have been recorded through the ages, ever since the first millennia of human activity.

Our Palaeolithic ancestors painted hybrids on the walls of their caves: creatures that were part human, part bison, bird, deer, goat or wolf. The Ancient Greeks told stories of unruly centaurs, half man half horse, and terrible winged birdwomen known as harpies, who were the harbingers of death. Then there was the famous minotaur

– half bull, half man – who hunted his victims to death in his underground labyrinth.

The Egyptians also recognised a hybrid bird-human that crossed the boundaries between the living world and the underworld. More benign than the harpies, Ba, the human-headed bird, was one of the eight immortal parts of the soul. In the daytime it flitted round the tomb, bringing food to the dead person; in the evenings it travelled with the sun god Ra on his celestial barge.

The Celtic underworld was ruled by the horned god Cernunnos, who was depicted as various forms of beast-human, most often a stag-man, but also with parts of serpent, bull and ram. Cernunnos could ascend into the world of the living to hunt people down, sweeping them back with him over death's threshold.

In shamanic religions – which still exist today and indeed are being rediscovered in Western societies – the shaman dresses up as a man-beast in order to enter a trance. Having put on the skin of his animal 'twin' (often a horned animal or a large bird of prey like an eagle or osprey), he doesn't merely mimic the animal but conjoins with its essence. A third being is created, at once animal and human, which can travel in the spirit world and cross the boundary between life and death.

You get the picture. Not only do these hybrids tend to combine similar physical features (wings, horns, human faces and/or limbs), but they share one key existential fact: they are all liminal beings, or creatures of the threshold. They belong in both life and death. They are a part of 'Deep Nature', if you like, where death, birth and life are endlessly recycling.

And they are very material. Their physical attributes are exact as well as bizarre. Look at the Palaeolithic hybrid painted in the French cave of Les Trois Frères: it has human calves and feet, hindquarters that seem to combine horse, lion and deer, and antlers, while its long head is at once staglike, manlike, and with the brow and direct gaze of an owl. The features shouldn't belong together yet they're utterly convincing. You could almost believe that the local people had seen such a being. Perhaps they came across it unexpectedly by the side of a track, or when they were hunting in the forest, going about their daily lives, just as those people in Point Pleasant and Mexico were doing when they saw the apparently impossible . . .

Brazil

Stories of ghosts and the paranormal wrap themselves around daily life in Brazil like creepers cover trees in the rain forest.

Deep in the interior, villages come under sustained paranormal – or UFO – attack. The forests are full of mysterious creatures: centaurs can carry you off to hell, mermen and mermaids infest the great rivers, and women in white, or possibly even the same woman in white, can be seen haunting jungle clearings and the vast barrios of Rio de Janeiro and São Paulo.

But if one thing sums up the spirit of this vast, diverse land, it is the carnival where all cultures meet in a riot of music, sound and dancing. A young British tourist attended carnival a few years ago and joined in the dancing. Soon he was surrounded by strangers wearing animal masks, butterfly wings, outrageous headgear . . . and a strange group dressed as zombies. He felt quite at home dancing with them – they didn't seem to move with the easy rhythm of the other carnival-goers and he was impressed by their costumes, which looked appropriately deathly, and the make-up, which had the real bloated appearance of rotting flesh. But did they really have to cover themselves in the smell of rotting meat, he wondered, and how did they see when their eyes had shrunk back into their heads – or seemed to be melting down their cheeks? Suddenly he realised. These were not costumes; he was dancing with the dead. He tried to run but they surrounded him. He tried to break away but they pulled him back. They closed in on him, the stench of death so thick he could barely breathe . . . and he blacked out.

He woke up in a cemetery on the edge of town. There was no trace of his supernatural abductors, just the sight of an old man patting down some earth that been recently disturbed. When he looked at his own fingernails, he saw they were filthy with grave dirt, as if he had been trying to follow the revellers back into their graves.

In the pre-Enlightenment past, people didn't reject what they couldn't understand. They were able to accept the idea that they had experienced things they had no way of explaining. Of course, they tried to fit them into their understanding of the world, but if they couldn't – well, they still recognised their power. They worshipped them as gods or gave them wary acknowledgement as denizens of the underworld. They marked their existence with symbols and contact with them was managed by rituals, usually performed by a spiritual leader.

Now, though, the world has moved away from the natural cycles. The two dominant religions of recent centuries, Christianity and Islam, are centralised and monotheistic and tend to cast these creatures as evil.

Search the Web for material on liminal creatures, for example, and you'll find commentaries identifying them as Lucifer's fallen angels, banished from the third heavens (where God lives) at the time of Lucifer's rebellion. According to the Bible's book of Revelation, they were then confined to the second heavens (the planets) and the first heavens (the earth and its upper atmosphere). Which would at least clear up the earthly-or-extraterrestrial debate about the Mothman sightings, because it would make them denizens (indeed prisoners) of both space and earth.

One theory popular among those who regard liminal creatures as evil is that they are currently manifesting more often and more randomly because we are entering the End Times. The fallen angels know the Second Coming is at hand, this argument goes, and that they will soon be cast into hell, so they are wreaking havoc on earth while they can. The collapse of the Silver Bridge certainly fits this apocalyptic vision.

And after the swine flu pandemic broke out in Mexico in 2009, some people began been looking back on the '*bruja*' hybrid sightings of 2004 and 2006 and wondering.

However, there are other places where hybrids have been appearing regularly in recent years and no disaster has yet ensued.

The Russian Almasty

In the Northern Caucasus, the small town of Elbrus is surrounded by woods and mountains. The undergrowth has claimed back many barns and farmsteads and, in these derelict places, the people of Elbrus see the almasty. Wild, apelike and covered with dark fur, the males shun human company, but the females have quite an appetite for human men. Elbrus is a farming community and the men are often out alone, sometimes spending nights camping. Several have awoken to see a female almasty close to them. She is usually large – six or seven feet tall – and covered with hair; she stands upright like a human but with curiously curved legs and very heavy breasts. Sometimes, as she approaches the man, she seems to transform into a beautiful, seductive being, and he finds himself submitting to her embrace and making love to her.

Adilgery Tilov is one of the most recent to encounter an almasty female. In 2008 he told *Pravda* newspaper that he had been asleep in a disused barn and had lit a fire just outside for warmth and to keep wild beasts away. Just before dawn he opened his eyes and saw a hairy, humanlike figure sitting by the fire. Tilov had grown up hearing his father's and grandfather's stories, so he recognised the almasty, but he was surprised by how small she was – only about a metre high. Her skin was black and her fur was matted and she was gazing intently at Tilov. Terrified, he slitted his eyes so she would think he was still asleep, and lay motionless. The almasty sat on, gazing, for about another ten minutes, then suddenly stood up and disappeared into the woods.

In their behaviour, the almasty bear more than a passing resemblance to a creature the ancient Mesopotamians knew and feared – the Lilutu. These were winged female demons with bird's feet and talons, beautiful but savage, who lived in deserts and wastelands. They would prey on travellers, bringing sickness and death to women and seducing men in erotic dreams.

The Mesopotamians also recorded their struggles with a similar female demon, the Lamashtu. This one killed women in childbirth, stole babies and brought disease. She was no seductress, though: with her hairy body, lioness's head, donkey's teeth and ears, long clawed hands and bird's talons, she was too terrifying.

This pattern of strong generic resemblances, yet differences in the detail of what each person sees, holds good for almost all sightings of liminal creatures. We try to fit them into our own experience and to find logical interpretations for the impossible thing confronting us. So the details vary, but there are some powerful constants running through the reports of sightings, even though they take place on different continents and may be separated by millennia.

For instance, many of these creatures are winged. And when they have no wings, they have strangely long arms or wide shoulders, suggestive of inhuman power.

Interestingly, you often find that at the same time as a winged creature starts appearing, some people in the neighbourhood will report seeing unfamiliar humans in cloaks or oddly draped clothes. They often report that people have broad shoulders or even a hunch. Could it be that these witnesses are seeing the same essential features as those who report seeing winged man-beasts, but their minds are reformatting them, adapting them into something less outrageous and more acceptable?

In T. S. Eliot's words: 'Humankind cannot bear very much reality.' So outspread wings become cloaks; folded wings are hunched shoulders; fur or hair-covered bodies transmute into dark skins. Yet, even in disguise, the truth about the creatures makes itself felt. For instance, many of the Point Pleasant townspeople who reported seeing strangers in cloaks or coats also added that their skin was reddish brown and they had bony features and slanting eyes. John Keel identified these as Asian characteristics, but in fact they point to a much more indigenous connection – Native Americans. One of the most powerful and widespread legends shared by different Native American peoples was that of the thunderbirds – huge birds or winged bird-man creatures with red eyes, whose appearance was considered an ill omen. Incidentally, in some tribes, including those of West Virginia, thunderbirds were also known as 'flying heads' because their heads and torsos seemed to be merged. The people who would later report seeing Mothman often faltered when trying to describe its head. 'Its eyes seemed to be set straight into its body,' they would say, or, 'It didn't seem to have an ordinary head.'

So the resemblances recur, patterns and similarities matching up suggestively, like DNA showing through.

And now, with new advances in analytical and imaging techniques, evidence of this DNA is beginning to sneak in by the scientific back door. An intriguing story emerged from Russia in 2004, when two scientific researchers scanned an old drawing of an almasty, made by a geologist in 1955. The geologist had been on an expedition in the Caucasus when he awoke one night, in pain from a leg injury, and saw a thickset human creature standing a few yards from his tent, with its arms braced on boulders. The creature vanished, but the geologist drew a picture of it, a vivid silhouette that showed powerful shoulders and arms, the classic pendulous breasts of the female almasty, and muscular legs. He sent it to the Russian society of cryptozoology, where it was filed in the archive. In 2004, as the society was transferring its records on to computer, two researchers scanned the drawing. To their surprise, many previously undetectable details showed up on screen. What had been simply a shaded outline on paper now emerged with a face, a loincloth, details of body hair and musculature. Concluding that what was logged as a drawing must in fact have been an indistinctly printed photograph, the researchers wrote to the geologist asking for the negative: they were excited at the prospect of magnifying it to reveal even more detail. The reply confounded them. The geologist said he had no negative because there had never been a photograph. The image he'd sent them had indeed been a drawing, a sketch he had done hurriedly, before his memory had faded. He'd put in no 'secret' details; the shaded silhouette was what he'd drawn because it was what he'd seen, and he couldn't understand how any new details could be appearing.

By the laws of known science, there is, of course, no ready explanation. But once you've tracked the appearances of liminal creatures elsewhere, you can't help but be struck by the persistent, ingenious ways that they continue to manifest their true natures, no matter how determined modern society seems to be to reject them. No wonder that in so many cultures (Greek, Roman, Norse, Celtic, to name but four) they've lent their shapes to trickster gods.

Since the Enlightenment of the eighteenth century ushered in the rationalist society, we have consigned such gods to literature or history. Yet curious and powerful figures have continued to roam our streets.

Just don't call her Bigfoot. The Almasty comes from Russia and beguiles men into thinking she's beautiful.

In Victorian Britain, for instance, while the Industrial Revolution was reshaping the country, Springheeled Jack leapt to notoriety in the popular press. First seen when he jumped a ten-foot-high cemetery wall and landed in the path of a Victorian businessman, this cloaked, red-eyed, clawed man terrorised suburban England in the mid-1800s. Often appearing as if out of nowhere, he could jump great heights, run at inhuman speeds, and would sometimes push or grab people, or else charge past them, knocking them to the ground. He tended to avoid the towns and was most often seen by women in quiet suburban areas, or on the very edge of settlements, where dwellings gave way to the countryside.

Then there is the antlered man who periodically walks the dark woods of Windsor Great Park. This royal hunting ground was once the heart of a forest that spread over three counties and many hundreds of square miles. A hybrid creature variously known as the stag man, the Huntsman or the antlered man has been seen by hundreds of people down the centuries – and at different epochs, different stories have swirled around him. Sometimes he stalks the ground on foot; at others he rides a black horse at the head of a baying pack of hounds. Elizabethan legends made him the ghost of the royal park's first keeper, wrongly hanged and out for vengeance. Others have seen him as the European metabeing Herne the Hunter, leader of the Wild Hunt, whose quarry is human souls; as an embodiment of Cernunnos himself, or as a portent of doom for the British royal family. Interestingly, though these IDs have all evidently grown out of different traditions, they share the central idea of the antlered man as a psychopomp, someone who will carry humans from life to death. It seems that whatever label is put on him, the denizen of Windsor Great Park is instinctively recognised as dwelling on the threshold between worlds.

Another noticeable coincidence is that sightings of the Huntsman – and indeed other liminal creatures – have tended to increase at periods of social change. Could it be that the weakening of the status quo sharpens people's vision so that amidst the upheaval they glimpse older, more elemental realities?

So with the Huntsman, for instance, you have an outbreak of sightings in the sixteenth-century, when England's religious, economic and political nature is being transformed; another at the time of the eighteenth-century Enlightenment; still more during the Industrial Revolution.

During the past fifty years, the antlered man has been more elusive, making his presence felt only twice. The first story, from 1962, sounds suspiciously folkloric, but let's tell it anyway. In 1962 some teenage boys were in Windsor Great Park, playing truant from school, when they found an old-fashioned huntsman's horn hanging from a tree. Several of them, who knew local legends about the Huntsman, wouldn't touch it, but the third took it off the branch and blew into it. At once they heard the sound of dogs baying and hooves thudding, distant but coming rapidly – impossibly rapidly – closer. The boys threw themselves flat and covered their eyes while the howls and crashes of the hunt burst over them. The noise was savage, and hoofbeats shook the ground. Afterwards they could never agree on how long it lasted or how close it had been, only that they were terrified and, once the sound faded, they all jumped up and ran for open ground. The terror and confusion sound more convincing than the other details, frankly – which is not to say that nothing happened. In fact, it suggests that whatever did happen was so inchoate and hard to grasp that the teenagers ended up reaching for a local legend to explain it.

Fourteen years later, in the mid-1970s, a soldier saw the antlered man, and this incident bears all the marks of a classic hybrid encounter. For Britain, the summer of 1976 was an intense one. The economy was nose-diving, punk rock was breaking out in pub back rooms and garages, and the country was in the grip of a fierce heatwave. Rivers and reservoirs dried up. Tarmac melted on roads and people cracked eggs on to the pavements to see if they'd fry. Strange beasts were sighted on land and sea (including a feathered man, of which more in a minute), and a Coldstream Guard on duty in Windsor Great Park was found unconscious, among trees and some way from his original guard post. When he came round, he said that, before passing out, he'd seen one of the park's ornamental statues come to life. As it did so, it sprouted horns from its head and, when it approached him, he thought it was wearing animal skins. The guard had no memory of what happened next and couldn't say how he had come to be deeper in the forest.

We might dismiss this story as the ramblings of a deluded squaddie, were it not for the fact that it has intriguing echoes of another incident – or rather, of a series of incidents – in which the antlered man, a stone carving and a mysterious stranger link up down the centuries. In 1856, when Windsor was a thriving town, dominated by the royal castle, two boys, William Butterworth and William Fenwick, were offered a lift by a man they didn't know, driving a horse and carriage. They were keen to ride in the carriage and, besides, there was something compelling about the stranger that made refusal impossible, so they climbed in. As the carriage went alongside the Home Park (the part of Windsor Great Park just north of the castle), the boys were both overcome with drowsiness and fell asleep. When they came to, they were no longer in the carriage but in the park itself, a long way from the gate they remembered passing on Park Street. Stumbling back into town, they found several hours had passed. Confused and frightened, they told the police, but as they'd come to no harm, and no one else had made any complaints against an unfamiliar coachman, it was taken no further.

More than seventy years later, in the early 1930s, the parish of Windsor decided to move its vicarage. The existing house, opposite the church on Windsor High Street, had been donated back in the fifteenth century by William Evingdon, then keeper of Windsor Great Park, and so there were many fittings and historical artefacts to be moved. One of them, discovered half buried in the cellar, was a stone head like a gargoyle; it had a stag's antlers but a man's face, with cold, commanding eyes. The local newspaper reported the find, along with various experts' ideas about what it might be. Some thought it might have come from the church, whereas others thought it more likely that it had belonged to William Evingdon and was a totem of the keeper's job and powers, with pagan associations like the Green Man. It was a small local story, not considered very important at a time when fascism was beginning to close in on Europe, and the head was placed in the garden of the new vicarage on Park Street. After the war it would be moved to the church museum, from where it vanished in the early 1960s, presumed stolen.

By this time both William Butterworth and William Fenwick had died. But William Fenwick had lived long enough to hear of the carved head in the 1930s, and some details of the find struck him. Park Street was the last place he and his friend remembered seeing before they fell asleep. There was the coincidence of the names – three Williams. He had never forgotten the stranger's face. And when he managed to get hold of a photograph of the stone head, he knew he was looking at it again.

Afghanistan

The special forces of the British Army are not known for their squeamish or superstitious disposition. They are practical, ruthless, focused and trained observers, which makes the following story all the more remarkable.

It was just after the invasion of Afghanistan in 2001. An SAS fighting group had been inserted into the country to keep watch on the main road linking the capital Kabul and the stronghold of the northern alliance in Mazar-e Sharif. There were rumours that a convoy of Taliban

fighters had eluded roadblocks and was aiming to escape the allies by cutting across the mountainous land to the east and escaping into the lawless Pakistan hill country on the other side of the border.

Reconnaissance is exacting work: the men had dug themselves into a position above the road and were quite capable of staying in position, without moving, for the next forty-eight or even sixty hours. One day passed, and then halfway through the second day, one of the men saw movement. It wasn't on the road but on the hillside above it, across the valley from where they lay. A shepherd? Dressed wrong. An enemy combatant? But why was it wearing jeans and wasn't there something wrong about its silhouette? The soldier dug his companion in the ribs and handed him the telescopic sight he was using. His friend took a look, went pale and retched. Face screwed up in consternation, he handed the telescopic sight back. His hand was trembling. When the soldier looked again, he understood why. The figure on the other side of the valley was dressed like an old hippy in sandals, jeans and a rough, local cotton shirt. The only problem was, he had no head and seemed to be floating above the rough ground as he moved slowly to and fro.

Later they heard from a local militiaman that the convoy had been intercepted up the road and the soldier asked if there were any legends attached to that particular area. 'Back in the 1960s it was notorious,' the militiaman said. 'A hippy had been hitching to Mazar-e Sharif and had made the mistake of going to sleep with the soles of his feet pointing to Mecca. A wandering tribesman, a fanatic, had found him, and had cut off his head and placed it on his feet. The ghost never understood why he had been murdered, and that's why he wanders that piece of ground, looking for an answer or looking for his head.'

In the same year the antlered man last appeared, two young girls in the little village of Mawnan in Cornwall saw an impossible creature hovering round the church tower. They had come from Preston, Lancashire with their family and were spending the weekend out in the Cornish countryside. The old church at Mawnan was built in 1231, a small, strong building of grey stone, dedicated to St Mawnan, a monk. The church is built on a pagan earthwork and sacred landscape cartologists have mapped a leyline running through the site. Woods cluster close behind the church while, in front of the tower, the land falls away to the Helston estuary, so that in fine weather the old stones are bathed in sunlight reflected from the sea in a conjunction of the four elements: fire, earth, air, water. However, on Easter Saturday 1976, 9-year-old Vicky Melling and her 11-year-old sister June had no thoughts of sacred landscapes or ancient sites of power: they were simply playing in the meadows near the church when they looked up and saw a huge feathered creature hovering over the church tower. Terrified, they ran to find their parents. Their father, Don Melling, couldn't make much sense of their description, and when June drew him a picture of a man with owl-like wings, head and legs, he was flummoxed. Realising that the girls were too afraid to enjoy playing out of doors any more, their parents packed up and returned to Lancashire, but not before Don had confided in local man Tony Shiels. Shiels was interested in the paranormal and was keen to speak to the girls, but Don refused to let him interview them, though he did hand over the drawing.

The Owlman was not the only strange occurrence in Cornwall that year. Since the previous autumn there had been a series of freak weather events – floods and sudden freezes, an unseasonal meteor shower, and, beginning soon after Owlman's appearance, a heatwave that was to last three months. Animals were behaving oddly: dolphins attacked swimmers; feral cats had converged on an isolated house, trapping its owner inside; a flock of birds had surrounded another, many of them battering themselves to death against its walls. People thought they'd seen big cats roaming wild on the moors, and the legendary *morgawr*, the Cornish sea serpent, was spotted off the coast. It was as though the energies were turbulent.

On 3 July, two 14-year-old girls, Sally Chapman and Barbara

Perry, were camping in the woods behind Mawnan church. It was dusk: shadows were gathering and colours taking on a blue tinge. At first they thought the figure standing among the trees was someone playing a practical joke – it appeared to be a man wearing a grey feathered bird costume, complete with owl's head and peculiarly glowing red eyes. Refusing to be scared, they rallied each other by jeering at it. At which it rose straight into the air, wings outspread but not flapping, and disappeared into the tree canopy. As it flew upwards, Sally and Barbara, who were now both screaming, saw that it had black talons for feet.

The next day Sally and Barbara went to find Shiels and told him what they'd seen. He asked them each to draw a picture, separately, and was interested to note that they registered slight but definite differences – they showed the wings differently, and Barbara gave the creature a prominent black mouth. (Police experience suggests that such minor discrepancies indicate truthfulness, as witnesses individually prioritise and interpret what they see.)

The creature appeared several times in the following weeks, sometimes to lone people, more often to pairs or groups. It would usually be seen standing quietly among the trees, and several people had the impression of a curious watchfulness. It had silver-grey feathers, a fierce owl's face with red eyes and tufted ears, but a human's mouth. Almost every witness noticed that its legs bent backwards like a bird's, and it had large black claws. Although it seemed to embody an elemental violence, it never attacked and, if confronted, would hurl itself back into the dimness of the woods.

Towards the end of August 1976, the heat faded from summer, and so, apparently, did the Owlman.[3] It did not vanish for ever, though: in 1978, a woman reported seeing 'a monster, like a devil' flying high up in the woods near Mawnan church. The same year, a great bird-like creature was seen flying over the River Helston. Meanwhile, Tony Shiels achieved a certain amount of fame as an Owlman commentator and never gave up hope of seeing the hybrid himself. In 1986, to the outrage of the press and the Bishop of Truro, he organised a ritual invocation in Mawnan church. Whether it had any effect is debatable; certainly nothing appeared immediately afterwards. But in 1989 a young couple walking in Mawnan

3 An account of the sightings is given in *The Owlman and Others* by Jonathan Downes (cfz, 1997).

woods at dusk were stricken with shock when their torchbeam lit up a figure standing silently on a branch above their heads. It was tall, its man's body grey-feathered, with wings half folded and strange, backwards-bending legs. As it saw them, it lifted its wings and half flew, half leapt backwards.

Since then, sightings have continued, though they are rare. In 1996 the local paper, the *Western Morning News*, received a letter from an American student describing how she had seen 'a monstrous man-bird "thing"' in the woods near Mawnan church. When it rose into the air and glided towards her, she was terrified and fled. More phlegmatically, one evening in 2001 a young man was relaxing in the churchyard when he realised he wasn't alone: a large, feathered shape had appeared and was resting, or roosting, over by the trees. Unable to see it clearly in the dusk, he tried to edge towards it, but as soon as he moved, it vanished.

Then there have been the lights. In 1996 (the same year the American saw her man-bird), a woman saw a ball of orange-red light floating over the church tower at night; as she watched, it faded away and reappeared a little further off. And late one night in 2003, two teenage girls who were sitting in their car chatting and listening to music, saw a miasma of light hovering above the church, pulsating gently.

Remember the Point Pleasant orbs? It is a curious fact, quietly noted by paranormal watchers, that wherever hybrids are seen, so – sooner or later – are orbs of light. Sometimes silvery-white, sometimes glowing with reds and greens, they hover, bob, drift, pulse – in fact, they behave like energy transmuting from one form to another.

Paraphysicists (scientists who apply their skills to the paranormal as well as to mainstream phenomena) have long been interested in orbs. As well as investigating them from the point of view of space travel and psychokinesis (some orbs seem to respond to human thoughts), they are also considering whether certain orbs indicate a liminal creature in the process of manifesting. Entities that could exist in two or more dimensions would by definition pass between different material forms. When we see these glowing lights, we might be observing a by-product of intense electromagnetic activity as they coalesce into their strange animal–human hybrid matter or resolve back out of it.

In Russia, the Caucasus is renowned as an area where such mysterious lights frequently appear. Centuries ago, people soothed their children with stories of an old woman who lived inside the mountain and who kept forgetting to shut her door, letting the light escape. In our technological age, people think nervously about secret military tests; indeed, since the turn of the millennium, so many orbs have been seen in the Caucasus that rumours now circulate of alien bases being established there. Several websites name-check Mount Elbrus as a place of intense orb activity; it also, of course, happens to be the home of the almasty.

Similarly in Mexico, balls of light are often seen over the hills of Monterrey, the region where the winged hybrid appeared, and where the UFO club captured its puzzling footage. The locals are so used to them that they often call them by their nickname – '*brujas*'. This, you'll recall, also means underworld witch or ghoul, and was the same word that leapt into the mind of Lieutenant Samaniego when he saw the clawed, cloaked creature fall from the tree.

Coincidence? Well it could be. But the name-sharing could also be a clue, language storing a connection that we have forgotten how to recognise.

Chile

Chupacabra, or goat-sucker, is a liminal or threshold creature that has the ability to kill in our world and then slip into another dimension. About four feet tall, it shares certain features with other liminal creatures, such as glowing red eyes and wings, but has characteristics all of its own, such as an insatiable taste for blood. Its attacks have also been verified by the international news agency Reuters and Chile's Ecology Department, a government agency, who have confirmed that its tracks do not match any earthly animal.

One unfortunate truck driver met one. Having swerved to avoid a dead animal in the middle of the road, he ran over some debris and got a puncture. It was too dark to see, so he decided to sleep in his truck and wait for dawn.

Halfway through the night he heard scratching on his cab door, opened the window and shone his torch down. There, trying to crawl up the side of his truck, was a strange creature with spines up its back and huge red eyes. He closed the window and lay down shivering on the seat. In the morning, when he plucked up courage to look outside, there were gouges scored deep into the metal of the door and strange tracks in the dust by the side of the road.

Sightings continue of these strange human-beasts – winged, horned, hoofed – with their peculiar mixture of characteristics varying from one individual to another, yet always carrying the same charge of overpowering physicality, of irrefutable being.

As already mentioned, they seem to appear at moments when society is in upheaval. Perhaps that's why there have been recent sightings in many different parts of the world. Globalisation and the Internet are bringing change to more places, at a faster rate, than ever before. We talk about the fabric of society being stretched. What if the fabric of matter itself becomes thinner, even tears, so that we have momentary glimpses of what we normally cannot see?

Then you get glimpses like these very recent ones.

When America was reeling from the 9/11 attacks and a new sense of insecurity, a hybrid with huge leathery wings and a horse's head and hoofs was seen in Jersey. The Jersey Devil had been sighted before, by Native Americans centuries ago, and by shocked European settlers in the eighteenth century. Now, at another time of trauma, a new generation of Jersey residents confronted the apparently impossible.

In Orlando, Florida, shortly before Hurricane Louise struck in 2004, a hybrid approached a man fishing in a lake. It walked upright on stork-like legs, with a thin body and inhuman head. Later, during the hurricane, a woman saw a slate-grey creature perched in a tree in her garden, unmoved by the battering of the storm. It had unwieldy arm-like wings, or wing-like arms, and was a curious blend of bird and human, with something reptilian about its features.

The year 2000 in Poland: a paramedic was cycling through a wood with his friend on the way home from a late shift at work, when a figure shaped like a man appeared, moving rapidly, just above the trees. It lay on its side with its face turned towards the young men. Its body was grey-coloured and something long, either hair or horns, streamed from its head.

And on YouTube you can see footage captured in Hamburg, Germany, 2006. A large, pale-winged creature apparently jumps off the top of a tall office building, falls without beating its wings, then glides away in mid-air . . .

CHAPTER THREE

POSSESSED

A New Look at the Ancient Foe

Thirty-six Chase Street, West Pittston looks like a good home. Built in 1896 and two storeys high, it stands gable-end to the road, with raised porches front and rear. Having bought it for $18,000 as a single house in 1972, John and Mary Smurl converted it into two apartments when their son and his family were washed out of their home in Wilkes Barr, Pennsylvania by Hurricane Agnes. It was a good arrangement: the families did most of the work themselves and then settled themselves in, the older generation, John and Mary, living in one half of the building, Jack and his wife Janet in the other with their two daughters, Dawn and Heather.

Jack worked as a neuropsychiatric technician, the girls went to the local high school and, if God blessed Jack and Janet, there would be more children on the way who would be brought up in the Roman Catholic faith like their parents and grandparents before them.

Like everyone starting a new life in an old home, they had a few problems with the property over the first eighteen months, but none of them proved to be long-standing or, as they thought, significant. A few creaks and groans were sorted out – nothing more serious – but then in January of 1974, a stain appeared on a brand-new carpet that they had laid in their brand-new home. No one owned up to it – the children indignantly denied all knowledge of it – and it proved to be stubborn, resisting the efforts of Jack and Janet plus a battery of cleaning products. Of course, these things happen, and the Smurls got on with their lives. Next, the television burst into flames. The Smurls commented on their bad luck but, in a new house with new wiring, perhaps something had gone wrong – a short circuit or a surge, for example. Certainly no one was linking the two events.

More teething pains followed – new pipework leaked, was resoldered and leaked again. By this stage, it was beginning to look as if the Smurls were unlucky: accidents that under normal circumstances might happen over a period of years had hit them over the space of a few months. The next event was altogether more disturbing. There might have been no immediate explanation as to why the pipes leaked or an indelible stain appeared, but when deep scratch marks were found on the walls, bath and wash basin, the Smurls had to ask the question: What in the world could have done that? It looked as if a wild beast had dug its claws in and left deep score marks in the surface, but what manner of beast could actually score porcelain or enamel? And where did it come from?

If the family was disturbed, it was not enough to make them actually do anything. When faced with the unusual, humans are programmed to come up with rational explanations (we can always find reasons for carpet stains or leaking pipes), but when faced with the truly impossible, we simply shrug our shoulders and get on with lives, because, after all, what else can we do? Our entire existence – from performing day-to-day chores to building a life of hopes and dreams – is based on being able to cope with what comes along. When something genuinely inexplicable happens, we would rather close our eyes than accept that much of the rational underpinning of our existence needs to be called into question.

So we can picture the Smurl family on a typical weekday night. Jack has come home from work, Janet has cooked, and the family has eaten. The kids have done their homework and gone up to bed. Lights go out, the house settles down; one by one they drop off to sleep.

Then Dawn, the older of the two girls, wakes up. Something is different in her room. Perhaps the temperature is not quite what she expected – it's a bit colder than she thought. Perhaps it is something as intangible as the arrangements of molecules around her bed. Whatever it is, she wakes up and sees a human figure at the foot of her bed. The first prickle of surprise jerks her awake with bright clarity, then the rational brain kicks in. It's Mum, Dad, Heather ... but no, it's the wrong height, the wrong shape ... it's wrong altogether. Is it a burglar? A cold rush of thoughts floods her mind. What's the best thing to do? Call out and hope to scare him away? No, suppose he comes at her. Stay still then, keep quiet. But what if he's not after her teenage jewellery or the few dollars in the sock drawer? Suppose he's really after her?

Terror builds. Her eyes open wider. She can't look away. It's as if she is hypnotised by the figure, by the strange, smooth way it moves around her room. Then her eyes are drawn to his feet, and in the dim light her mind is forced to accept the impossible. The thing in her room is not touching the floor. It is floating above it. She screws her eyes tight shut but the fear of the darkness is too strong and she forces them open to see . . . nothing.

The spectre has gone.

Ecuador

An Ecuadorian widow went to her priest in a state of acute distress.

She had woken in the middle of the night and had felt invisible hands caressing her. She felt powerless to resist and then, to make matters even worse, the ghost had started making love to her. Was this a sin, she wanted to know, especially as she was certain that it was her late husband's spirit.

The situation was not unknown to the priest: the husband had died in a state of sin and his spirit had become a gagone. *These are restless spirits whose behaviour is determined by the sin – in other words, her husband had probably been adulterous. She had to do three things: one, she had to confess because* gagones *were only visible to the pure of heart; two, she had to draw a cross on his forehead with soot to render him visible; three, she had to hold him to her until daylight.*

She confessed, was shriven and went to bed. In the early hours of the morning her husband came into her bed and started caressing her. Carefully, so as not to alarm him, she reached to the side of the bed where she had

hidden a bowl of soot, dipped her finger in it and drew the cross on his forehead. Instantly he was visible and started to writhe. She held on for hours as he struggled to escape then, at the first light, he quietened. As the room grew lighter, he grew less and less substantial and, as the first rays of the sun entered her bedroom, he disappeared completely.

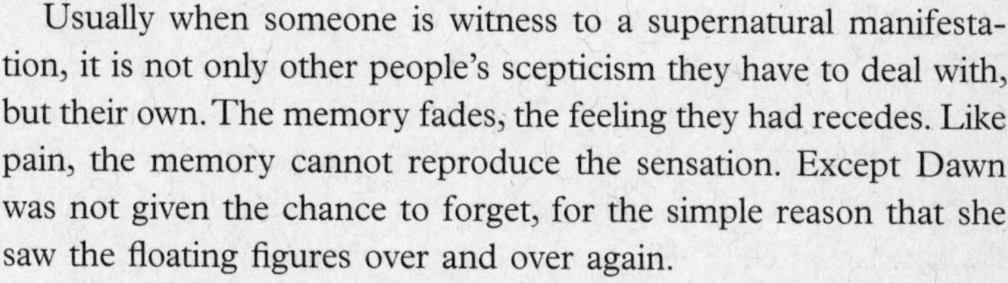

Usually when someone is witness to a supernatural manifestation, it is not only other people's scepticism they have to deal with, but their own. The memory fades, the feeling they had recedes. Like pain, the memory cannot reproduce the sensation. Except Dawn was not given the chance to forget, for the simple reason that she saw the floating figures over and over again.

The Smurl family was, and is, staunch in its Roman Catholic faith. It's possible that Catholicism, with its panoply of saints and its strong emphasis on spiritual intervention, better prepares its followers for the supernatural than other religions, or maybe their faith provided the necessary armour to allow them to deal confidently with the dawning knowledge that they were not alone in their home. Over the next two years they logged a number of phenomena normally filed under the heading 'unexplained', but which they were brave enough to recognise as supernatural in origin: toilets flushed when no one was near them, footsteps rushed up and down stairs, unplugged radios would switch themselves on and blare out noise, and rocking chairs not only rocked, but creaked with the weight of an unknown sitter.

What could they do?

The answer is: not much. As long as the happenings were harmless, life in the Smurl household could carry on pretty much as normal – so much so that the family now numbered six, with the arrival of girl twins, Shannon and Carin, in 1980. Hindsight, as they say, gives 20/20 vision, and with hindsight it is clear that everything that happened up until this point was just a prelude – an exploratory period maybe when the various inhabitants of the house explored coexistence. The only problem was that the unseen members of the household were starting to get more intrusive. You can divide the Smurl's experiences into two distinct phases. The first was noninvasive; the second reveals a growing will to disrupt, disturb and ultimately to destroy.

If the first wave of occurrences concentrated in the main on the Smurls' house, the second wave was focused for the most part on the home. When we think of a good home, we automatically associate it with various qualities: warmth, comfort, peace and a measure of privacy. In the Smurls' case, this was underpinned by a faithful and faith-based marriage. All these qualities now began to be stripped away from the family, first with stealth and then with an extraordinary and mounting savagery.

To give some idea of the timescale, the occurrences started to become intrusive in about 1977 and built slowly through the end of the 1970s and into the mid-1980s. The temperature would drop inexplicably so that the entire home suddenly became icy cold. Then the smells started. Smell is one of the signatures of a house – it is no coincidence that real-estate agents urge prospective sellers to make their house 'smell welcoming' to help possible buyers imagine themselves living there. If the smell of your house changes, it is as if you are being pushed out and someone, or something else, is taking over. In the case of 36 Chase Street, this phenomenon could not have been clearer. A sour and sickening stench started to drift through the rooms, lingering no matter what the family did.

Then someone or something began to manifest itself more aggressively to Jack and Janet in their own home, and John and Mary next door.

While she was in the basement doing her laundry, Janet heard her name being called. She answered and was called again. Worried that someone needed her, she left the laundry and searched the house, only to find that she was alone.

Then one evening Jack's parents were dismayed to hear loud and obscene language bellowing through the walls that separated the houses. Jack's family are not people who swear, and his parents were rightly concerned to find out what had happened to have prompted such an outburst. But when they approached Jack, he said it could not have been them. They were in but they were definitely not arguing and certainly not swearing. Neighbours heard arguments as well, and assumed the Smurls were going through a rough patch. They were, but not in the way the neighbours assumed. And anyway, on many of the occasions the sounds were heard, the Smurls were out.

But the most worrying events concerned Jack and Janet.

While standing in the kitchen, Jack felt an invisible hand reach through his trousers and caress his genitals. It's possible that some men might have been excited or even aroused by an event such as this. For a devout Catholic, however, it was an assault not just on his person but on his marriage, and by extension on his God, who had sanctified his union.

Two days after Janet had heard her name being called, she was working the kitchen when the temperature suddenly dropped. She shivered in the icy cold, but this was by no means a new phenomenon and she knew it would pass. However, she was not prepared for what happened next. A faceless, black human shape suddenly materialised in front of her. Terrified, she stared as the figure hovered in the air, before passing slowly through the wall that separated her kitchen from her mother-in-law's. Conquering her fear, and frightened for her mother-in-law, she ran round to the other apartment. Yes, Mary had seen it too. No, she didn't know what do to. What could a person do?

Life had to go on, but it was as if the faceless figure in the kitchen were a herald for a series of events that grew in intensity and danger. Heather had now turned 13, and one landmark the family had been looking forward to for months was her confirmation. The confirmation of Heather's acceptance into the Church passed happily and uneventfully. But when they returned to the house, near-disaster: her younger sister Shannon was passing under a ceiling fan when it detached itself from its fittings and crashed to the floor, missing her by inches.

The violence then escalated at an astonishing rate. Shannon was lifted from her bed and thrown down a flight of stairs, Jack and Heather were lifted and dropped and the family dog, an Alsatian, was repeatedly picked up and thrown down. These were events of a different order from what had gone before, but soon things were to get even worse.

Jack and Janet Smurl are a loving couple, and throughout their ordeal had managed to keep their love life alive. In a sense it was their pledge to each other that, come what may, their souls and bodies were their own and each other's. What happened next showed all too clearly just how destructive the entity in their home was, and where it was going to focus its energies.

It was night and Jack and Janet had just made love when they noticed a terrible stench in the bedroom. They had experienced such smells before, but this one was different. The smell was vile, strong and thick, so strong and thick that it was literally acting like a pressure on Jack's chest and blocking his throat so he could not move. But this was nothing compared to what happened to Janet. Struggling and crying, she was yanked from the bed and dumped on the floor. Only then did the smell disperse and Jack was free to stand up and comfort his wife.

Over the next few days the scraping and scrabbling inside the walls went on unrelentingly and neighbours were treated to the screams and shouts and groans coming from the house, noticeably when the Smurls were out.

It was now January 1986 and the family accepted that it was time to take action. Demonologists were called in and they brought with them a nurse and psychic. Between them, they identified four separate entities within the house: three were minor spirits – ghosts in common parlance, and the fourth was a demon.

But their investigations were frustrating.

The house itself provided no leads, there was no evidence of prior supernatural activity and the Smurls themselves, devout Catholics all, had certainly not been calling on spirits to visit them, nor summoning demons. The next step was to try and draw the demon out. After prayers were said and holy water sprinkled, Jack saw two women in colonial-era clothing standing in the room. Then the mirror shook and a voice called out: 'Leave me alone, you filthy bastard.' In other words, they got a response but no result.

And if they thought things had been bad before, they now became horrendous.

As if sensing a challenge, or perhaps even drawing energy from it, the demon now made an all-out assault. Although its attacks had been clearly concentrated on family life before, now it focused its attentions on the keystone of the Smurl household, Jack and Janet's marriage.

Once again, it chose the bedroom as its playground, but this time it left the children alone and went for the parents.

It is a hot summer night, the temperature up in the 80s and the

Smurls' bedroom feels airless. Both Jack and Janet are restless and, as she often does, Janet goes downstairs to sleep on a couch in the sitting room. Eventually Jack drops off in a restless, summer sleep.

Suddenly Jack wakes with a sudden jolt – he didn't even realise he was asleep but knows he must have been because he is confused and for a brief moment, panic-stricken. Where is he? Why is he on his own? Why are the sheets all twisted like this?

Gradually he comes to his senses. He's in his bedroom. The sheets are twisted because he's kicked them off in the heat. He's alone because Janet is sleeping downstairs – she often does when the nights get hot.

He takes a breath, looks around and sees a figure in the corner. No, there she is. She must have decided to come back up after all.

She moves towards him out of the darkness and then Jack realises that it is not Janet. It is a woman but she is naked, and there is something odd about her face. She moves closer and now he sees more clearly. Her paper-white skin is covered in scales, although dark sores that ooze pus have broken through in places. Her hair is wild, white and straggly, her gums so rotten that the broken, putrefying flesh has turned green, and her few teeth are long and yellow.

His cry of terror dies in his throat. He is petrified and, as she glides closer and closer to the bed, he notices something even stranger: although she has the face of a hag, her body has the firm, fleshy contours of a young woman and it is this body that straddles him as he lies helpless on the bed, and it is this flesh that arouses him so that as she lowers herself on to him, he enters her.

She moves, slowly at first, then faster. Still paralysed, he feels his body respond even as he is transfixed by the horror of her face. Her lips move, pulling back from the long teeth. Is she smiling – no, it is something more. Her mouth opens in a rictus of ecstasy and he realises that she is working herself to orgasm. Her body moves faster, faster, then it is jerking and spasming. He tries to look away, to get away but he is still helpless, then . . .

She is gone, vanished into thin air. Jack lies still , too shocked to move, too horrified to react. His genitals are rubbed raw, although the intercourse only lasted a few, awful minutes. Even worse, when the demon came, it released a sticky substance, the equivalent of semen, over his genitals and body. It stinks, and he staggers to the shower, where he stands under the jet of water to rid himself of the stench.

Philippines

Over the years, Japanese, Spanish and Americans have invaded and colonised the Philippines. The brutality of their behaviour finds an echo in the Ghost of Balete Drive, where a woman, brutally raped and then murdered, wanders the road.

Drivers are urged not to pick up lone women dressed in white seen wandering down the road at night. If they catch sight of her face in the rear-view mirror of the car, the horror of her injuries will make them swerve off the road? Who is she? It seems she is a sort of universal victim, first of the Spanish invaders, then of the Japanese, and lastly of the Americans. If anyone does talk to her, she will tell them of her lost love, now long dead, while she is condemned to walk the road on her own.

Unwary visitors should watch out for the horrible manananggal. *It can look like an attractive man or woman, but at night it splits in half and the top half goes in search of victims – it loves to suck out human innards. If you ever find the bottom half of a* mananangaal, *do the world a favour and pour ashes, salt or vinegar down it. It's the only way to kill it.*

The Smurls decided that it was time to get the Church involved. They contacted officials at the diocese of Scranton, but all they received was an offer of help with no immediate action, so they turned to the demonologists for help again. They recommended a traditionalist priest who ignored the Vatican Two rulings and insisted on conducting services in Latin. However, his exorcism failed and, once again, the powers in the house grew in strength, with a demon that retaliated with an attempted rape on their daughter Dawn, and slashed and bit Janet and Mary on the arms. More worryingly, it seemed to be winning. Worn down by years of attacks and made to feel hopeless by the way the demon, or demons, seemed to feed off their attempts to control it, the Smurls were psychically exhausted. If they were to avoid full-scale possession, they had to attempt another exorcism. This had exactly the same effect as the first – the attacks became stronger. Jack was molested by the demon at work and, when he and Janet attempted to take the family away on a camping trip, the demon followed them there as well. They gave an interview to a television station and that made things worse still.

The Smurls had heard the sound of grunting before but had never seen the pig. Not even the Gadarene swine, the herd of pigs into which Jesus sent the madman's demons, could have looked like the creature that Jack encountered when he was reading quietly in his sitting room.

He heard the footsteps first, but that was nothing new, so he hardly bothered to look up from his book, but as they got closer and closer, he felt he had to.

And was pinned back in his chair by the horror. A pig? A pig that walked towards him on two legs? What did he take in first? The questing snout, the small, dark eyes, the yellow dripping fangs, rough, flaking, bare pink skin, short, stubby arms that ended in blunt trotters? Or was it the final obscenity: below the upper body of the pig, with its barrel chest and rows of dugs, were the legs and sexual organs of a woman.

He rose and tried to run. The pig knocked him down and then kicked him over. He lay on his back as the pig straddled him, then squatted over him. The snout drew closer to his face so he could feel its cold, fetid breath. He felt the pressure of the body as it lowered itself on to his crotch and slowly, very slowly, began to rub him up and down.

No, he thought. This can't be happening! But it was. It was as if his body remembered the last rape and, in remembering, responded. He felt blood rush into his member as it stiffened. Then he understood the true horror of his situation was worse even than being raped; he now realised that his body was not his. It was controlled by this monster. The reality was too much for him to bear and he passed out.

When he came to, he was sore and stank of pig. Like the last time, he could only stagger to the shower and try to wash the foulness away. He was close to breaking point.

A demon, probably a succubus. Once objects of terror, you can now find spells to summon them on the web. (Fortean Picture Library)

As if it had taken on a new lease of life, the house was now filled with the sound of the demon's harsh grunting. Press attention grew. Tourists had their photographs taken at the Smurl house and finally the official Roman Catholic diocese agreed to perform an exorcism at the house at an unspecified time in the future.

By then, however, the Smurls had identified two of the minor spirits – a man who had been mob-lynched after killing his wife and her lover, and an old woman called Abigail – but the main demon remained shrouded in mystery. The traditional exorcist performed a third exorcism. As before, it had the effects of drawing the demon out but not expelling it. The shadowy figure that had first appeared to Janet in the kitchen now appeared to Jack and beckoned him.

Jack knew that there were four stages of possession and that he had been through three of them. Initial manifestations are followed by infestation which is followed in turn by oppression. The purpose of oppression is to weaken the subject so much that the demon can initiate the fourth and final phase: total possession of mind, body and spirit. So Jack understood all too well what the demon was doing. It was saying: we've won, come and join us.

Perhaps Jack Smurl knew that he was too exhausted at this stage to resist a full-scale assault, and so did the only thing he could. He gave his house over to the Church for a full exorcism and left, taking his family with him.

This time, the exorcism worked. Today the house on Chase Street is quiet and the Smurl family has been left in peace, but the big questions remain: what happened, and why them?

Before we go any further, we need to understand the nature of the enemy and try to pin down exactly what a demon is.

Christianity is clear on the subject. When Satan was cast out of heaven by God, following his failed rebellion, a number of angels were expelled with him and sent into the pit of hell. There they sat and festered and plotted the downfall of mankind, God's new favourites. This is the crucial point of the Christian version: demons hate us. The second point is less easy to explore but it seems self-evident: demons are fascinated by flesh and horribly attracted to it. All through the Christian era, demons have been associated with sexual urges, from St Antony being tempted in the desert with sins of the flesh to the sexual panic surrounding the witchcraft trials from the medieval period onwards. What distinguished the devil and demons and made their possession so real was the sexual interest they showed in humans.

So there would seem to be a clear motive for demons to attack Christians, and matters would be much simpler if they concentrated their attacks on the religious cult that showed particular animosity towards them. Unfortunately, the situation is more complex than that. Supernatural beings that perform aggressive sexual attacks certainly do not limit their activities to any particular group, cult or denomination.

One of the best-known victims of a sexual attack was not a practising Christian and at no point did she invite representatives of any church to intervene to help her. Instead, she looked for help from more contemporary sources: counselling, a neuroscientist, photographers and psychic investigators who took a scientific approach to the problem. The case formed the basis of a successful film and novel, both called *The Entity*, both of which made no bones about being a fictionalised account of the true story. This is harder to pin down: no one is even sure what the name of the real victim was, or even if she is still alive. Some say her real name is Carlotta Moran (the name used in the film as Carla Moran), but Dr Barry Taff, who investigated the case in the first instance, calls her Doris Bither.

Doris's circumstances were very different from those of the Smurls. She was a single mother who lived with her four children in a condemned house in Culver City, California. So where the Smurls were comfortably off, she was struggling financially. Where they were Mr and Mrs Average, with an orderly way of life, she was emotional and inclined to drink, both for pleasure and comfort. Which she needed more than ever after she began to be physically pushed and attacked by forces that started off as invisible presences, but then began to take the shape of men. Her children could see them too and one was so familiar that they even had a name for him: Taff reports this as Mr Whose-It, but surely this is a misinterpretation of Mr Who's It? Whatever the case, he was large, well over six foot tall and semi-solid. As well as him, there were two other entities described as evil-looking. These two had been fighting each other on one occasion and had knocked one of the sons out of the way when they passed in the corridor. But this was nothing compared to what they did to Doris.

She was in her bed when she became aware of other people in the room. Anyone with children will tell you that a parent's bedroom is irresistible to children, so Doris was not too alarmed at first to see the small figures at the bottom of her bed. She grew worried when one grabbed her ankles and pulled her legs apart, and she started to scream and struggle when the other grabbed her by the wrists and pressed her back into the mattress. But her torment had only just begun. There was a third entity in the room, and this one raped her.

It did not just happen once but on many occasions. Doris was battered and bruised by the violation; on one occasion, her 13-year-old son was thrown across the room when he tried to intervene, breaking his arm. He saw her being physically pressed down into her mattress so she left an indentation in it by . . . something.

What could Doris do? She felt trapped: she was worried the police would dismiss her as a fantasist; if she went to hospital, there would be more questions and the possibility of incurring expenses she could not afford. So she did nothing – she just suffered the abuse from the entities in exactly the same way she had suffered abuse earlier in life at the hands of humans.

Until one day she was browsing in a bookshop for a book that might throw light on her predicament and she heard two men talking about ghosts. She approached them shyly and told them that they might be interested in her house. It was haunted, the ghost was violent and, above all, she wanted help.

One of the men was Kerry Gaynor, associate to the paranormal investigator Barry Taff, and he arranged a visit. Unsurprisingly, nothing happened.

Although they did not let on, when Doris first told them about the attacks, they were disbelieving. As paranormal investigators, they were more conscious than most of how important it is to nail down experiences and sightings with hard evidence. Here, they thought they might be dealing with a fantasist and that all parties would be better off if they put her in touch with professional therapists. In fact, the only thing that stopped them was the thought of their embarrassment as they tried to explain the case to a professional. What brought them round to Doris's house a second time was a phone call from her when she told them something she'd forgotten: the entities did not only appear to her and her children. Five people at least had seen them. If Barry and Kerry came round again, they would be sure to see something.

In fact, this time they saw, smelled and felt quite a lot.

The first thing that struck them was the stink. They had not picked up on this before, but realised it occurred in clearly defined 'stench spots'.

The second thing was the temperature, which was noticeably lower in Doris's bedroom than in the rest of the house – and this was in summer in a house without air conditioning.

The third thing was a sense of pressure on the inner ear – rather like the feeling of diving into deep water. Experience taught both of them that this could be a sign of a poltergeist haunting.

Fourthly, their Polaroid – a camera that developed pictures there and then – kept on picking up anomalies. These varied from orbs to mysterious fogs to bleaching. Doris had invited a psychic to meet Kerry and Barry and they photographed her when she said she felt a presence. On each occasion, the photograph was heavily fogged, as if the Polaroid had picked up an energy field.

It was certainly enough to bring them back and over the weeks that followed, they introduced into the house photographers, students and psychiatrists, including the head of UCLA's Neuropsychiatric

Institute. All witnessed extraordinary phenomena, from stenches so strong that people vomited, to three-dimensional floating lights which on one occasion coalesced into a faceless human torso. The lights showed intelligence – flashing yes or no in prearranged patterns and even hovering over words on a board.

Unlike in the case of the Smurls, where the demonic activity intensified after exorcisms, and became more focused on Jack, here the investigators' arrival seemed to afford Doris some protection. It was as if the demon became distracted by them, and determined to put on a show. Doris remained central to the phenomena: the investigators noted that her mood affected the intensity of the occurrences. When she drank and became emotional, abusing the demon (and she had a lot to abuse it about), the lights and smells would be at their most spectacular, whereas on several occasions when she was not there, all the investigators had to report were mild temperature swings and the odd lingering smell. But there were no more rapes; Doris became calmer, and her sense of the demon's physical presence gradually tailed off.

Doris/Carla eventually vanishes from investigators' records, after having moved house. Did she manage to stay free of her demon? We can't know, but it's clear that the interplay between demon, victim and investigator/exorcist is a complex one.

Take the case reported in Sacramento, where a woman invited exorcists to expel a spirit from her favourite doll. Although they succeeded, the spirit grew so angry that it attacked the woman, throwing her down to the ground and raping her. Disturbingly, the woman seems to have come to an accommodation with the spirit because when another exorcist offered to help, she refused. Perhaps she was worried that another botched exorcism would make the situation even worse?

Germany

A housewife from Germany experienced a full-scale seduction from an incubus, which made its move on her when she was married. It started with small caresses while she was watching television, then moved on to visiting her

when her husband was away on business trips, lifting the blankets, getting into bed beside her, getting her aroused before moving her on to her back and penetrating her. The incubus grew bolder, making love to her around the house in broad daylight, even taking her when she was gardening out in the open. While she felt some moral worries about this (she was not sure if making love to a ghost constituted infidelity), she was so enraptured by this creature and the sex was so powerful that she let things carry on until the day her husband had a near fatal accident in his car – just as he was turning into the road by their house, he saw a figure appear in front of him. His first instinct was to swerve away from it – straight into the path of bus, which fortunately managed to avoid him. Worse was to come – he was nearly electrocuted by a kettle and a house tile slipped from the roof just as he was walking past. If it had hit him, it could have cut his head off.

Alarmed, the woman confessed what had been going on. Her husband, to her dismay, started divorce proceedings and the incubus left her, never to be felt again.

Anna Nicole Smith, the tragically flawed pin-up girl who fought with psychological demons all her life, had sexual encounters with a spirit in the days before she became famous. She woke up believing her boyfriend was making love to her, only to discover that he was not even in the bed but a supernatural entity was. 'A ghost would crawl up my leg and have sex with me at an apartment a long time ago in Texas. I used to think it was my boyfriend, then one day I woke up and found that it wasn't.' Although she was scared at first, she then realised that she was finding the experience so enjoyable that she didn't want it to stop, she told *FHM* magazine. 'He never hurt me and he just gave me amazing sex, so I have no problem.'

One psychic investigator claims that these encounters are almost commonplace in graveyards and one of her colleagues says that a ghost actually fellated him during a funeral in New Orleans, while plenty of other psychics talk of being stimulated while giving ghost tours.

Clearly, it is a rich area for investigation.

Going back in history, we can see that there has always been this uncomfortable, highly transgressive element to natural/supernatural relationships. The earliest written record concerns a Sumerian demon god called Lillu who made love to women while they slept. He has rather fallen by the wayside, but his female equivalent, Lilitu, who lavished her charms on men, has gone from strength to strength, adapting to each new era and turning up in new cultural clothing. First, she changed her name to Lilith and gained notoriety as the supernatural prostitute of the god Ishtar. Later, she evolved into a barren, aggressively sexual nightmare figure, who left men drained and weakened. She is found again in Jewish mythology, as Adam's seducer after he separates from Eve, leaves the Garden of Eden and wanders the world on his own.

In an alternative, folkish spin on Genesis, written in or around the sixth century CE, she is Adam's self-assertive and sexually adventurous first wife, who sprouts wings and flies off in a high dudgeon when he insists that they make love in the missionary position. Eve, presumably, was more accommodating. She is rediscovered and re-eroticised by the Pre-Raphaelite Brotherhood, a British artistic movement whose members achieved near superstar status in high Victorian times. Her eroticism combined with her edge of danger made her a perfect sexual dream partner in an era driven to sexual frenzy by repression, yet terrified of sexually transmitted diseases. Today, of course, she is a central figure in ceremonial sex magic ('Her lips are as red as the rose, kissing the universe. She is the irresistible fulfiller of lust, seer of desire!'), and in contemporary Luciferianism and Wicca. Google Lilith and you will see all the evidence you need that her spirit is alive and well in the modern world.

While Lilitu/Lilith is undoubtedly the mother of all sex demons, the father was the demon Asmodeus, whom we find mentioned in the Book of Tobit, one of the books of the apocryphal Old Testament. Believed to be particularly potent in November, he fell in love with Sarah, daughter of Raguel, killing each of her seven husbands before they could sleep with her. Only the last, Tobias, was able to escape this dreadful fate. The archangel Raphael advised him to place a fish liver on hot coals, and the smell so disgusted Asmodeus that he fled to Egypt, where Raphael dealt with him.

While it is not stated in the story, we get a strong impression that Asmodeus's jealous rage was heightened by the fact that he could not sleep with Sarah himself and, if he couldn't, he would not allow anyone else to either. His relationship with Solomon the Great suggests he is more like a frat party friend than a partner in crime, egging the king on to greater indulgence but only able to enjoy it vicariously.

However, if Jewish records remain sketchy, Christian records more than make up for this with the medieval church recording ever-increasing levels of intercourse between humans and demons, both female and male: succubi and incubi respectively. It was their practice to seduce men and women while they slept. St Augustine argued that since they could not conceive, they could have no desire or lust as such – only a desire to lead humans into harm's way; that did not stop sex with demons – or with the devil himself – developing into a pan-European obsession. Thomas Aquinas delved even more deeply into the subject. Since the devil was not human, he argued, he could not produce human semen. If he wanted to people the world with his hell-spawn, he would have to transform himself into a woman, seduce a man, keep the semen in his vagina, transform himself into a man and impregnate the woman with the semen. By holding on to the semen, something of the devil's spirit would have transferred to it, so the offspring would be his half-children, at least. This explains the obsessive desire of witch hunters to find out if men and women had had full, penetrative sex with the devil. It was not just a question of saving their souls; it was a question of saving the world from being overrun with Satan's offspring.

Not that the experience was necessarily fun. Witch finders and devil hunters compiled volumes of first-hand accounts of what sex with the devil was like, and predictably found out that it was not very nice. As well as having to perform the 'abominable kiss', that is, on his anus, the devil's member was 'scaley and causes pain . . . his semen is extremely cold'. But that didn't stop people wanting more. Another seventeenth-century researcher into the subject, Sister Madelaine de Demandolx, identified a pattern to such events that went: copulation on Sunday with incubi and succubi; sodomy on Thursdays; bestiality on Saturdays; Mondays, Tuesdays, Wednesdays, Fridays – anything you wanted. Mind you, that was just one Saint's view. Father Sinistari, writing in the seventeenth century, thought that sexual intercourse with an incubus 'does not degrade, but rather dignifies' – because demons were fallen angels and so retained a vestige of grace.

All through history and up into the modern times, the devil has been spurred on by the feeling that, however hard he tries, he is less potent than God, who had, after all, effortlessly impregnated the Virgin Mary through the Holy Ghost – no complicated gender switches for Him. The example of the Virgin Mary is of course emblematic of the Christian Church's teaching that the only tolerable spiritual contact is with God – everything else is dangerous. Thus saints, as they fasted in the desert, were beset with seductive demons to tempt them from the only supernatural power they were permitted to have congress with. In fiction, this split is powerfully represented in the vampire myth: sexually potent demons will condemn you to eternal damnation. Only the power of the cross will save you.

It's been worthwhile looking into the early relations between devils and humans because it throws such an interesting light on what is happening today. On message boards throughout the world, people are asking the question: is it permissible to have sex with demons?

Let's look at some examples.

A girl wakes up in her bedroom when a weird feeling prompts her to open her eyes. There is a man at the end of her bed but he is not a normal man. He is floating and she can see through him but instead of feeling scared she feels relaxed and happy. He pins her down and starts to touch her. She does not struggle and he takes off her pyjamas. She feels him enter her, blacks out and, when she wakes up, he is gone.

Internet reaction is mixed. Allegations that this is a classic date-rape scenario are angrily rebuffed by the writer and, after that, the majority of contributors to the thread suggest that the writer must be very careful in future. Everything from prayers and wearing a cross to watching comedy films last thing at night are suggested, but there are dissenting voices, with some people telling her to embrace her experience and judge her night-visitor lover as she would judge a human – in other words, go along with him if it works for her, send him away if it doesn't.

Another case: a man has been reading the threads about incubi and succubi and writes in to confess that, when he was seventeen, he was raped by a demon that manifested as a grey cloud. He wants to know if there are other people out there who have experienced the same thing. He discovers that he is not alone. Loads of respondents have been raped, some while wearing clothes, others in bed. All confess to feeling a deep sense of shame that has stopped them sharing the humiliation with others. Another thread prompts a number of heterosexual men who have been raped by incubi to say that it is nothing to feel ashamed of but it can be stopped with the correct psychic weapons: positive thinking, a refusal to let it steal energy, even reason. One contributor advises admonishing the incubus: 'You are not here and I will no longer allow you do to do such things to me . . .'

Another man, writing from California, is in a loving, 'heterosexual' relationship with a succubus. It started when he was living on his own in a cabin and woke up in a state of total, all-consuming, transcendent lust. Thinking it was just a rush of hormones, he masturbated and thought no more about it although, with hindsight, he realises that it was the start of a number of paranormal experiences – doors opening and closing, voices in empty rooms, other noises that he could not identify but which were not of this world. These manifestations grew in intensity, especially when the man moved in with a drug-addicted girl who, he now thinks, meant him harm. It was at this stage that the succubus started manifesting as a solid. She was black in colour and had physical presence, being able to slam doors. She also terrified the man's cats.

Eventually the man left his girlfriend and began to develop a relationship with the spirit. The arousal she created in him was similar to the feelings he had when he was living alone in the cabin, and he realised that she had been with him all this time. At the time of writing, he is still in a relationship with her. His cats are no longer terrified, but do leave the room when she visits him at night, and he has found out that he can talk to her. Inspired by these experiences, he has even set up his own forum devoted specifically to people in sexual relationships with incubi and succubi. Here people discuss their nonmaterial lovers: what is the better way to communicate with them, pendulums or Ouija boards?; sexual techniques and positions; how best to stop the incubus/succubus asking for sex at inappropriate times; how to fight off bigoted denouncements from Christians and take the debate forwards. Some people argue that those who condemn relationships between discarnate and incarnate beings should be denounced as racists. Within living memory, this argument goes, people were denounced for having relationships with people of different races; prejudice against spirit sex is exactly the same, but with churches taking the place of kangaroo courts, Christians taking the place of the Ku Klux Klan and exorcisms taking the place of lynchings.

Within Christian countries, religion does colour the debate. Around the world, reactions vary, as does the interpretation of the night visitor. In the Far East, for example, the visitor is far more likely to be identified as a ghost rather than a demon. An Indonesian man is reported to be asking for help in warding off the advances of a lustful ghost that has been plaguing him for sixteen years. The ghost is long haired, insatiable, has stopped him getting married and, worst of all, keeps on getting him fired as he is too tired to concentrate on his work. A medium suggests he arrange a 'netherworld' marriage for the ghost, complete with doll groom, toy car and miniature snacks and, by all accounts, this is successful.

From a Western viewpoint, it is fascinating that the main thrust of the article is not about the ghost or about the sex but about the work – a fact that is backed up by the final paragraph in the piece concerning a commune in China that has been set up where men can live without having to worry about the pressures of the modern world. The spirit too is treated differently. Although it is never quite explained why the man waited sixteen years before getting help, when help does come, the clear implication is that this is not the devil in disguise, nor some entity devoted to having sex with humans, but an unhappy ghost. And how does one make an unhappy, unfulfilled ghost leave? Offer it what it wants: a groom and decent wedding. In China and Japan also, possession is more likely to be from an unhappy, dissatisfied or angry ghost, and the solution to the haunting is always the same: find out what the ghost wants, give it to them and they will go away.

It works the other way around. A Japanese woman, married to a salaryman, found solace with an unhappy male ghost. He was shy – the first indications of his presence were when she was in the shower and the shower curtain twitched, as if a wind had caught it.

Not long after, her husband complained that someone was following them on one of the rare occasions when they went out together.

At cherry blossom time, the woman was particularly miserable as she compared the current state of her marriage with her courtship. She went out to walk under the blossom and happened to turn around just as a gust of wind shook the petals off a tree. For an instant, a shape had appeared in the blossom, the silhouette of a slim man. But when she blinked he was gone. She remembered how she had walked with her husband when they were young lovers, how he had given her a sprig of cherry blossom and how she had frozen the petals in an ice cube to keep them forever. They were still there in a ziplock bag in her freezer and, really, she should throw them away.

The next night her husband called from the office to say that he would have to stay so late entertaining clients that he might as well book into a hotel overnight. The woman agreed and for the first time did not feel resentful. She felt nervous but at the same time excited at the thought of her first night alone for years – and by the thought that she might at last find out a bit more about this mysterious, ghostly man. So that night, in the full knowledge that her husband was going to be away, she set the table for two and ate a semi-formal supper, serving both places, eating politely, and clearing away quietly. After supper, she poured some whisky into a tumbler and very deliberately put it by an armchair while she sat demurely in another and played music. She chose Western, melodic music: bossa nova followed by romantic love songs.

Later, she laid out the sleeping mats and sheets, turned off the lights and went into the bathroom to wash. When she came out, she saw a shape beneath the sheets. She checked the sitting room: the whisky had not been touched but had obviously done its job! Although it was what she had wanted and prepared for, her heart nearly stopped beating, then began to pound. What could she do? She had effectively summoned this spirit and to reject it now might make it angry. On the other hand, what might it do to her when she got into bed next to it? She looked around the apartment that was so bland, so modern and so familiar. There were the Venetian blinds, drawn. There was the vase her sister had given her. There was the CD player, the flatscreen TV, the stack of DVDs and there, in the bed, was the ghost.

But then she thought: what could be worse than my life now

and, taking a deep breath, she slipped off her robe and lay down under the thin cotton sheet.

At first nothing happened, and then she felt the lightest touch of a hand on her cheek, on her neck, on her shoulder, on her arm, in the dip of her waist. Her husband had never touched her so lightly, and with such sensitivity. She moved slightly and the hand moved to her back, and then her breasts. It was like an electric shock passing through her. Instinctively she arched her back, and reached out, to grip the ghost and hold it – and found it was a woman. She felt the hair – it was cut short – but the rest of the ghost's shape was female. Reacting to her shock, the ghost withdrew. The woman sat up, her legs tucked up under her knees, and then she started to laugh. She had been quite prepared to have sex with a ghost: why should she care whether it was a man or a woman? The whole thing was ridiculous. She lay back down and relaxed, giving herself over to a range of sensations she had not known she was capable of feeling.

Her affair lasted a month. During this time, her husband was away more than he was at home and, while the woman did not get to know her ghostly lover, she came to care about her and wonder, so she went to see a priest.

The priest was unruffled. It was rare, he admitted, to find a ghostly lover, rarer still to find one of the same sex, and almost unheard for that to develop into something like a relationship. However, she had to accept that what she was doing might not be right for the ghost. She had to let it go, if she could, and he would hold a ceremony in her house. It might be inappropriate to offer the ghost a marriage ceremony, but perhaps some other token?

Then the woman remembered how the ghost had followed her through the cherry blossoms, had stood under the tree while the petals fell and how she had some stored in her freezer.

That evening, instead of setting out the sleeping mat, the woman put out her most precious bowl, and in the bowl she put the ice cube with the petals inside. The priest chanted, the ice melted, and the petals floated on the surface, just for a second. Then they withered, turned brown and sank.

The ghost had gone.

Iceland

In Iceland some people complain that elf-watching and elf-belief has become a sort of craze, and singer Björk has commented on rumours that record companies like to check musicians' positive attitude to elves before signing the latest Icelandic prog rock band. And indeed elves are closely linked to the other kind of rock. In a town close to Reykjavik, a road was diverted so the builders did not have to blow up an elf rock, and in nearby Kopavogur, Elfhill Road actually narrows to one lane because of another prominent elf rock. Perhaps those road builders knew a thing or two. Efforts to flatten an elf hill in the same town came to grief after repeated equipment failure. News crews who tried to report on the anomaly found that all footage in their cameras was hopelessly fogged, even though they worked perfectly well when pointed away from the elf hill.

The Philippines are a rich source of ghostly lovers. A woman writes that a clever ghost raised the temperature in the room so she lay on her back to try and get cool, then it raped her. It has returned on various occasions, sometimes to have sex, sometimes simply to cuddle her and stroke her hair. While the experience is not painful, in the mornings she is drained of energy and has flu-like symptoms, prompting one correspondent to the thread to suggest that she has met a *kitsune*, or a fox demon. Another suggests she try to get rid of it, but not to break its heart, as it sounds like a gentle spirit.

Some local spirits are much less pleasant, however. In the spice island of Zanzibar, a cultural crossroads where Islam, animist African religion and Christianity mix into a potent brew, a local sheikh was engaged in a boundary dispute with his neighbours. Knowing a bit of elementary magic, he decided to enlist supernatural help in the form of a djinn, but being canny decided to set limits on its powers. Firstly, he wanted the whole affair to be kept secret, so he would tell the djinn only to terrorise the neighbours indoors. Secondly, he was determined that they would be punished whatever steps they took, so he would also instruct the djinn on how to enter locked and shuttered properties. But then the sheikh had an attack of conscience. Up until now, he and his neighbours had limited their dispute to words and gestures. As a moral man of God, he really had to warn them that he was upping the stakes and that they should take his warnings seriously. So the next time he saw them, he told them that unless they settled the dispute in his favour, he would summon up a djinn to help him. The neighbour just laughed at him. 'You may believe in nonsense like that, and everyone else might too, but we're living in the modern world, my friend. All your talk of djinn doesn't frighten me, for the simple reason that you know and I know that such things don't exist.'

'That does it,' the sheikh said, and decided to add another instruction: only attack people who don't believe in you. Then he set to work and called up a hideous creature. It was small, leathery, with a single red eye and enormously powerful. It had claws, bat wings and an insatiable desire for human bodies. The sheikh bound it with the conditions he had set and sent it on its way, only realising after it had gone that he had forgotten to bind it with the most important instruction of all: that when it had finished terrorising the neighbours it would return to the dimension it had come from.

And so began a reign of terror in Zanzibar and the neighbouring island of Pemba. Popo Bawa, 'Bat Wing' in Swahili, has driven whole communities to sleep outdoors because he is known only to attack people inside.

If anyone is foolish enough to ignore the warnings of the community, the first they know of Popo Bawa is the clatter of his leathery wings as he lands on the roof of their hut. Next they hear the sound of his powerful, clawed feet and hands scrabbling at the thatch or tugging at the corrugated-iron roofing. Next comes the smell – powerful and rank – and a change in the atmosphere which becomes cold and clammy. A terrible weakness then grips the victim as they hear the scratch of his claws on the floor and the rustle of his dry wings as he moves slowly across the floor towards them. Then he leaps on to the bed and assaults them, men and women, for anything up to an hour. Only when he is satisfied does he crawl out of the house and fly away into the night.

Kenya

A prankster ghost haunts two rooms of a safari lodge in the Masai Mara. Clients staying in rooms 153 and 154 have seen curtains swaying when the windows are closed and there's no draught, and have returned from their rooms after brief absences to find their luggage opened and their belongings strewn round. Their nights are disturbed by knocks on the door; no matter how quick they are to answer, they can never find any trace of anyone outside. They feel cold spots and tickles on their spines, as if they're being teased. The ghost is thought to be that of a 9- or 10-year-old boy who was killed on the reserve by a leopard in the 1950s.

Throughout history, mankind has consorted with supernatural beings. In the Book of Enoch, it is told that angels slept with human women and gave birth to a race of monsters. Medieval Japan is storehouse of stories of people sleeping with unhappy ghosts. In Europe, witches called down the devil and demons for orgies. Today there are rumours of supernatural sex tourism in South East Asia and the ghosts of former communist torturers offering supernatural S&M in abandoned Siberian prison camps. So perhaps it isn't that surprising the instructions for calling down a demon lover are only a couple of mouse clicks away on the Net.

The difference between summoning a demon and being approached by one is the difference between meeting someone at random and calling a specific person on the telephone. To call up a human, we need a telephone, the technical knowledge of how to use it and, importantly, a number. To summon a demon, equipment might come in the form of a Ouija board or simply a piece of chalk for drawing a circle. Instead of technical knowledge, you will need to know a ritual, and instead of a number, you need to know the demon's name. After that, people can pick and choose off a smorgasbord of ghostly opportunity.

Artist and magician Austin Osman Spare, who believed that desires are spirits that wished to find a realisation in flesh, used meditation, masturbation and small clay phials that he filled with semen and buried. The techniques he used were taught to him by an elderly lady called Mrs Paterson, a descendant of Salem witches who had escaped persecution, and had the rare gift of making thoughts materialise. Spare developed this ability and used it to conjure up spirits with whom he would copulate. Sometimes the figure would be Mrs Paterson herself, in the form of a nubile young girl. He was able to induce a state of incredible sexual energy, some of which he poured into his art, some of which ended in copulation, eighteen times in one night. In the course of his life, he created a magical alphabet with which he was able to awaken desire, especially when it was accompanied by certain spells:

O mighty Rehctaw! Thou who exists in all erogenousness,
We evoke Thee!
By the power of the meanings arising from these forms I make,
We evoke Thee!

By the Talismans that speak the secret leitmotif of desire,
We evoke Thee!

By the sacrifices, abstinences and transvaluations we make,
We evoke Thee!

By the sacred inbetweenness concepts, Give us the flesh!

By the quadriga sexualis, Give us unvarying desire!

By the conquest of fatigue, Give us eternal resurgence!

By the most sacred Word-graph of Heaven, We invoke Thee!

For Aleister Crowley, sex magick was a difficult ritual that involved discipline, meditation and an appetite for the extreme: the greatest magical ecstasy was achieved through union with the ugliest and most grotesque subject. However, his practices went beyond simple self-gratification: he argued that the personal transformation achieved this way led to great improvements in health, well-being and raised levels of tolerance and understanding. Crowley's ritualistic approach is short-circuited by much of the freewheeling advice you get today on the Web: you can buy special herbs on eBay for summoning an incubus ($30.00) or spirit stones for male or female nymphs ($45.00).

'Spirit sex is real,' one website states. 'It requires some psychic work in order to open your mind to senses not normally accessible to the average person, but the way to do this is much easier than with other methods and a lot more pleasurable. Demon friends and lovers are wonderful for those who are in prison or incarcerated in any way.'

It then goes on to describe just why demon sex is better than any other – being disembodied they can reach parts of the body that physical lovers cannot; how to begin – tell 'Father Satan' just what sort of relationship you want; how to choose your demon – they're much better looking than people would have you believe; and finally, a health warning: users might feel slightly tingly, as in a mild case of sunburn.

On another forum, the advice is hedged around with warnings, but then goes on to give pretty detailed and highly practical advice, from why certain 'magickians' like to wear robes, and why black is the colour of choice, to the use of the pentagram. It discusses the use of wands, images, ritual candles (demons are colour sensitive) before going on to describe the ritual itself: clear your mind, design the right altar, draw your pentagram, align your mind with the forces of hell, summon the demon and, once he has arrived, state your business politely and firmly. Elsewhere you can find ten easy steps for summoning a succubus (easier to banish than an incubus) and a shrine to Lilitu, praised as being the ultimate role model for the modern, dynamic Jewish woman.

There's an old saying in parts of Lincolnshire – a very rural county in the east of England – that the best way to cure your fear of the dark is to get out of the light. This is not to say that things do not live in darkness, it is just to say that when you make the effort to enter into that world, they are not as bad as you think. And it's true that if you are walking down a country lane on a moonless night when the wind is rustling the leaves and you have an impression of shadows shifting beyond the hedgerow, as if something is stalking you, the quickest way to banish your fear is probably to go round the other side and see for yourself.

But to do that with demons . . . ?

Throughout the millennia, almost all of recorded history, mankind has been terrified of the dark world of shadows, the world of the occult. What we are learning today is that while this world is real, there are many people out there who are exploring methods of coexistence, cooperation and even cohabitation. Does this devalue or call into question the undoubted torment and suffering that a family such as the Smurls had to endure?

Emphatically not. Just as there are good humans and bad humans, sexual deviants and careful, considerate lovers, there are rapist demons and those that would not dream of violating a potential lover. The Smurls were targeted by an entity, or small gang of entities, that were attracted by the Smurls' respectable, god-fearing souls in the same way a playground bully is attracted to the nicely brought-up child who comes to school in their Sunday best. When the Smurls reacted, it was ineffective, and only succeeded in enflaming the demon's anger; the more they fought against it, the more energy they gave it, until it eventually had the power to materialise as a pig monster and take Jack Smurl against his will.

But it really is a case of different strokes for different folks. When humans encounter an incubus or a succubus, they respond with the full gamut of reactions, and while it is hard truly to believe that a deep and meaningful relationship can be had with your demon lover, there are clearly people out there who are serious, committed and deeply involved with entities in ways that are satisfying to both parties.

China

In Shaanxi, a western province of China, an undertaker called Li Longsheng was faced with a problem. In line with local tradition, an elderly client who had just died was refusing to go quietly into the afterlife. The reason? He had died single and his spirit was looking for a ghost wife. At the same time, nearby, a peasant who was unhappy with his wife wanted to recoup some of his outlay; he got in touch with the undertaker who said he would buy her corpse for 16,000 yuan, so his client could get married in the afterlife.

The plan worked so well and the dead client was so happy with his ghost wife, that the undertaker let it be known he was in the market for other corpses. The murderer formed a working partnership with a friend and they duly provided one, luring a prostitute to a deserted courtyard and strangling her. It was at this stage that the police caught up with the criminals and stopped a lucrative trade in ghostwives.

CHAPTER FOUR

SOUNDS IN THE SUBURBS

Poltergeists at Work

It began on 31 August 1977 in the bedroom of a semi-detached house in the London suburb of Enfield. Eleven-year-old Janet Hodgson and her 10-year-old brother Johnny had been wondering what was making the shuffling noise – from their beds they could see that everything in the small room was still and yet there was that sound again, as if something was being dragged. Their mother Peggy heard it too. She assumed the children were playing – they were a lively and mischievous pair – and she went upstairs to tell them to settle down. As she stood in their room, a loud knocking sounded on the wall. Then the chest of drawers slid away from the wall into the middle of the room. Peggy, not quite able to believe what had happened, calmly pushed it back. It moved again, this time sliding into the doorway, and now when Peggy tried to move it back, it resisted her.

Peggy was suddenly overcome with fear. Her panic infected Janet and Johnny, and also the other two children, 13-year-old Margaret and 7-year-old Billy, who had rushed in to see what the fuss was about. The family called the next-door neighbours, who duly came in to reassure them. They too could hear knocking from the walls. Indeed, as the neighbours went from room to room, checking for rats or intruders, the knocking followed them. It was loud and insistent, with a hollow ring. They checked the alley and the garden, but there was no sign of anyone outside.

To be on the safe side, they called the police, reporting a disturbance. The local patrol – a man and a woman – went round and, realising the family was genuinely scared, searched the house. The most likely explanation seemed to be that an airlock in the pipes was making the noises, so the male police constable went to look at the plumbing, while the woman constable inspected the living room. At which point she saw a chair vibrate, rise up slightly off the floor and glide several feet to the right. She immediately inspected it, picking it up and turning it upside down to see if a trick had been played on her, but there were no wires or strings attached. Replacing it, she wondered if perhaps the floor sloped, so she borrowed one of the Hodgsons' marbles and placed it in different spots under and around the chair, but it stayed put – the floor appeared to be quite level.

So far, so inexplicable. The noises died down, the police and neighbours left and the Hodgsons, thoroughly unnerved, decided they'd all sleep together in the living room. They awoke to a peaceful house – but normality didn't last long. That afternoon, a Lego brick hurtled through the air. Then another. Then a marble dropped from above, as if it had been stuck to the ceiling.

Throughout the next few days, the family continued to hear bangs, knocks and sighs. Furniture tipped over when no one was near and small objects kept tumbling from places they should not have been. And the atmosphere in the house changed – everyone was agitated and jumpy, not surprisingly, but it was more than that: the family began to have a sensation of being watched. Janet felt it most strongly – she had the feeling not just of unseen eyes on her but of a physical presence very close.

The Hodgsons were bewildered by what was happening to them. At that stage, they had never heard the term 'poltergeist'. This was about to change: within a few weeks, the media had taken an interest, closely followed by experts in paranormal research, with the result that during the next nine months, many different people were to witness an intensifying cycle of noises, movements, voices, physical assaults, and even self-igniting fires – all the marks of a major poltergeist infestation.

Poltergeists have disturbed humans throughout history. An Ancient Egyptian scribe recorded a violent attack in which the beds of the household shook and stones showered out of the air. Ancient Romans called them *lemures* and believed them to be unhappy and mischievous spirits of the dead. In sixteenth-century France, the servants of a wealthy merchant were repeatedly attacked by an invisible force that hurled stones at them; in keeping with the preoccupations of the times, they believed it was a demon. Eventually they retaliated by throwing stones back, at which point fires broke out and the house burned down. In seventeenth-century Europe and America, disembodied noises and inexplicably moving objects were often considered evidence of black magic and spelt the death of many women at the hands of witch finders.

In the past hundred years, these forces have become known as poltergeists – a German term which means 'racketing ghost'. The name captures the noisy, disruptive, often violent side of the entity, but there is another aspect as well: an insidious, menacing quality . . .

This was well to the fore when the journalists turned up in Enfield. *Daily Mirror* journalist Douglas Bence and photographer Graham Morris arrived in sceptical mood. They were used to hearing stories of things that went bump in the night and had decided to investigate this report only because the police had confirmed it. However, as soon as they entered the house, on Sunday 4 September, they felt the tension in the atmosphere, and as the evening wore on (uneventfully) they realised that Peggy Hodgson was truly frightened. They soon discovered why. In the early hours, just as they had decided to give up and leave, they heard a commotion from the living room. Running back in, they saw toys flying past at incredible speed. Graham Morris backed into a corner and started clicking his camera shutter; as he did so, a Lego brick hit him hard on the forehead. Douglas Bence, observing, was baffled as to where the toys were coming from. As they continued hurtling round, he abandoned his professional detachment and helped the family seize loose toys and pack them hurriedly in drawers and cupboards.

Bence's report and Morris's pictures were intriguing enough to give the story legs, and they rapidly became repeat visitors to the house. Meanwhile, the disturbances continued night after night. Peggy and the children became increasingly frightened and bewildered and the Society for Psychical Research was called in.

The SPR was (and is) a highly respectable society. It was founded in 1882, right at the dawn of the modern technological age, to study evidence of paranormal and supernatural events and it has always numbered many doctors and scientists among its members. Maurice Grosse, who was to spend the next twelve months investigating the Enfield Poltergeist, was a retired businessman with a systematic and businesslike approach. In late September he and a writer colleague, Guy Lyon Playfair, moved in to the Enfield house with notebooks, cameras and tape recorders, and began documenting the disturbances.[4]

It soon became clear these were centred on Janet. Drawers slid open as she passed; chairs jumped and flipped over. One day the kitchen table turned upside down. Rappings sounded on the walls and floors of rooms she was in. Electrical equipment regularly malfunctioned near Janet – photographer Graham Morris would arrive at the house with fully charged flashguns, only to find them registering no power once inside. And there were other, odd incidents that seemed to disobey the laws of physics. Marbles would drop from unseen perches high up in the house and stay motionless where they'd landed, no bouncing or rolling. In October, pools of water appeared on the kitchen floor: they had sharp outlines and resembled human silhouettes.

With the family near breaking point, Maurice Grosse tried to intervene by opening communications. Next time knocks sounded on the walls, he spoke to them, suggesting that they answered his questions using a 'one knock for no, two for yes' system. The response was a long pause followed by an outbreak of raps that sounded almost jeering. Grosse persevered, asking if this was a joke. In answer, a cardboard box and a pillow rose up from the far corner of the room and flew into his face.

Grosse was a patient, methodical man and he persisted in trying to communicate with what he thought of as 'the entity', setting it simple sums, and on several occasions getting the right answer back. If he was trying to distract its attention from Janet, he was disappointed: on the night of 12 November, Janet was hurled out of bed and landed on the floor, with her mattress on top of her. From then on she was main focus of the unseen force's energies. She began crying and moaning in her sleep, was repeatedly thrown out of bed and across the floor, and one night was thrashing round so violently that a doctor was called to sedate her. Later the same night she was pulled from her bed and hurled through the air, landing on top of the wireless set on the chest of drawers.

4 A first-hand account of the family's experiences is told in *This House Is Haunted: The Investigation into the Enfield Poltergeist* by Guy Lyon Playfair (Sutton Publishing, 2007; first published 1980).

Other people in the house were affected too. One night Playfair, Grosse and Peggy discovered Margaret at the top of the stairs, balanced on one leg, with the other stretched out behind her like a ballerina. She was crying for help: her leg was being pulled and she was locked into position. When the adults reached her, they found her peculiarly rigid and stable, as if held in a clamp. It was only after they turned her whole body around that she suddenly went limp.

The children's uncle (Peggy's brother) was catapulted out of his chair, an experience he reported as being pulled rather than pushed, like being sucked into an airlock.

But Janet was definitely the focus. Metal objects began to bend near her, as if she were exerting a forcefield: a teapot lid curved out of shape on a shelf above her head and a magazine rack buckled while she was sitting close to it, reading.

She also began making alarming noises – whistling and barking, and talking in a deep hoarse male voice.

The deep voice expressed an angry, unhappy personality. It swore a lot and referred to Janet as if she was in the way. 'I was sleeping here!' it explained when Grosse asked why it was shaking Janet's bed. 'Get Janet out.' Janet and Margaret had bizarre conversations with it, in which there definitely seemed to be three people present, even though two of them were using Janet's vocal chords.

Or rather, in the case of the male voice, her 'false vocal fold'. Because when experts were consulted, they said the voice came from above the larynx, and couldn't be sustained without injury to the throat. Anyone doing it for more than a few minutes would get an inflamed throat and have to speak huskily. Yet the voice would come out of Janet for up to three hours at a time, alternating with her own voice, and she'd suffer no ill effects.

Moreover, Janet didn't need to move her lips to allow the voice to speak. When Maurice Grosse, ever methodical and cautious, made her hold water in her mouth and then taped her lips, the voice still spoke. Janet said it felt as though someone had their hands on the back of her head and was transferring the voice into her from behind.

Her sister Margaret had a similar impression: she said it seemed as if Janet always had an invisible person with her.

Throughout these events, Maurice Grosse consulted doctors and scientists, keen to have as much independent scrutiny as possible. When put under light hypnosis, Janet was able to talk about the disturbances quite calmly, but remained puzzled about why they were happening. She said she and her sister and 'I don't know who' were causing the disturbances, and that sometimes when she was physically thrown around she felt she was being gripped by something cold.

A physicist using a strain gauge and pulse counters measured abnormal activity in metal objects close to Janet, registering a spike of activity at the moment when the objects finally buckled.

BBC journalists heard the startling hoarse voice emerging from Janet (it joked with them, claiming to be called 'Tom' and 'Dick'), and when Maurice invited his lawyer son Richard to conduct an independent interview, the voice sparred with him for a while, and at several points unnerved him by seeming able to read his mind. Eventually the voice told Richard his name was Bill and that he'd died of a haemorrhage in the chair in the corner of the living room.

At this point, it would be tempting for many psychic investigators to think in terms of possession. But it seemed to Maurice Grosse that the 'personality' speaking through Janet was unreliable. He was beginning to feel that he was witnessing a display of stunts and mimicry. What distinguished him from other sceptics, though, was that he didn't hold Janet responsible. He'd experienced enough in the Hodgson house to be convinced she wasn't faking it. Instead he felt they were being toyed with by a wayward supernatural force, 'some psychic joker'.

On 14 December two people passing by in the street – a baker's delivery man and a lollipop lady – thought they must be imagining things. A cushion appeared on the roof of the house. Then, behind the windowpane of the main bedroom, objects started whirling in mid-air. Books, dolls and clothes appeared to be floating rapidly, circling the room clockwise, bouncing off the window and then returning again at the same height. Amid the whirling objects was Janet, lying on her back and apparently being tossed up and down, her arms and legs flailing. To the spectators, the scene defied possibility, no matter how they tried to rationalise it. (The lollipop lady even went home and tried vainly to bounce on her bed while lying down.) To Janet, it was just one more onslaught from the poltergeist, though even she was shocked by its next trick: she found herself propelled through the dividing wall, into the next-door neighbour's bedroom.

For another six months, the poltergeist wrought havoc. Janet was pushed, thrown and levitated (and so, occasionally, were other family members). Furniture and household objects continued to move without warning. Foul smells arose; a box of matches ignited; human-shaped shadows appeared where there was nothing to cast them. Newspapers, TV and radio ran regular stories, and soon people were suggesting that the house, or Janet herself, should be exorcised.

Worried for Janet's well-being, the family, at Maurice Grosse's suggestion, got her admitted to the Maudsley psychiatric hospital for assessment. During the three months she was there, she experienced only a few small disturbances which quickly tailed off. In the Enfield house, they continued for a while but less dramatically and less often; it was as if, now Janet was removed from the house, the poltergeist had lost its source of energy and couldn't recharge. It showed signs of trying to transfer to Janet's younger brother Johnny: he would moan and cry in his sleep and awaken frightened, and once or twice the familiar gravelly voice erupted out of him. However, the force definitely seemed to be weakening. After Janet came home in September 1978, having been pronounced psychologically and physically normal, the whole family held its breath, but the downward trend continued. For a few months, there were intermittent manifestations – furniture falling over and Janet and the other children seeing people who weren't really there – but by spring 1979 the house was quiet.

To those who'd studied poltergeist cases, this came as no surprise. Poltergeist activity classically follows this pattern. It is a form of energy that has a recognisable cycle; in fact, you can plot the stages of a typical poltergeist cycle as below:

It starts with bizarre and inexplicable physical disturbances, apparently connected to one place (usually a building). In reality, while these are drawing on the energy of the place, they are almost always associated with a particular person who frequents it. Raps on walls, small objects moving on their own, lights flicking on and off are typical phenomena. Also changes in temperature, especially cold spots, and a sense of being watched.

The activity intensifies: larger objects move, including furniture;

disembodied sounds become louder and more insistent, and electronic equipment – especially TVs, computers and musical equipment – malfunctions.

The sense of being watched grows. People experience direct physical sensations, as if they are being touched or pushed. Doors and windows may open and close; taps turn on and off of their own accord.

An element of mockery enters in. The poltergeist seems to be enjoying playing tricks. These may involve arranging objects in stacks or geometric patterns or hiding them in weird places (on tops of doors, inside shoes). Beds and chairs shake when people are sitting in them. The tricks often become quite personal, with certain phenomena being repeated around particular individuals. One person might keep seeing faces at the window, while another finds that books seem to jump off the shelves when they pass. The more the individuals react, especially with fear, the more dramatic the tricks become. To an outsider, the activity can look playful and quite funny, but to the people involved it feels malevolent. There is a growing sense of a personality at work. By this time it's usually very clear that one person is attracting most of the activity.

There are direct physical assaults on the people in the house, especially the focal person. The invisible entity may push them, slap them, pull their hair, tip them out of bed. They may float through the air or levitate, or find their limbs contorting into unnatural positions. The sensations of being tugged by invisible hands, and of being pulled from the inside out are common. They may speak in an unfamiliar voice as if they are possessed. The atmosphere is menacing and now, when objects move, they create danger: knives fly across rooms, mirrors shatter; boxes of matches burst into flames. Electrical wires short-circuit.

Weakening activity: the manifestations become sporadic and die away. Sometimes they stop abruptly; more usually they tail off, with the decline interrupted by a few incidents that often seem like pale imitations of earlier ones.

Each poltergeist is unique. You'll find different details in each case: a different selection of phenomena, coming in a different order. But across the hundreds of different cases that have been recorded, the main pattern holds true: energy builds up and the phenomena become more dramatic, powerful and dangerous, before falling away.

In the face of so much consistent evidence, the ideas of the past, that poltergeists are ghosts of place or possessing spirits, have been widely discarded. Modern poltergeist theory concentrates on psychokinesis (PK in the jargon), the ability of the mind to affect matter. It suggests that the poltergeist is an unstable psychic force, an entity that gathers will, powers and personality from the humans whose lives it affects. It often seems to manifest in situations where there's emotional tension, and to be associated with one particular individual, usually an adolescent girl.

Where the psychic energy comes from is a matter of hot debate. Is it generated from within humans, a sort of exteriorisation of strong emotion?

Does it come from outside, a force latent but unformed, which responds to emotional turbulence and feeds on it?

As importantly, we need to ask whether or not it contains the remnants of human consciousness. Though poltergeists are not ghosts in the classic sense, they sometimes mimic or make references to people who have died. When this happens, the listeners usually have an overpowering sense of another personality being present. The Enfield Poltergeist was particularly hyperactive in this respect. It spoke as several different old men, as well as appearing as a silent little boy, as if there were competing signals on its wavelength.

Okinawa

Okinawa, a small, subtropical island midway between Japan and Taiwan, has more than its fair share of ghosts. Part of Japan, it still has a huge US military presence and its troubled history seems to create a setting in which the paranormal is normal. In World War II, threatened with American invasion, many of the inhabitants threw themselves off the cliffs of the island rather than face the foreign devils.

Building 2283 of the United States Organization Airbase at Kadena is an ordinary nondescript structure, originally designed to house US military families. So far, the fathers of two American families living there have gone

mad and killed their wives and children. One room was considered too damp to be used and was knocked down. The house was then converted into a storage shed, but passers-by began to notice a green glow emanating from it.

Fascinated by the rumours, a psychic held a séance in it and contacted the spirits of two children who appeared as ghostly images in photographs. Later, service personnel who re-enacted one of the murders in the house suffered near fatal accidents shortly afterwards and staff on the base refused even to enter the building for the stores that were kept there.

Irritated by these stories, the authorities ordered the building to be torn down but, after the demolition contractors started seeing ghosts, they left. Today, the house remains empty, home only to the entities that live in it.

Are poltergeists more likely to manifest in certain environmental conditions? The case of Tina Resch, which became famous in the 1980s and then notorious in the early 1990s, offers some intriguing clues. In 1984, 14-year-old Tina's home in Columbus, Ohio, erupted into a chaos of crashing glasses, tumbling furniture and photographs, pens and kitchen knives hurtling through the air. The press latched on to the story and it became a huge controversy, dividing people over whether she was a trickster or for real. James Randi, the magician, was loudly sceptical; her family and paranormal investigator William Roll were convinced.

When the press furore had died down, Roll took Tina to be assessed neurologically. The findings showed she might have a mild form of Tourette's Syndrome, in which minuscule electrical discharges in the brain cause physical jerks and tics, as well as verbal outbursts. This set Roll thinking.

Of course Tourette's doesn't give people psychokinetic powers. But the tiny electrical impulses we experience in our brain are on a continuum with electrical activity of a much more dramatic kind – like artificially administered electric shocks and violent electrical storms in the atmosphere. In the 1970s, research showed that psychokinesis is more common at times of geomagnetic disturbance.

And when Canadian university neuropsychologist Michael Persinger investigated the background to Tina's poltergeist manifestation, he found that it had begun immediately after a three-day geomagnetic storm.

Could it be that the high level of electrical impulses in Tina's brain predisposed her to attracting poltergeist forces? And that when the geomagnetic storm passed through Ohio, it charged her up even higher, turning her into a human generator of psychic energy, ready for exploiting by unseen forces?

Such a phenomenon would certainly fit with the latest thinking on a question that has long puzzled poltergeist-watchers: why poltergeists so often attach themselves to adolescent girls.

Recent discoveries in neuroscience have revealed that adolescence is a time of extraordinary development within the brain. Whole areas become more active as new synaptical pathways are laid down, creating new connections; electrical impulses race along these in ever more complex patterns, dazzling the owner of the brain, giving starbursts of insight and rushes of excitement. In girls, the monthly hormonal cycle further boosts the activity, intensifying it even more. Italian physicists Pierro Brovetto and Vera Maxia are working on a theory that in some adolescent girls (and a few boys), the fluctuations in electron activity are so great that they disturb the quantum field for up to several metres around the brain.

And this, of course, would create an invaluable source of energy for restless, untethered entities. From their point of view, the adolescents have helpfully turned into walking, talking, psychic power stations.

Tina Resch's poltergeist activity died away after a few months, as does most people's. Unhappily, though, her life had been troubled before the poltergeist and continued to be so afterwards. Within a few years, relations broke down with her family and she left home; soon afterwards she was in trouble with the police. In 1994, at the age of 25, she was convicted of contributing to the death of her young daughter by failing to procure medical treatment for injuries, and imprisoned for life.

No one knows whether there was a connection between Tina Resch's poltergeist and circumstances that led to the death of her child. (Tina took a plea-bargain deal that maintained her innocence while accepting a jail sentence, in order to avoid the possibility of execution.) If there was a direct link, it would make Tina a rare exception. Most poltergeist infestations don't lead to serious harm. They are often terrifying and at their peak can create truly dangerous situations, but it's a remarkable fact that few people are injured during them.

Once the disturbances die down, the people at the centre of the activity usually go on to lead ordinary lives. Unless, that is, they find themselves being blamed for what's happened and accused of witchcraft, devil worship or wilful acts of violence. Take the case of Carole Compton.

In May 1982, 19-year-old Carole left her native Scotland for Italy. She had fallen in love with an Italian and when he was called up to do military service she decided to follow him to Italy and get to know the country. She took a job as a nanny with a rich Roman family but, although she and the children got on well, the family's maid was uncertain about the newcomer. Within a few days of Carole's arrival she had noticed a picture apparently jump off the wall while Carole was walking past. The maid had been unnerved, especially because the picture was a religious one, and insisted on saying a blessing while Carole crossed herself.

As the summer heat intensified, the family decamped to the grandparents' house in the Alps, taking Carole with them. One evening, when Carole was taking a stroll with the young son and the grandfather's nurse, a fire broke out. Seeing smoke pour from the windows as they returned, Carole ran into the house and roused the grandfather, who was obliviously watching TV downstairs. They got out safely, but by the time the fire brigade arrived, the upper floor was wrecked. The fire service, unable to find an obvious starting point for the fire, suggested it might have been an electrical fault. The family, Nicole and Carole all moved into a vacant flat in the village. Two mornings later, the grandmother smelled burning and, after a frantic hunt, they discovered some paper smouldering in the rubbish bin under the kitchen sink. The following day, her employers' bed burst into flames while her employer was having a shower. The atmosphere became strained. No one openly suggested Carole was to blame, but shortly afterwards she found herself out of a job.

At the end of July 1982 she went to work for another family, and again followed the Italian custom of going with them to stay with their grandparents, this time on the island of Elba. Things did not get off to a good start: Carole felt the grandmother was reluctant to have her there and she felt jumpy and anxious that the family were going to blame her for any mishap. This was soon put to the test: the day after they arrived, smoke started billowing from the grandparents' bedroom at lunchtime and they found the mattress smouldering down one side. Then a statue toppled over when Carole and the grandmother were both nearby but out of reach. The next day, first a cake stand, then a glass vase, fell inexplicably from high surfaces while Carole was in the room. With each incident, tension grew, and Carole heard the grandmother talking about her, mentioning the word '*strega*' – the Sardinian term for witch.

That same afternoon, as the family's 3-year-old daughter was having a nap in the parents' bedroom, Carole heard peculiar scratching noises. They sounded as if they were behind the walls, either in the living room or the bedroom. When the girl's mother and grandfather opened the door, smoke billowed out: once again, the mattress was smouldering. The little girl was pulled to safety and the mattress thrown outside, but the incident was far from over. The grandmother seized Carole and furiously accused her of starting the fires. When Carole ran into the courtyard, she was locked out of the house and found that the neighbours had been alerted by the uproar and were congregating, staring at her in horror. Shaken and terrified, she hoped that when everyone had calmed down, she might be able to talk things over with them. Instead, the police arrived. They handcuffed Carole and drove her to the police station where she was interrogated and imprisoned.

Carole was held for seventeen months while the police explored allegations of arson and attempted murder; meanwhile, lurid press coverage both in Italy and the UK fuelled speculation that Carole was a witch. These rumours were rife within the prison too, making life very hard.

Carole is a logical person, without superstitious beliefs herself, and she felt that the best way to clear herself was simply to tell the truth and allow the events to be seen for what she believed they were – coincidences. She didn't think the unidentifiable scrabbling sounds or the falling objects could be important, and when she was contacted by various paranormal experts offering theories of psychokinesis and poltergeists, she was alarmed rather than reassured.

To the experts, of course, the poltergeist features of the case were only too evident. Chemist and SPR member Dr Hugh Pincott and Guy Lyon Playfair (see Enfield Poltergeist, page 95) compiled a dossier of testimonies and expert witness statements for submission to the court. Many of these drew parallels with other recent instances of spontaneous fires and associated paranormal happenings, and pointed out that just because these phenomena were not understood, it did not mean they did not exist. However, Carole and her defence team would not use the dossier. Carole insisted she had no psychic powers. Knowing that many Italians were only too ready to believe she was a witch, she thought it would be dangerous to cite any kind of paranormal explanation in her defence.

So she put her faith in the courts to separate fact from superstition. After seventeen months in prison, Carole Compton was tried for arson and attempted murder.[5] Faced with a range of eyewitness accounts that differed from what she remembered (and that often contradicted themselves), she doggedly defended herself, protesting her innocence and pointing out that no one had ever witnessed her starting a fire or trying to harm the children in any way. Much of the forensic evidence supported her: there was no trace of lighter fuel or any other kind of inflammatory aid at any of the points where fires had broken out. What was more, the forensic team was puzzled by the way the fires appeared to have caught and burned. The mattress fires appeared to have been caused by fierce heat but not by a naked flame. It hadn't been possible to recreate them in the way and during the time that had been established for them; indeed, a chief fire officer said that in his career he had never seen fires follow this pattern before.

Surely, Carole thought, these testimonies, together with the lack of direct evidence against her, would lead to an acquittal. She was wrong. Hysteria had taken root in certain sections of the population: an old lady approached her in the courtroom brandishing a crucifix and tried to 'save' her by throwing holy water on her. Even those who didn't accuse her of witchcraft were unwilling to accept that so many fires could be coincidental. They sensed a mind at

5 For her own account of the incidents and trial, see *Superstition: The True Story of the Nanny They Called a Witch* by Carole Compton with Gerald Cole (Ebury Press, 1990).

work behind the outbreaks, a personality struggling to express itself, and they assumed it must be Caróle's. The charge of attempted murder was held to be not proven, but she was convicted of arson and sentenced to two and a half years in prison. Because of the time she'd already served, the remainder of the sentence was suspended; Carole was released and fled back to Scotland, desperate to put distance between herself and the country where she had been branded 'evil'. A year later the case went to appeal (though without Carole, who refused to return to Italy). In fact it was a double appeal – Carole's defence appealed against the convictions, while the prosecutor appealed against the sentence, demanding it be increased and Carole returned to jail. Both appeals failed.

Carole has never come to a firm conclusion about what happened in Italy. She now knows more than she used to – and more than she ever wanted to – about poltergeist behaviour, but she prefers not to think about it too much. She is married with a family and living happily in Yorkshire; she has experienced no more poltergeist manifestations. In 2004, when a series of unexplained fires broke out in a village in Sicily, the press remembered her and tracked her down. What did she think was causing the fires? Did she have any advice or warnings for the people of Canneto di Caronia? Had she heard that the Vatican had mentioned demonic forces and exorcism? Carole returned a firm no comment. One thing she has definitely decided is that it's better to let sleeping poltergeists lie.

In fact, spontaneous fires occur in only a minority of poltergeist cases. But when they do, they are frequently dramatic. In the town of Suzano, Brazil, the de Souza family suffered an extraordinary concentrated outbreak of fires during one week in May 1970. It focused the attention of the police and scientists, though it had not come out of the blue. On closer analysis, it turned out that the family had been experiencing a lower level of poltergeist phenomena over a long period before it suddenly escalated.

It began in 1968, just after the father, Ezequias Valeria de Souza, returned to his family after a period spent living with another woman. He and his wife, Judith, both worked, and their eldest daughter Ivanil looked after her younger brothers and sisters and kept house. Ivanil was 13, which is of course a prime age for being receptive to emotional and psychic forces. One day her mother,

Judith, met the other woman in the street and an aggressive confrontation ensued. Shortly afterwards a shower of stones fell on the roof of the house.

From then on, stones often struck the roof, apparently materialising out of nowhere and falling with such force that they broke the tiles. The attacks became more regular and powerful until, in the month of May 1970, nearly 200 tiles were broken and Ezequias reported it to the police. Then the fires began. The first one broke out in a locked wardrobe in the main bedroom in the middle of the day. The house was empty at the time; the first to reach it were Ivanil and some neighbours, after they'd heard a loud bang from inside. They put out the fire, packed the burnt clothes into a bag and stowed it in the outdoor lavatory. That evening, the bag combusted.

Around midnight on 22 May, four of the children were lying in bed together. There were two beds in their room but they were all sharing one because they were afraid to split up. Two had fallen asleep, the others were too frightened, and while they lay awake one of them was startled to hear a noise like a dog's bark. It seemed to come from just beyond the wall but sounded quite different from the family dog. Shortly afterwards, a ball of flame seemed to fall from the ceiling on to the empty bed and its mattress ignited. The fire spread fast while the children were waking their siblings and rousing the rest of the house, and was hard to douse; even after they had dragged the mattress outdoors and soaked it, it smouldered.

A passing police patrol reported the incident and a senior officer, recognising the address from the complaint about the stones, took a colleague to investigate. They found the family moving other furniture outside, afraid that the house would continue to burn. It seemed they were right: while the officers examined the house, the mattress that had been removed from the main bed caught fire, rapidly followed by the sheets draped over the bed's frame. The officers had the impression the second fire hadn't spread from the first but had ignited from within the sheets.

Then they saw tiny flames begin to curl the paper of the calendar on the kitchen wall. Baffled and intrigued, the officers found another calendar and hung it on a hook in the bedroom. They retreated to the door and watched: blue flames appeared and burnt the calendar – also singeing the hand of one of the officers who wanted to check they were not an illusion. They repeated the experiment by fixing a newspaper page to the wall (it burnt) and cheques (they didn't).

Next, smoke seeped out of the closed wardrobe. Several police officers were present to see that when the door was opened, there was no naked flame inside but one of the wooden struts in the wardrobe was glowing with heat. Meanwhile a stack of notes on the kitchen table burst into flames.

Stones were also falling: a shower fell in the kitchen, a single stone hurtled into the main bedroom and then one of the stones rose from the kitchen floor and flew through the kitchen window, smashing the pane.

The police, having duly noted it all down, decided the only wise course of action was to say prayers. It seemed to work: at any rate the phenomena stopped and the children went off to stay with neighbours, while a police officer kept watch.

A priest was called in to exorcise the house. Sensing that the forces at work were focused on Ivanil, he recommended that she go to stay with relations. There was one small conflagration in a kitchen cupboard, and then quiet, until Ivanil's return on 28 May. There were two more outbreaks the day Ivanil came home – first an empty bed smouldered, then in the evening the baby's bedding caught fire. But these turned out to be a final spasm: just as in the case of the Enfield Poltergeist, removing the entity's focus seemed to have robbed it of its power and after that night there were no more fires.[6]

Wales

A disruptive paranormal entity is behind the closure of a Welsh pub, the Thirsty Scholar in Wrexham. Even though a blessing by the local vicar calmed the entity down, it had changed the temperature in the bar, smashed glasses in people's hands, knocked beer mats off tables and opened and closed doors.

6 Information taken from the report given by Mr Hernani Guimaraes Andrade to the second International Conference for Psychotronic Research at Monte Carlo, Monaco, 1975.

The testimony of the last landlady is backed up by plenty of other people, largely those who had tried to make a go of the business. Pipes banged, and a dark presence was seen following people through the building. One child of the owners was terrified every night as she believed that the bedroom was occupied by someone else. In spite of a benevolent spirit called Arthur, one landlady was scratched across the face by an unseen force as she went to investigate noises in the tunnels below the building.

Emotional tension is a key factor in all these cases. Tina Resch had recurrent arguments with her parents; Carole Compton was living among strangers, missing home and her boyfriend, and struggling to fit in with her employers' ways of life; Ivanil was caught in the aftermath of her father's relationship with another woman. In Enfield, too, the Hodgsons had had a difficult year in the run-up to the poltergeist. The parents' marriage had broken down and the family had to deal with the loss of its father, and a fraught atmosphere on the occasions he visited.

Many paranormal investigators believe that unhappiness and psychic stress are prerequisites for poltergeists – that they simply don't manifest in happy environments. What's more, an individual's unhappiness doesn't seem to offer the same psychic opportunities. Poltergeists need the group dynamic to thrive. Very often this is a family, but poltergeists have also been recorded in schools, hospitals and offices.

Beginning in Germany during the summer of 1967, the usually well-ordered office of lawyer Sigmund Adam experienced a run of equipment glitches. Photocopiers malfunctioned, lights turned themselves on and off and, most irritatingly, the office phones went haywire, ringing repeatedly only to be silent when answered. The telephone company investigated but could find no fault, so they monitored the line with special equipment. During the next five weeks it registered hundreds of calls to the speaking clock. Adam and his employees knew the calls couldn't have been made from the office as they had been present during the periods in question. But what really puzzled the engineers was that many of the calls were shown as coming in spates, and registering at speeds beyond the capabilities of the exchange.

When the power company was called to discover why the lights kept flashing, it was equally puzzled. So Sigmund Adam allowed a team of external investigators to monitor events. One of them was Dr Hans Bender, a psychologist with experience of paranormal cases, and he quickly identified a 19-year-old employee, Annemarie Schneider, as the key person. He established that the glitches only happened when she was in the office and also monitored her actions to ensure that she wasn't physically causing them. By this time, the phenomena had expanded into other classic poltergeist manoeuvres: pictures falling off walls, drawers opening and light fittings rotating.

Annemarie, it turned out, was in an unhappy phase of her life. Psychological tests indicated that she was often frustrated and angry, and that she was finding it hard to deal with personal interactions. She wasn't enjoying her job, though she tried to hide her feelings. All of which, Dr Bender theorised, was likely to make her a highly attractive focus for a poltergeist force.

Sure enough, when Annemarie was given time off to go on holiday, the disturbances stopped. When she returned, so did they. She left the firm soon afterwards, by mutual consent.

Dr Hans Bender went on to investigate and study many more poltergeist cases, and became Professor Emeritus of Psychology and Border Areas of Psychology at the University of Freiburg. He was one of the parapsychology experts who offered testimony in support of Carole Compton's innocence.

While various experts were puzzling over the Rosenheim poltergeist, a similar episode was taking place across the Atlantic, in a Miami novelties store. Boxes fell off shelves, glass and china merchandise crashed on to the floor and broke and the damage became so persistent that the store manager called the police. When no culprit could be found, American parapsychologists Dr J. G. Pratt and Dr William Roll (who would later investigate the Tina Resch case) entered the scene. They spent two weeks monitoring the store and recorded 120 instances of objects moving, 44 of which they witnessed in person. From the pattern of events and their observation of behaviour and personalities, they zeroed in on 19-year-old Julio Vasquez, a clerk, as the focal person.

From their psychological profiling, they theorised that the clerk was frustrated and unhappy, and in particular had difficulties expressing his resentments to authority figures, including his parents and his boss. Julio apparently acknowledged that he quite enjoyed the disturbances at the store, though he denied that he had ever knowingly caused them. He soon left his job, after which the disturbances there duly ceased. There was a postscript to this story, however: a while later he cooperated with Roll in taking part in some controlled tests, and these experiments, including one where Julio tried to throw dice with his mind, suggested that he still had some powers of psychokinesis, though they were no longer creating mayhem.

Which raises the question: do those people who become poltergeist agents keep hold of latent psychokinetic powers after the disturbances have died down? And can they learn to control and even develop them?

Matthew Manning would say yes. Born and brought up in Cambridgeshire, England, he had his first experience of poltergeist forces in 1967 at the age of 11. It began mildly enough: a silver mug that usually stood on a shelf was found on the floor, two mornings in a row. It had fallen in exactly the same spot, which seemed odd; the family was also puzzled by the fact that, though it had fallen quite a distance, it wasn't dented. Then other objects – ornaments, books and cutlery – began to move. Matthew's parents contacted the Cambridge Psychical Research Society and Dr George Owen suggested that of all their children, Matthew was the most likely to be attracting the activity.

All went quiet for a while and it seemed the episode was over. Then, when Matthew was 14, the Mannings moved to an eighteenth-century house in a village a few miles away. And there the activity began again. Doors opened and slammed shut; and objects moved of their own accord. Matthew was woken up one night by his bed shaking, then lifting right off the floor to drop down again in a different position. Although he was used to things moving inexplicably, this incident frightened him, and that night he insisted on sleeping on the floor in his parents' room. During the winter of 1971 the disturbances increased. Classic poltergeist phenomena occurred: knocks sounded in walls; furniture levitated in front of people's eyes or was found stacked in towers; objects seemed to appear out of nowhere. Some of the phenomena seemed connected to the history of the house, just as Janet Hodgson's voices seemed connected to the history of hers. For instance, the spontaneously materialising objects included two bread rolls. When one of them was later analysed, it was found to have been baked in the late nineteenth or very early twentieth century. And when writing appeared on the walls (sometimes of locked rooms), it frequently spelled out the names of the house's previous inhabitants.

When Matthew returned to his boarding school, the poltergeist activity followed him. It often manifested at night in the dormitory he shared with twenty-five other boys. His bed frequently shook and moved out of its place towards the other beds. Stones, plates and cutlery would appear and fly through the air. Some of the other boys were frightened at first, but because by this time Matthew took it pretty much for granted, they also adapted to it. All the same, news of it spread through the school and it was extremely disruptive. Many of the staff witnessed incidents too. One evening, several of them saw a strange patch of light glow on the wall of a room near Matthew. When they held out their hands towards it, they could feel heat.

At this point, the headmaster was reluctantly considering expelling Matthew. But then the activity took a new course. One evening Matthew was sitting at his desk writing a homework essay when his mind drifted. As he was groping for what to say next, he felt his hand begin to write, very fast, as if it was moving by someone else's volition. He didn't know what he was writing until he stopped. When he read it back, it was in unfamiliar handwriting, and had no connection with his essay.

Fear did grip him then: he had a powerful sense that something separate from him had broken through and was directing his actions. He tore up the paper and threw it away, trying to wipe the incident from his mind.

However, it brought him (and his classmates) an unexpected benefit. He noticed that the next few days were calm. No objects hurled themselves through the air; he slept without his bed shaking. The automatic writing seemed to have given the restless energies a more satisfying form of expression. So when he found himself doing automatic writing again, he didn't fight it. Matthew was soon writing in dozens of unfamiliar styles, often using archaic expressions or writing in languages he didn't know. The content was like fragments of messages or accounts from other people. They often seemed to be from people who had died unhappily, or else from people who were dead but didn't realise it.

Dr Owen, then a scientist at Cambridge University, encouraged him to develop his automatic writing prowess, theorising that this was a constructive channel for the extraordinary psychokinetic energies he seemed to possess. Sure enough, as Matthew researched the names and references that appeared in the writing, and managed to identify a few actual historical figures, the random disturbances grew fewer. He also found that, besides writing, he could draw in the style of Old Masters when in a trance state. He finished school and in 1974 he published a book about his experiences, which made him a celebrity. By now he had established a rapport with one particular communicant who 'wrote' through him – a doctor who identified himself as Dr Penn, and who would pass on to Matthew diagnoses of illnesses and conditions suffered by the people around him.

Matthew himself was never sure what to make of Dr Penn and the other personalities. Were they genuine and well-intentioned, or were they part of the trickery that characterised the whole poltergeist experience? His misgivings were sharpened when, on a German TV show, he was asked to make a diagnosis of the show's producer, who had just had a hospital consultation. He duly went into his automatic writing trance and received a detailed analysis in Dr Penn's handwriting which the producer, astonished, confirmed as accurate. But when the producer's medical consultant was brought on as a surprise guest and asked to comment, he disagreed. The actual diagnosis, he said, was significantly different, though the producer's confusion was understandable – he had misunderstood the complexities of his own condition. This gave Matthew serious pause. What exactly was 'Dr Penn' providing here? An understanding of people's medical conditions, or a glimpse of their thoughts and fears?

Could it be that Dr Penn was simply a persona being adopted by the psychokinetic forces centred on him, forging a link between his psyche and those of the anxious people around him? Alarmed at the idea that he might be feeding off people's fears, Matthew gave up his partnership with Dr Penn and stopped doing automatic writing in public. Instead he decided to investigate whether he could develop his energies to help people. Over the next four years he underwent a series of laboratory tests to see if he could influence matter with his mind. The results show that when external objects near Matthew are moving or undergoing molecular change, Matthew experiences increased brainwave activity in areas dormant in most people. One particularly interesting experiment has suggested that by focusing his concentration on samples of blood, he can strengthen the resilience of the cells.

Ever since then, Matthew has concentrated on developing his powers of touch and communication and today he works as a healer. Note – he doesn't call himself a faith healer and he doesn't promise cures. He prefers to describe himself, rather cautiously, as someone who can channel energies. After being at the heart of a poltergeist storm for so long, he obviously has a wary respect for the unseen forces he is still able to attract. And people who consult him – including sceptical journalists – testify to the extraordinary heat that seems to emanate from his hands.

So who – or what – was Dr Penn? Not to mention all the other people who made their presence felt through Matthew's automatic writing and drawing. Were they simply aliases adopted by the poltergeist forces, or were they truly the spirits of dead people, somehow caught up in the whirl of psychic energy?

Or perhaps a mixture of both? Modern poltergeist watchers suspect that poltergeist forces and poltergeist phenomena may be separate things, working in a complex relationship. Psychokinetic forces are opportunistic, the theory goes, and just as they like to channel themselves through receptive adolescents undergoing emotional turmoil, so they will also manipulate any available matter, both physical (three-dimensional objects, sound waves, heat and light) and psychic – the imprints of human consciousness.

At one point in Matthew's teenage years, he would repeatedly wake in the morning to find signatures of unknown people written all over his bedroom walls. His father counted more than 200 signatures, almost all of them in old-fashioned script. Some incorporated fragments of information, incomplete but full of personality and detail. Such a jumble of communication is characteristic of poltergeists, and so is the fact that, later on, key facts may often be corroborated.

Remember 'Bill', one of several old men who spoke through Janet Hodgson in Enfield? 'Bill' was particularly aggrieved that Janet was taking up his space in the house and often tried to throw her off the furniture. He was an awkward person to have talking through you: opinionated, with strong likes and dislikes and prone to bursts of raucous humour. Among many remarks (including insisting that doors were closed and demanding to hear jazz), he said he had died downstairs in a chair in the living room, of a haemorrhage, and that he'd come from the graveyard to see his family. Several months after the poltergeist disturbances had died down, a man named Terry contacted the Hodgsons. He'd read about their experiences in the press and the address had piqued his interest because his father had lived there for many years; indeed, his father had actually died there, in his favourite chair in the living room, of a haemorrhage.

These 'ghosts' often seem to break through during poltergeist infestations, but they aren't true hauntings. They don't have the persistence of genuine human ghosts, who haunt because they are tied to a place or a memory or a particular event. Compared to classic ghosts, they tend to be confused and temperamental. One of the most famous American poltergeists of the nineteenth century, the 'Bellwitch', which infested a Tennessee farmhouse, threw up a range of invisible characters that swore, hit and kicked visitors' backsides. One theory now being developed is that some people leave imprints of their personalities when they die, especially in places that have been important to them, and during poltergeist activity these are charged up into temporary life.

Of course, poltergeist activity also gives form to hidden sides of living people's characters. Frustration and rebellion tend to be the most striking. But sometimes, in place of mayhem, gentler aspects emerge. In summer 2008, Soraya Rahman was paying her third visit to a peaceful monastery in the Canary Islands. This was an annual trip for her, a conference she attended as part of her job, and she had come to love the visits, relishing the calm atmosphere and the austerely beautiful surroundings. The monks continued to live in the monastery while the conference was on, combining their daily worship with housekeeping and catering for the guests.

That year, she noticed, the number of monks had grown. A new intake had joined and among them were several young men. The atmosphere was slightly different too. It was still ordered and friendly but she felt there was an intensity hidden away in it. Several times, Soraya had the sense of being watched. She wasn't too astonished by this: after all, she was an attractive young woman in a monastery, and there was nothing threatening in the atmosphere. If anything, she thought some of the new monks looked rather lost.

The night before she was due to leave, Soraya awoke suddenly. It was the early hours of the morning, her room and the whole monastery was dark, and there was someone by her bed. She could feel their presence, and yet she knew at the same time that in logical, physical terms, she was alone. While one part of her mind wondered if she should be afraid, she felt a strong urge to help the unseen visitor, and she asked in a friendly voice, 'What do you want?' The next moment she felt hands take hold of her upper arms and hold her firmly for several long seconds. It was a very definite physical sensation, a clasp that was steady and warm.

Soraya went home the next day and said nothing to anyone at the monastery about her experience. As a psychotherapist, she had some knowledge of poltergeist phenomena, and she believes that in those quiet hours the accumulated loneliness and longing of the young monks took physical shape, reaching across empty corridors and through thick stone walls to draw comfort from a hug.

A very different agenda made itself felt in the South Shields poltergeist of 2006. In the northeast of England, a young couple, who tell their stories under the assumed names of Marianne and Marc, were the victims of a peculiarly vicious poltergeist infestation. From the outset the entity was hostile rather than playful, and manifested in what amounted to a campaign of persecution against Marianne. Sinister symbols and the words 'RIP' and 'Die bitch' appeared on their young son's message board, and were quickly followed by threatening texts on her mobile: 'Going to die today.' 'I'll come for you when you asleep, bitch.' When she tried to trace the texts, she could get no number. On the other hand, there was no mystery about who was making the many silent calls to her mobile – it was her own landline number popping up on the screen. The trouble was, these calls would come in at times when Marianne knew the house was empty, because she had just left it deserted and locked behind her.

The fact that so many of the outbreaks involved Marianne's mobile is a sign of the times. Although mobiles have been around for twenty years, it's only recently that poltergeists have started exploiting them. At first, this seems odd – surely poltergeists, attracted as they are to electrical fields and circuits, should have been early adopters? But in fact poltergeists attach themselves to people first and foremost and tend to manipulate objects and equipment that are an everyday part of their lives. Now that mobile phones are indispensable for many of us, we can expect to see poltergeists playing havoc with them more and more.

Marianne relied on her mobile to keep her in touch with Marc, with friends and family, and to reassure her about her young son when she was away from him. These hateful messages and sinister silent calls struck at the roots of her security. They also ensured that she couldn't escape the poltergeist by leaving the house.

The claustrophobic atmosphere mounted. Like the Hodgsons, Marianne and Marc had a neighbour in whom they confided. What little relief this afforded, however, was soon cut off when he too received a call from their landline, made when no one was in. It was as if the infestation had learned how to disrupt all their lines of communication, blocking their exits. Meanwhile within the house the disturbances reached a peak of violence. Objects were hurled. Bangs and cracks sounded. A dark shape, like the silhouette of a man, appeared, emanating cold dislike. Marc now became a physical target: he would feel an invisible presence touch his back and a sharp, burning pain move across it. Wherever he'd felt the touch, his skin would erupt into livid scratches, some so deep they bled.

The infestation lasted for nearly a year, and several phenomena were caught on camera by psychic investigators Michael Hallowell and Darren Ritson. The activity eventually petered out, but not before the couple's nerves had been shredded. This poltergeist played the usual tricks with household objects and toys, but almost always with an unpleasant twist – one day, Marianne and Marc found their son's large toy rabbit perched on a chair at the top of the stairs, with a box cutter balanced on it. Just as with Janet Hodgson, the entity took to moving the boy himself. Twice his parents found him inexplicably out of bed, once on the bedroom floor and once – after a terrified search – in a cupboard. Both times he was fast asleep, and wrapped up so tightly in bedlinen or clothes that he couldn't move.

And yet for all the vindictiveness, no one was seriously hurt. The activity eventually died down and has not resumed. Hallowell and Ritson wrote a book[7] about it which attracted a good deal of media attention and quite a lot of scepticism, partly because of the uncompromising approach they took to defining the infestation as an attack from outside: the book is subtitled, 'One Family's Fight Against an Invisible Intruder'.

That is, of course, how it felt to Marianne and Marc. That is always how a poltergeist infestation feels – as if an uncanny presence, at once intimate and foreign, has inserted itself into your life and home. But as this chapter shows, it's likely to be a more complex process than that. Poltergeists are drawn to people in emotional and hormonal flux. They feed off their energy, are partially shaped by their personality and grow into uncontrollable forces that create bizarre, frightening disturbances. Many of their antics can be recorded and measured scientifically. Increasingly, parascientists are able to offer explanations for how the energy build-up occurs. As to the why, they can only speculate, like the rest of us. Perhaps soon they will be able to capture some of those fragmentary personalities that seem to whirl inside certain poltergeist manifestations, and question them. Not that they would necessarily get reliable answers.

Meanwhile, in unassuming households in ordinary streets, someone seems to be playing tricks . . .

England

In England, ghost sightings and paranormal events are woven into the humdrum cycle of everyday life. In County Durham, in the north of the country, the local council took a pragmatic decision to pay for the spiritual cleansing of a flat – it was cheaper to get rid of the ghost than rehouse the terrified occupants!

7 Michael Hallowell and Darren Ritson, *The South Shields Poltergeist – One Family's Fight Against an Invisible Intruder* (The History Press Ltd, 2008)

English towns are made up, for the most part, of long rows of identical houses, drab enough from the outside but each one home to a family . . . and a story. This haunting from the future took place in the red-brick terraced streets of Manchester, England. A woman wakes at the dead hour – between 2.30 and 3.00 in the morning – to give her newborn baby a feed. She is sitting up, sleepily, when she sees the doorknob to the closed bedroom door turn, once, twice, and then begin to rattle as if someone is in a hurry to get in. She is petrified but her husband, startled into action by the noise, leaps to his feet and throws the door open.

No one is there and the couple's daughters, the only other people in the house at the time, are both sound asleep in their room.

The husband prowls through the house while the woman calms herself down, gives her baby a feed and the family goes back to bed.

In the morning, the husband gets up and goes to work while his wife stays in bed with the baby. The other two children join her for a cuddle but then, inexplicably, she feels the weight of something pressing down on the mattress at the end of the bed as if another, invisible child has joined them in the room. Terrified, but unwilling to frighten her children, she gets out of bed and holding her baby in her arms and with her two young daughters trailing behind, she looks down the stairs. There, at the bottom, the children's rocking horse is rocking to and fro, as if someone has just got off it . . . but who?

Then she sees. A little boy of about 6 years old walks out of the sitting room and climbs the stairs. He is tall for his age, fair-haired. Too startled to talk, the woman stands back as he walks towards her but her daughter doesn't and the boy walks straight through her and disappears.

The woman screams, throws some things into a suitcase and dashes out of the house with her family to stay with her mother. To her mingled horror and relief, later that

day she hears the extraordinary news that just after midday a freak bolt of lightning smashed through the window of her front room and incinerated the sofa where her two daughters would sit after lunch every day. The appearance of the little boy has saved them.

Six years later she is looking at her son, the baby in her arms when the events took place. He has grown up tall, has a shock of blond hair – and then she realises: he is the spitting image of the child that appeared in her house on that life-changing day.

CHAPTER FIVE

RITUAL KILLING IN THE TWENTY-FIRST CENTURY

In these days of mass tourism, any part of the world that can claim a supernatural or occult heritage exploits it to the hilt. Ghost tours of old towns abound, and haunted hotel rooms command premium prices. You can even buy a voodoo package tour of Haiti to see the dark arts in practice: roll up for a live zombie experience in the flesh!

The west of England is no exception. As the land tapers into the Cornish peninsular and the narrow sunken lanes seem designed specifically to clog up with summer traffic, shops selling crystals, Tarot cards and dream-catchers crowd the narrow streets of market towns and ancient fishing villages. The area's claim to a Celtic heritage somehow make it the natural refuge for witches and druids, and this in turn has brought in the fortune-tellers and spiritual healers. Today, the village hall is as likely to host courses on astral projection as jam-making.

Although the world of magick is decked out with traditional trappings, this is a typically modern phenomenon. Supply follows demand with dizzying speed as containers of newly printed Tarot cards are shipped in from China and the world's mines are scoured for semi-precious stones. But inevitably, behind the charming façade of occult-lite, sometimes one can sense something far older and much darker that feeds off the energies of innocent crystal gazers and naïve astral voyagers.

At first it seemed like a little local tragedy. The crab boat *Clairvoyant* was pulling in its catch in the western reaches of the English Channel, about ten miles west of Lizard Point, the famous Cornish beauty spot. It was a fine morning, with a gentle swell and good visibility, otherwise they might never have seen the body, floating face down in the water. In the words of the *Clairvoyant*'s skipper, it looked for all the world like a big crab.

They pulled the body from the sea and laid him on the deck. Although he was stone-cold dead, it was clear from the general condition of the corpse that he had not been in the water long. He had injuries, but that was common enough with drownings, especially where people had been swept on to rocks or caught in a ship's propeller. Neither was it odd that he was shoeless – the sea would often strip its victims bare. But that was slightly at odds with the way the corpse was dressed. He was still wearing a boiler suit – the sea and rocks had not ripped it away from the body – and there was ring on his finger and a necklace around his neck. Both carried the distinctive pattern of the sort you could pick up in almost any of the Celtic craft shops that serve Cornwall's tourist trade: the pentagram.

An RAF helicopter swept the area but there was no sign of the drowned man's boat; still, the sea could have taken that and there was no reason that day to think the death was anything other than an unfortunate accident.

It was when the body was finally identified that the police became more interested. The corpse was that of Peter Solheim, a local man from the village of Carnkie a few miles inland from Falmouth. Soon suspicions began to pile up. His boat, the *Izzwizz*, was found floating close to its mooring in Mylor Harbour, thirteen miles from where his body was found. There was no chance it could have floated back. Next, the autopsy threw up some disturbing facts. There were traces of sleeping pills in his stomach and bloodstream and the injuries bore no resemblance to chance collisions with a rock or even a propeller. Rather, they were consistent with blows from a machete or axe. There were eighteen in all, including four to the head and what looked like attempts to amputate a leg and a toe. Graze marks suggested that Solheim had been dragged along the ground at some stage, and a reconstruction of his last movements suggested he had been held captive for around two days before being drugged and thrown into the sea, where he drowned.

Peter Solheim's girlfriend, Margaret James, informed the police that Solheim had been planning to go fishing with a friend called Charlie, somewhere out in the English Channel. Anyone with the slightest knowledge of drug slang immediately saw a possible shape of the case emerging. Of course Charlie is slang for cocaine, and Cornwall has never entirely shrugged off its traditional reputation as a smuggler's paradise. More than that, although Solheim was a former local councillor, he was far from being a pillar of the community. He collected firearms and knives, did drugs and dealt in pirated hardcore porn DVDs. People also suspected that he was involved in a scam dating back to the 1980s when a local man fraudulently claimed that ancient Stannary Law would exempt Cornish residents from the hated poll tax if they could prove ownership of a tin mine. Solheim set himself up as intermediary, took the cash that flooded in, but when people discovered the exemption was a complete fiction, it was discovered that £200,000 had gone missing. Peter Solheim was implicated.

The police also discovered that Solheim was in what Britain's tabloid newspapers gleefully recognised as a love triangle. As well as Margaret James, Solheim was in close contact with his ex-girlfriend Jean Knowles. When Jean received a text from Solheim, telling her that he was fishing near the French coast after his body was recovered from the sea, the police were able to narrow their search. They traced the text's point of origin to Margaret James's mother's cottage, where Margaret had been staying.

They searched her house, found a large stash of cash, and a poison-pen note. Not only that, but the ex-girlfriend, Jean Knowles, claimed that Solheim was on the point of dumping Margaret James and coming back to her. On top of all this, the police found out that Solheim had been threatening James with exposure of some dark and dreadful secret. Putting all this together took time and Margaret James was not arrested until February, when she was charged with murder and conspiracy to murder.

But the love triangle was far from the only unconventional thing about Solheim and James. Peter Solheim and Margaret James were both occultists, sensation-seeking black magicians who had been brought together by a shared interest in 'pills, potions, spells and sex'. Not only that, but Solheim's obnoxious behaviour had already seen him thrown out of a druidic group based in St Merryn, North Cornwall. The druids disapproved of his obsession with sex; his habit of hitting on female druids whenever he had the opportunity; his dress, which included a rather undruidic Viking helmet and sword; and his habit of ritually cursing people who crossed him. Another Wiccan group made it clear that he was unwelcome with them as well. His endless talk of sex made other people uncomfortable. One pagan priestess commented: 'He was a boaster. He described himself as hot stuff. He felt he was very attractive to women and had no trouble attracting them.'

In the west of England, covens are almost as common as cream teas, and witchcraft has a habit of cropping up in the most unexpected places. Take the case of Vixen Tor and the Ramblers – a series of strange events that took place on Dartmoor in the neighbouring county of Devon. Most of Dartmoor is a National Park and so open to all walkers and ramblers, but Vixen Tor, a spectacular pile of weathered granite on the western moor, is surrounded by good grazing land and so subject to different regulations. When the land around Vixen Tor changed hands recently and the new owner decided to ban access altogether, all hell broke loose – literally. On two occasions, sheep have been slaughtered nearby, their throats slit and their eyeballs removed. On one occasion they were arranged in a circle (some describe this as a seven-pointed star); on another they were laid out in square with two left by an ancient sacrificial stone. Although local ramblers and hikers have been active in protesting about the ban, police don't suspect them. The tor is named after the witch Vixana and indications were that police were investigating links to pagan activity.

Dedicated to Vixiana, a famous witch, today Vixen Tor is walled off and access is forbidden to members of the public.

And the further west you go on into Cornwall, the more mysterious things become. The reasons for this are relatively straightforward. Cornwall, cut off on three sides from the rest of England, holds itself apart. It is Celtic in character, as opposed to Anglo-Saxon; it has its own language and, until relatively recent times, a degree of autonomy. Although wealthy once from its tin mines, today development appears to be passing the county by. The locals hold themselves apart from the yearly invasion of summer tourists – incomers, or emmets as the Cornish call them, find it notoriously hard to integrate with local village life. In other words, if there was one place in the crowded, industrialised, fast-moving United Kingdom where a local religion – based on local lore and sustained by a web of long-term, local relationships – could exist, Cornwall would be it. In the county's Witchcraft Museum, situated in the delightful, picture postcard fishing village of Boscastle, you can see recent examples of witchcraft on display: potions in bottles and crude little dollies with pins or nails sticking in them, for example. Today Cornish witches advertise on the Web, and local newspapers advertise pagan circles, pagan healing, and charm-making.

Although it's difficult to make hard and fast judgements, most of the Cornish covens are entirely benign and practise Wicca in all its gentle forms. The movement was founded (or revived) in the 1950s by Gerald Gardner, a retired colonial administrator with a highly developed interest in local customs, folklore and, some claim, nudism. He always claimed that central tenets of Wicca had been passed down orally over the millennia and finally came to him by way of long evenings spent in the company of a country witch from the New Forest in Hampshire. Gardner was the first to compile these teachings in book form, taking advantage of new legislation that had recently decriminalised witchcraft.

Wiccans tend to be respectful of people and nature, like to bless rather than curse, and feel a strong and emotional bond with the rocks, stones, trees and hedgerows of the countryside. With its bare moors and fields enclosed with ancient dry-stone walls, Cornwall is the perfect place for its practice. The landscape is not overtly dramatic; it reveals it secrets slowly. There are sacred wells, stone circles and standing stones. Mists often roll in from the sea and cloak the landscape but, when the sun shines, something about the light is truly enchanting.

Although Solheim was Cornish born and bred, he never fitted in.

A childhood friend commented on how he liked to 'push things to the limit'. His magic was aggressive, angry and sex-centred. Solheim tried to use the force of his gaze (he had a pronounced cast in one eye) to get people into bed with him. This behaviour would disrupt the subtle harmony of Wiccan ceremonies which depend on finding a balance between eroticism and formality. When Wiccan's go 'sky-clad', their rather beautiful term for being naked, it's to help transmit and receive natural energy. When they perform the 'Great Rite' – sanctified, ritual sexual intercourse – almost as much attention is paid to the symbolic aspects of the act as the act itself. There's the fivefold kiss, which involves a moving incantation, ritually determined embraces, and much opening and closing of magic circles. Wiccans thought Solheim was into satanism, which might have been the case, or he could have been trying out Crowley-ite sex magick, where energy is generated and released during various forms of sexual activity: intercourse, sodomy, bestiality and masturbation. The High Priest of a Falmouth Coven summed it up: 'Members of my group thought he was off his head. He always had a great big sword and a helmet. He caused a lot of trouble.'

The sword and helmet were Solheim's signal that he was different, and an advertisement of his Nordic stock – his largely absent father had been chief engineer on a Norwegian whaler. He liked to refer to himself as 'Thor's hammer' and may have experimented with Nordic pagan ritual. Asatru, its most common contemporary form, is somewhat meatier than Wicca. Without actively encouraging the uptake of swords, helmets and hammers, it extols warrior virtues and emphasises the importance of victory, without too much emphasis on a strict moral framework. It is easy to see how a loner like Solheim, with an inflated sense of his own importance, would find justification in a Nordic cult like this to continue ploughing his own solitary furrow.

Whatever the case, he found a fellow spirit and willing partner in Margaret James, and their relationship deepened as he grew more fascinated with darker aspects of the occult. But although the relationship was sexually fulfilling, it was shot through with jealousy and darkness, with explosive rows that were compounded by the couple's weirdly chilling habit of referring to each other as 'it'. As the midsummer solstice of 2004 approached, Solheim contacted his ex-girlfriend Jean with two pieces of startling news. He was leaving Margaret and he wanted to marry her that very December, at around the time of the midwinter solstice.

Peter Solheim's death was sensational enough to attract the attention of the UK's tabloid press, while his life was sufficiently weird for it to be reported almost completely without embellishment. All the salient points of the story as reported – druids, witches, black magic, murder – correspond pretty accurately to his life in reality. But amidst the strangeness, one thing has been missed. Underneath the fabric of the Peter Solheim tale lies a very old, very dark shape that strongly suggests that, consciously or not, powerful forces had somehow broken through and were influencing events in the twenty-first century. The modern, eclectic form of pick-'n'-mix occultism that he embraced out of self-interest and self-gratification was about to shake itself down, re-form and take an altogether more substantial shape.

Leaving the obviously occult features of the story to one side for a minute, let's look at some of the astonishing coincidences that frame the story – and ask whether they are coincidences at all. For example, the boat that found Solheim floating in the middle of the Channel and brought him back to land was called *Clairvoyant*. He was killed a few days away from the summer solstice and was due to get married just before the winter solstice – key events in the natural cycle and the pagan calendar.

Things become much darker when we start to look at his death. Solheim was drugged, bludgeoned, stabbed, mutilated and drowned. Not surprisingly, the police saw this as a frenzied, sadistic attack and based their lines of investigation on that. What they seem to have overlooked was the ritualistic aspects of the murder. In other words, seen in another context, Solheim was not killed as much as sacrificed – and the assault on his person, leading to his death, can be seen as anything but frenzied.

USA

The paranormal and the law make uneasy bedfellows, but in Nevada, in the southwest of the USA, an attorney has filed legal papers against a Navaho witch. It all centred around a custody dispute in the 1970s when a Navaho woman hired a lawyer to help her limit her estranged husband's access to

their son and claim unpaid child support. During the hearing, the son returned from an evening with his father and said something rather strange had happened. He had been taken to a wood near a cemetery by his father and a Navaho witch where a ceremony had taken place that involved the burying of two dolls in the ground following hours of chanting. The mother reported this to the lawyer who in turn consulted a Native American professor. This man told him that he was certain that a very rare ceremony had taken place – one so powerful that witches were able to perform them only four times in their lives. The purpose was simple: the dolls represented the lawyer and the mother and the burial was to ensure that they both died soon, to be interred in the local cemetery.

Alarmed, the lawyer took out an injunction against the father and the unknown witch – named in the papers as John Doe, a Witch – arguing that the ceremony was not a blessing as the father's attorney claimed, but a lethal curse. The Native American judge agreed, the court recessed, and that very evening the father dropped his claim – knowing his reputation would be forever compromised if it became more widely known that he had resorted to witchcraft.

As we have seen with Gerald Gardner and his great Wiccan revival, witchcraft claims an unbroken heritage that goes back to the days before Christianity reached Europe. There is still some debate about this: Margaret Murray, the British anthropologist who first called it the 'Old Religion', believed she had found evidence of a pan-European cult based around small congregations of twelve or thirteen practitioners who worshipped the Horned God – a male fertility god with obvious parallels with Pan and whose main characteristics European Christians appropriated for the devil. There was clear cross-fertilisation between Murray's work and Gardner's ideas (Murray wrote the introduction to Gardner's famous *Witchcraft Today*) and while few people now would go as far as Murray did in their claims, there is evidence of pan-European religious practice, particularly where ritual slaying is involved. We know this for one stark reason: while so much of the Iron Age's oral culture has been lost to us, the remains of some of the people they killed have survived from Denmark to Ireland, almost perfectly preserved in bogs.

So meet Clonycavan Man, Grauballe Man, Haraldskaer Woman, Lindow Man, Old Croghan Man, Tollund Man and Bocksten Man, Yde Girl, Windeby Boy and Windeby Man. Between 2000 BCE and 250 CE, all of these people were beaten, bludgeoned, stabbed, hanged, strangled and drowned, in any number of variations, and left in water. Some had bits of them cut off.

Now think about Peter Solheim. The Cornishman was beaten, bludgeoned, stabbed, and left to drown in water. There's evidence that some of the bog-men and -women were given drugs just before dying. So was Solheim. All of them were sacrifices, willing or otherwise, of the Old Religion. Peter Solheim followed the Old Religion. This method of execution, often called the Triple, or Threefold Death, is closely linked with British witchcraft, and there are examples, well documented in British criminal history, that substantiate this. In other words, Peter Solheim is not the only witch to have been sacrificed in modern times and, as such, he can be said to be part of a British tradition.

The date is 14 February 1945, the place is Warwickshire, Shakespeare country, the heart of England. On the continent, the German army is preparing for its last, doomed offensive in the bitter winter chill – a last throw of the dice that would be known as the Battle of the Bulge and cost the two opposing forces over 100,000 lives in a white hell of mud and blood and bullets and bombs. Across the Atlantic, in the Los Alamos laboratory in New Mexico, the first atomic bomb is being built and will be detonated five months and two days later over the desert.

And in England, as a bitter winter is scouring the landscape, a witch is sacrificed in a muddy field on the flanks of Meon Hill, just outside the village of Lower Quinton.

The witch's name was Charles Walton. He set off from his cottage early in the morning carrying his trouncing tool, a long-handled billhook and a pitchfork, and walked to Firs Farm where he had been employed by Alfred Potter do some hedge-cutting in the fields. Then, at some point during the day, he was clubbed on the head, rolled into a ditch, mutilated with his trouncing tool and stabbed so hard with his pitchfork that the tines dug six inches into the earth. He was found that evening by his niece and employer. The police were called and a murder inquiry set up immediately.

From the outset, rumours of witchcraft, witch sacrifice and ritualised slaying were in the air. First, there was the man himself. While he was not a recluse, Charles Walton was a loner. He lived with his niece Edie, whom he had adopted, and did not drink. People claimed he could also see into the future. He was also well versed in natural lore and was said to be able to charm wild birds so they flocked around his head and ate from his hand.

But in case anyone mistook him for the reincarnation of St Francis of Assisi, others claimed he had owned a team of trained toads that he could send into an enemy's field and cause its crops to wither. He also kept a piece of coloured glass in the back of his pocket-watch, whose purpose was to absorb any bad thoughts or ill wishes directed towards him. Significantly, on the day of his death, he was not carrying his watch.

And what of that day: 14 February? It is, of course, well known as St Valentine's Day. Since the 1840s, it has been the custom of lovers to send cards in memory of an obscure Christian Roman soldier who was put to death for allowing his troops to marry – against army regulations – and subsequently elevated to sainthood for his pains. However, as is so often the case, Christianity overlays an older event, in this case the Roman spring festival of Lupercalia. Although associated with the wolf (*lupus*) that suckled Romulus and Remus, the founding fathers of Rome, the festival was linked to Lupercus, the Roman god of the countryside, better known by his Greek name of Pan. During his festival, lovers did not send each other flowers. Instead, two male goats and a dog had their throats cut before being flayed. The skins were then cut into thongs and revellers would run round the streets, striking anyone they met with the thongs. Young women would rush to the front of the crowds that lined the streets because being touched by the thongs encouraged fertility and easy childbirth. But the festival of Lupercalia, and the Greek festival of Lykaia it derived from, evolved out of much earlier sacrificial festivals in which the god king, a man selected from the tribe, was killed, his blood collected and spread on the earth to propitiate the gods, fertilise the soil and secure a good harvest for later in the year. The word February derives from the Latin *februa*, or cleansing, referring to spring rituals of purification, something which finds a faint echo in the habit of spring cleaning.

The anthropologist, Margaret Murray, whom we met earlier, claimed that a small adjustment of the calendar, to take into account the switch from Julian to Gregorian systems, put the date of Walton's murder back to 2 February, or Candlemas Day. Midway between the winter solstice and the spring equinox, Candlemas was both a festival of lights for Christians and one of the gathering days for witches. In America, 2 February is known as Groundhog Day – a key date which sets up the rest of the year. An auspicious day for a sacrifice, in other words or, in the words of the investigating officer, the famous Fabian of the Yard: 'the ghastly climax of a pagan rite'. In spite of bringing in the RAF to photograph the area and taking 4,000 statements, including from travellers from hundreds of miles away who might have passed through the village, no trace of Charles Walton's killer was ever found. To this day, the case files remain open.

But returning to the present day and Peter Solheim, we can find still more connective tissue between Solheim's death and witchcraft. When the police were searching Margaret James's house, they found a rather significant note and a small, sinister doll pierced by a single pin. People associate pierced dolls with voodoo (a relatively recent cult), but the practice is almost certainly universal and as old as magic itself. The Ancient Greek playwright Theocritus talks of wax dolls, or *kolossoi*, which could be used for a huge variety of purposes, such as binding loves or controlling demons. Today the tradition survives but is particularly strong in the western counties of Great Britain where the dolls are known as poppets. The theory informing poppet use is sympathetic magic – the idea is that where one thing is similar to another, it can have an influence over it. This is why people who make poppets go to great pains to include in the effigy something belonging to the person they wish to influence.

For example, in Boscastle's Museum of Witchcraft, there is a poppet with a human face, pubic hair sewn between the legs and a carefully carved dagger stuck into its abdomen. This was probably used to perform an abortion on the person who donated the pubic hair – at least one hopes the process was voluntary. Another darker possibility is that the pubic hair was stolen and the poppet used to cause a miscarriage. Poppets are still widely – even promiscuously – used

This poppet is now safe in Boscastle's Museum of Witchcraft, but others like it are still used to this day. (Photo John Hooper Hoopix/Museum of Witchcraft UK)

today, with poppet kits on sale in craft shops and advice that suggests, for example, that a good way to rid yourself of an unwanted friend is a simple two-step process that ends with tying the poppet's hands together and tossing it in a river! It is worth bearing in mind that two hundred years ago Margaret James's poppet could not only have been produced as evidence of a motive for killing Peter Solheim, but it could have been held up as the weapon itself.

What of the note found in James's home? Although mentioned in newspaper reports, its significance has been overlooked up until now, so much so that even the wording varies according to the different reports: 'what go around come around' in one, 'what goes around comes around' in another; 'what goes around must come around' in a third. Perhaps if the reporters knew of the Threefold Law of Wicca, they might have paid closer attention and treated the note less as a piece of whimsy and more like evidence of occult forces influencing events.

The Threefold Law is one of the key tenets of modern witchcraft, but only a practitioner of Wicca, or researcher into core faiths, would be able to apply it to Peter Solheim's death.

Ever Mind The Rule Of Three
Three Times Your Acts Return To Thee
This Lesson Well, Thou Must Learn
Thou Only Gets What Thee Dost Earn

In a Judeo/Christian tradition, this would be given a moral weight. The implication is clear: in a moral universe, bad actions have bad consequences and, on a personal level, your punishment for being bad, or for doing bad things to other people, is that bad things will then happen to you. The Wiccan interpretation is subtly different. Repercussions do not come about as a result of moral ordering; they just happen because everything is connected to everything else. In other words, Peter Solheim did not suffer the triple death as punishment for his wrongdoings. He suffered it as a result.

Occult forces are so called because they are hidden. Often the pattern is obscured and muffled. Nothing is quite straightforward and it's seldom that the workings of unseen forces can be seen as clearly as they are in the case of Peter Solheim. They seem to have infected everything, from the name of the trawler that discovered him, the *Clairvoyant*, to the ritualised manner of his death. Conspiracy theorists looking for further evidence (of the extent of the authorities' awareness, for example) might comment on the name the police gave to their investigation – Operation Tungsten, which was, incidentally, the longest murder inquiry ever carried out in Cornwall. Tungsten is, of course, one of the hardest metals known to man, and easy match for Solheim's Thor's hammer, which we must assume was made of iron. Another name for tungsten is wolfram – derived from the German *volf rahm*, or wolf's froth. Wolves play a central role in Scandinavian mythology, so beloved of Peter Solheim but, ominously for him, the wolf Fenrir, always depicted as a slavering monster, devours Odin at Ragnarök and brings destruction on the world. The police investigation did not devour anything, but it did a reasonably good job of ignoring the implications of the evidence.

In all the thousands of words written about the Peter Solheim mystery, there is one enormous gap. When you notice this absence, your first thought is that it's like not seeing the wood for the trees, but it's more than that. It is more like mistaking the wild wood for a recreational park. Oddly enough, the absence is the central core of most investigations: the death itself. It's almost as if the events surrounding the murder have cast a glamour over the event, when, over a two-day period, Peter Solheim was confined, drugged and tortured. Ultimately we don't know where it happened, we don't know why it happened and we don't who did it.

It's possible that Margaret James participated in the torture – it doesn't take much strength to hack at a drugged man with an axe or machete. What beggars belief is that she could have restrained Solheim single-handedly in the first place and then somehow manoeuvred his drugged body from the place where he was tortured and into a form of transport, driven him to a boat, lifted him into the boat, and then tossed him out of it in mid-channel. The judge himself acknowledged this and instructed the jury to find James not guilty of murder on the grounds that, if he died by drowning, she could not have lifted him out of the boat. She was convicted of conspiracy to murder and sentenced to twenty years at Truro Crown Court. When the judge commented that she showed no remorse, James shot back at him: 'How can I feel remorse for something I didn't do?'

While James did receive justice, the investigation and trial left wide open the question of who actually did kill Peter Solheim. James has never said, nor, as far as one can find out, did she offer to turn her accomplice in as part of a plea bargain. Three obvious possibilities fall out of this. One: she was totally innocent and the victim of a miscarriage of justice. Two: she was so frightened of her accomplice or accomplices that she did not dare give up their names. Three: she felt such a strong bond with her accomplice(s) that she simply did not want to give their names to the police. So what are we talking about here? A murderous death cult? Possibly, although these are more common on the continent, where regions and communities have been terrorised in recent years by satanic killing sprees. Perhaps this was local retribution – a stunningly violent response to a man who, by rejecting local religions in favour of his own, in effect insulted them. Perhaps he was misusing powers he had learned in local groups and was stopped to warn others.

The bog-men might point to another possibility. Although it was assumed originally that the dead men and women found in the bogs were sacrificial victims, there is no evidence that they went reluctantly to their deaths. Suppose they were willing sacrifices, volunteers even? Perhaps the triple death is the way to kill people of power – magicians, shamans, saviours – in such a way as to ensure the sacrifice is recognised. The presence of hallucinogenic grains in the stomach of at least one of the bog-men might suggest that the victim was looking for a transcendental experience. The noose, still on the necks of other bodies, suggests the same. Restricting the blood to the brain is a common way of achieving an altered state. Suppose Solheim himself was Margaret James's accomplice. For this driven outsider with the cast in one eye, thick glasses and Viking helmet, self-belief never quite translated into respect or influence. Suppose that he might not have seen his death as assisted suicide; that instead it could have been his attempt at immortality through invoking the dark powers, calling them down to him and then letting them do with him what they wanted. Water has always played a key role in pagan religions. It is material but not solid; vital to humans but dangerous to them, reflective and transparent. Gifts to the gods are thrown into water and, in choosing this way of death for himself, perhaps Solheim was making his own bid for immortality.

And finally, it might be karma. What goes around comes around. What comes around goes around. Put simply, Peter Solheim dabbled in the darkness and in the end the darkness found willing agents on earth to take him down . . .

Costa Rica

Traditionally, Latin American culture has been known for its machismo. However, women whose men have been unfaithful have traditionally found an ally in La Cegua. Along roads where horses are still the best form of transport, men with an eye for the ladies are stopped by a vulnerable-looking beauty. She has a voluptuous figure, tumbling black hair and huge, teary eyes. She will say that she has been walking for hours to reach her sick mother, or some other excuse, and could she please be carried on the man's horse for a while.

If he lets her up, he is doomed. If he looks over his shoulder at her, he will see her face transform into a rotting horse's skull, the flesh dropping off it and maggots crawling in and out of its eyes. The shock will sometimes kill him but, if it does not, the ghoul will bite a chunk out of his cheek and render him impotent for the rest of his miserable, haunted life.

How likely is it that sacrifice is practised in this day and age? The answer is: very. Since people developed a spiritual framework to their lives, sacrifice has played a vital part in their rituals. From Ancient Greece through the pre-Columbian massacres in South and Central America to the weekly consumption of the Christian god's blood and flesh in churches all over the world, we are reminded that the urge to sacrifice is hardwired into the human psyche. The motives are complex: sacrificial ritual is a means of binding communities together and, when death is involved, the bond is strengthened either by the need to keep the event secret or simply to not to break 'group rules' in case you end up the next victim. Another motive is propitiation: you offer something immensely valuable to the gods and in return ask for their protection from events beyond your control.

But what of sacrifice in a world where many of the ancient motives that drove the practice have been lost? Health, wealth, fertility, both of the soil and the womb . . . these are no longer controlled by fortune or the gods but by human application and science. One aspect of sacrifice that is often overlooked is that it confers enormous power into the hands of the person performing the rite, the priesthood, and it is this interest in personal power that has increasingly defined dark arts. This is the age of the individual and increasingly people define themselves not in terms of the society but in terms of their own levels of satisfaction. The question we must ask now is what happens when the 'Me Generation' turns to the occult.

The answer is disturbing. On the one hand we have the fairly harmless habit of people consulting the Tarot to increase their personal wealth or find out where to go on their next holiday. Hardly edifying in itself, but it does lead to deeper, darker practices. The old idea of sacrifice involved giving up something precious: the community would sacrifice its prized bull; the god king who was sacrificed in the spring was kept fat and happy with precious supplies the tribe could ill afford to spare. Christians believe that God gave up his beloved son to save the world. In other words, it wasn't only the victim that suffered. But in the modern world, our contemporary life-myth constantly reassures us that we can gain power and ensure happiness without individuals having to give up a thing. And the clearest example of this are a series of murders that took place in and around Florence, Italy, between 1968 and 1984, murders committed by a man who came to be known quite simply as '*Il monstro*'. The monster.

The story of the monster is depressingly familiar, a template for evil, cruelty and, once the occult elements have been factored in, pure and pointless waste.

There were sixteen murders, comprising eight couples killed between August 1968 and September 1985. The victims ranged in age from 18 to 36, and all were murdered at night while engaged in some form of sexual activity. The deaths took place in country lanes – at the time, young Italians tended to live with their families until they were married and so making love in cars was commonplace – and in all cases where the killer was undisturbed, they combined shooting, stabbing and mutilation.

The first murder took place on 21 August 1968 and involved a married woman and her lover, shot while making love in a cemetery with the woman's son asleep on the back seat. Following the murders, the boy was carried out of the car, it is assumed by the killer, and left on the doorstep of a nearby farmhouse. Eight .22 calibre cartridge cases were found at the scene. Although the woman's husband was arrested, many years later the crime would be seen as part of the series.

The next murders were committed six years later on 15 September 1974. Two bodies were discovered just north of Florence. Cartridge cases were scattered on the ground. In the car a man was discovered, shot. On the ground outside was his girlfriend. She had been dragged out, spreadeagled, stabbed, and a vine branch inserted into her vagina. The contents of her handbag were scattered in a nearby field. At this stage, no one connected the events – the first killing was thought be committed by a jealous husband who was safely locked up, while the second was clearly the work of a sex maniac.

Seven years passed until an off-duty policeman, out for a stroll with his son, came across a parked car with the contents of a woman's handbag scattered on the ground outside it. Inside the car was a dead man with his throat slit and, twenty yards away, down a bank, was the body of a woman, lying on her back, her legs apart and her vagina cut out with a sharp knife. In spite of the knife wounds, the autopsy revealed that cause of death was multiple shots – with a .22 calibre gun. When ballistics matched the bullets and cartridge cases to the 1974 double murder, the police realised they were dealing with a serial killer.

Months later, the killer struck again, this time murdering a couple at a beauty spot near Calenzano, outside Florence. This time, the coroner concluded, the couple had been shot through the window of their car, dragged out and stabbed before the killer hacked out the woman's vagina in a field of wild flowers.

Less than a year later, on 21 October 1982, there was another double killing in which the female was killed outright but her male companion managed to start the car engine after he had been shot. Although he drove the car into a ditch before finally perishing, the killer was too disturbed to carry on with his ritual and fled the scene. It was at this stage that the police connected the crimes to the very first murder twenty years previously, but it left them no closer to solving the murders.

And about a year later he struck again, on 9 September 1983, this time shooting two German tourists – two young men. Again, the bodies were not mutilated but in all likelihood it was because the killer had mistaken one of the men, who was slight and had long hair, for a girl. In other respects, the murders followed the same pattern as the previous ones: same gun, a car and a rural location. The police also noted that each killing had happened in similar weather – on a cloudy, moonlit night.

He waited a year before striking again, this time completing and even elaborating on his ritual. The couple were shot, stabbed, and the woman spreadeagled on the ground and her vagina removed, but this time, her left breast was hacked away as well. The same gun was used, the wounds and stabbings (the couple had been stabbed over a hundred times) indicated the same knife as well. With no breakthroughs, the police could only hope that the killer would stop of his own accord. They were disappointed.

The eighth and final murder took place on 8 September 1985. This time, a young French couple were killed: the man shot and stabbed; the woman shot and stabbed and mutilated in exactly the same way as the previous victims.

Myanmar/Burma

In Myanmar a repressive military dictatorship sometimes clashes with the vivid folk traditions of the people, sometimes just goes with the flow. For example, the generals have built themselves a new capital in the middle of a malarial swamp, allegedly because a fortune-teller told them that the old capital, Rangoon, was going to be destroyed in a flood. According to ancient Burmese tradition, new buildings must be protected by the ghosts of unfortunates buried alive in their foundations and rumours persist that political prisoners suffered that terrible fate in the foundations of the new parliament.

Theirs are not the only ghosts to haunt this unhappy country. After the devastating hurricanes and floods of 2008, villagers put on all their jewellery before fleeing the weather. When desperate survivors fished out the bodies from the floodwaters and stole their gold to buy food, they were screamed at by vengeful ghosts until they threw the gold back into the floods.

So, occult, ritual murder or psychopathic crime spree? Ultimately, of course, it does not matter to the victims or their families. What does matter, however, is clarity, and that is something that has been lacking in this case since the outset. The man who was finally arrested for the crimes, a labourer called Pietro Pacciani, was first convicted of the murders, then cleared on appeal by a judge on the grounds of unsound evidence. To compound this farcical sequence of events, he died of a heart attack brought on by a cocktail of drugs, just before the police were about to *rearrest* him. The police had arrested two other men, supposedly his accomplices, and one of them had allegedly confessed to carrying out the killings with Pacciani. Both men remain in prison for aiding and abetting him.

In spite of this, the case will not die down. Rumours of satanism have persisted, and police have investigated alleged members of a society black-magic circle that supposedly employed the three convicted men to collect body parts for their rituals. The religious historian, Massimo Introvigne, claims that the area had had a long tradition of occult practices but this did not necessarily point to satanists. This is wise, if uncontroversial advice. Almost every corner of the world has a long tradition of occult religious activity and the term satanist is so vague as to be practically useless; the case, if nothing else, shows how quickly and inaccurately the press labels any ritual killing 'satanic'. Other examples of similar inaccuracies can be found all over the world. In the Brazilian town of Altamira, between 1989 and 1993, up to nineteen boys were kidnapped and mutilated by members of a sect known as Superior Universal Alignment. Castrations, blindings, eye-gouging and organ removal were carried out on children by trained doctors who believed the cult's teachings that anyone born after 1981 was possessed by the devil and that cult members would be transported into the heavens by spacemen in 1988. In other words, it was an anti-satanic spaceman cult. Sadistic, cruel, ritualistic, yes, but not satanic by any stretch of the imagination.

As an aside, it's doubtful whether any of the self-proclaimed satanic groups are truly satanic in any meaningful sense of the word. Today, Satan is simply a marketing tool to increase sales of heavy metal music and chrome paraphernalia featuring snakes and skulls. There is no evidence that Beelzebub particularly likes hard rock – in fact, most music critics would associate the beast with the numbing effects of elevator music rather than anything else. An astonishing number of court cases where satanism and satanic abuse has been reported have collapsed under investigation, and it cannot be the case that every police force and judicial system in the Western hemisphere is infiltrated with agents of the dark lord, out to thwart any disclosure of his power.

And even where these youth cults have actually committed murder, analysis of their behaviour is generally way off the mark. The Beasts of Satan, a Milanese cult who claimed to worship the devil, murdered three of their own members – hardly a successful model for a religion, and although the killings were described as ritualised, they simply were not. Two of the victims were beaten to death with a hammer after an all-night drinking session in a Milanese heavy metal pub, while a third, the girlfriend of the cult leader, was shot and buried alive. These are vile murders but not cultic. It would be hard to imagine them conducting a series of ritual murders over a twenty-year period without being caught.

The mutilation and theft of the women's sexual organs inevitably drew the authorities' attention to some sort of sexual ritual, although exactly what these involved remains unclear. Sex magick, for example, as expounded by Aleister Crowley, was developed as a way of channelling the body's most powerful source of energy. Through sex, practitioners could enter an altered state and develop a higher form of consciousness, but only by following an elaborate ritual in a specially conducted service or mass. While the service drew on Judeo-Christian traditions for its structure and presentation, the philosophy behind it was Asian, combining Taoist thought from China and tantric teachings from India with a wholly Crowley-ite emphasis on secretions, male and female, and open-minded attitude to anal penetration.

While Crowley would have seen heavy metal satanists as his bastard offspring, he might have celebrated their lack of inhibition and shame and, like them, he made no efforts to hide his activities or belief. Even more significantly, his interest lay in living energy. Power derived from nonliving flesh, whether the brain, the sexual organs or any other part of the human anatomy, belongs to a different tradition altogether.

It was a failure to understand this that led the Italian police down their most unproductive blind alley. The killings followed a certain ritualised pattern. This, they reasoned, must be part of a greater ceremony. A greater ceremony was clearly beyond the imaginative powers of the three accused peasants, so it followed, clearly, that a high-society circle of black magicians was involved. The three convicted men were mere pawns in this greater, highfalutin, evil.

All they had to do now was find a group of suspects who were posh enough.

This was not so hard in the prosperous heartland of Italy. Following an anonymous tip-off that a satanic cult made up of successful professionals was active in the Tuscan hills, they swooped on the homes of a doctor and a retired chemist, both of whom were released, and muttered about an artist whose house contained newspaper clippings of the case and, allegedly, drawings of mutilated women. Nothing came of that either, and there the case remains to this day, with two men in prison and third dead by a drug overdose.

So what does lie behind the murders of the monster, or monsters of Florence? As in the cases of Peter Solheim and the unfortunate

Charles Walton, an old and disturbing pattern of blood, the elements: earth, air, fire and water.

Let's look at the key factors again. First and foremost, all the Italian murders were committed in the open air. Second, each murder took place on a night when there was a moon, but also cloud cover. Third, they all involved couples who had been out to clubs or discotheques, were unmarried and were engaged in some sort of sexual activity. Fourth, we must note that, although most were shot before they were stabbed, they were still alive when stabbed. In other words, we are talking about multiple killing methods. Fifth, when the killer was undisturbed, the woman was dragged away from the car and her blood was spilled on the earth. Sixth, there is emphasis on the woman's reproductive organs: vagina and breast. Seventh, having been cut out, these were removed from the scene.

The first thing we must dismiss is the satanic-trophy-hunting theory – that the three men accused of the crimes were mere hunting dogs sent out to bring back flesh for their masters or mistresses. This sort of cannibalism simply does not occur in Western occult traditions, and to link it to satanism is culturally illiterate. Satanism might involve sacrifice but – and this is the crucial point – it occurs as part of the ceremony. In other words, the ritual is driven by the taking of the life force while it is still present. Consuming body parts belongs to another tradition altogether – *mutu*, a form of witchcraft practised in Africa, and headhunting traditions in Asia and the South Pacific, where warriors believe they can absorb the positive qualities of their slaughtered enemies by consuming their freshly butchered remains.

For the monster of Florence, then, the murders weren't leading up to the ritual. The murders were the ritual. When all the extraneous details have been stripped away, this is a story about the earth and the moon, light and darkness, and while most modern interpretations of the rituals have concentrated on the psyche of the perpetrator, we should look beyond that at the pattern of the actions and their effects.

The sacrifices of ancient times were carried out in the open air and so were these. In each case, where the ritual was not disturbed, the killer even dragged the woman, the main focus of the sacrifice, a distance away from the car. Once away from the car, he made sure the woman was spreadeagled on the bare earth, her limbs carefully arranged. The connection with the earth is important. Letting blood flow into the soil was a key component of ancient sacrifice, although as religions became more skybound and moved into the controlled environment of the temple, this element grew less important. (Note that in ancient Jerusalem, blood from the Great Temple was sluiced from the sacrificial tables into a sewer and channelled into the Kidron brook, where it was collected by farmers and used as fertiliser.)

But the orientation of these rituals might not be the earth but the sky. Consider their dramatic imagining. The spreadeagling of the victims was a display, meant to be viewed, but on each occasion, who was there to see it? Only the night sky and, specifically, the moon. If these were ancient killings, dating from a thousand years ago, we would be quick to explore the significance of that. Remember that the killings took place on moonlit but cloudy nights. The moon's presence seems to have been important – otherwise, why not choose entirely moonless nights, which would be darker? But on these nights the moon was present, yet only intermittently visible, vanishing behind the clouds and reappearing at intervals. Could it be that the murderer saw the moon as some kind of partner, or mistress, and that he mutilated and staked out his victims as an offering to her? Again, if we were thinking in terms of ancient cultures, the clouds would have a dual function – to hide the murderer from human eyes, and to provide a screen between him and the moon while he worked. He would be able to prepare the sacrifice with the moon obscured, her light diffused; once he had finished, the next parting of the clouds would create a moment of terrible drama, revealing the moon herself, blazing coldly down on the body.

What of the other details? Almost all the victims had been killed after visiting nightclubs and all were murdered while engaged in sexual activity. The sequence of dance and ecstasy followed by sacrifice belongs to classical rituals. And of course the concentration on mutilating women's sexual organs suggests a chilling obsession with sex. Which brings us back to the moon: in Roman mythology, Diana, the moon goddess, is the goddess of chastity, as well as hunting and wild places. So determined is she to remain untouched and unseen that she turns Actaeon into a stag and sets her hunting dogs to tear him apart after he has spied on her bathing.

Hunting – with its traditions of cutting out body parts straight after the kill; wild plants and flowers; murderous fury as punishment for sex . . . the elements of the Diana myth are all there in the murders.

Is it feasible that an Italian farm worker would be involved in a classical ritual? Outside Italy, classical knowledge is the preserve of academia and occasionally explored in novels: Donna Tartt's novel *The Secret History* describes how a group of North American students, while studying the classics in an exclusive Ivy League university, get carried away and start to imitate the maenads – the followers of Silenus who drank and danced themselves into a trance before tearing animals and humans limb from limb.

In Italy, however, the old Classical religions still persist in a folk form – Stregheria – in which Diana, the moon goddess, is revered. Just like its north European cousin, Wicca, Stregheria has undergone a revival of late and its current form is as gentle and nature-orientated as Wicca. But all religions are built on blood and just as we saw darker forces breaking through the modern drapery of contemporary folk religions to kill Peter Solheim and Charles Walton, so here we seem to have something similar.

Pietro Pacciani, the man accused of being '*Il monstro*', had a long history of violence and sexual deviancy. He had served prison sentences for murdering his wife's lover and raping the corpse, and, more heinously, for raping his two daughters. If indeed he scoured the wild places of Tuscany looking for lovers to kill (and the evidence against him is strong), was he knowingly offering his desexed victims to the virginal moon? Or had he just stumbled ignorantly into Diana's grove, led further and further in by his own brutal acts?

As so often happens, the last death in this ritualised series was his own. He died suddenly one night of a heart attack, under the influence of drugs. He was discovered with his trousers round his ankles, exposed as the victims had been. One can imagine a shaft of moonlight, slanting through an uncurtained window, travelling across the floor, touching him, illuminating him.

Then moving relentlessly on.

In these last examples, we have seen evidence of dark, primeval forces pushing up through the fabric of the modern world, like rocks pushing upwards from the earth. In each case, however, the cause, or causes of death, have not been in doubt: bullets, knives, axes, pitchforks, water . . . these are familiar objects. But what of cases where the cause of death – or perhaps it would be more accurate to say the agency – is less easily explained? In the following account, names have been changed to protect the living relatives of the protagonists.

On an April morning in 1996, a young man called Timothy Renfrew was about to die, although he showed no sign of knowing it. He had been unhappy and disturbed recently, but had plans for later in the day and told a close friend that he was going for a walk 'to clear his mind' and would be back in about twenty minutes. Moments later, he was seen plunging over a cliff above the town, a look of terror on his face, screaming as he fell. There was no one at the top of the cliff and his behaviour – the note before he set off on his walk and the screams overheard as he fell – strongly suggests he did not commit suicide. Indeed, at his inquest, the coroner left the verdict open, even though there was no evidence that any other person was directly involved in his death. So what killed him?

Renfrew himself had felt he was under psychic attack in the weeks before his death. He reported to his girlfriend that he was being haunted in nightmares by a vision of a dark figure. He believed that people were trying to kill him and had been told in an anonymous phone call that he was being pursued by demons. When police entered his room after his death, they found pages from the Bible plastered to his wall. Underneath, scrawled in felt-tip, were the words: 'Please God. Somebody save me. Protect me from black magic.' Shortly after Renfrew's death, a local farmer came across something very disturbing in a remote barn on his farm. He found an altar, candles, a photograph and a note. The photograph was of Renfrew. The note said: 'I, Timothy Renfrew, completely renounce Christianity.' At this point it was tempting to conclude that Renfrew had killed himself after experimenting with the occult – except for one thing: when his friends were shown the scrawled note from the Bible pages in his bedroom, they said the handwriting was not his.

So exactly what was Timothy Renfrew's connection with the occult? Let's look at the location first. Although the place in question presents as a charming, historic English country town, it has a chequered history and an 'interesting' present. Ancient pagan festivals are still vigorously celebrated with processions and bonfires that draw crowds up to 60,000 people every year. More recently, however, the town has become associated with more disturbing events that began in 1995 and built up in the years leading up to Renfrew's death. Just before Christmas in 1995, the vicar of one church found that the crib had been desecrated and the figures smashed. Days later, mutilated cats were left on the vestry steps. At another church, close to the town castle, pages were torn from the Bible, the pulpit was damaged and curtains torn down and ripped. In a village nearby, stone crosses were broken off gravestones and stuck upside down in the earth and a grave was used as a sort of fire altar, with a trench dug around that was filled with inflammable liquid.

Attacks on churches are immediately associated with satanism, an issue that the local police themselves have had to deal with – inside their own organisation. Five years earlier, in 1990, a secretary for the Police Intelligence Unit admitted to having sadomasochistic sexual relations with 'dozens' of male witches. The press had a field day, the secretary was suspended and the police had to investigate, although in the end they had to admit that equal opportunities legislation meant that being a practising satanist could be no barrier to performing police duties.

And it seems that Renfrew himself had been on the edge of black magic circles. In 1995 he had met a young man called Tom Crowdon. Though just a teenager at the time, Crowdon was reported to have had a mesmeric effect on people who met him. When his home was raided on one occasion, police found a shrine with black painted walls, a star and a runic circle painted on the floor, and an upside-down cross hanging on the door. Chalices, candlesticks and priests' robes were also found at his home. Was he Renfrew's way into the world of the occult? Crowdon admitted sending Renfrew a cow's heart pierced with nails but claimed that it was just the sort of a thing a friend would do – and he was a good friend.

At Renfrew's inquest, Crowdon said that Renfrew had been irrevocably cursed by a group of black magicians he had met in a pub; while the rest of the evidence was being given he sat, protected by a bodyguard he had hired for the event, cracking his knuckles and grinning at the Renfrew family. An experienced police officer compared Crowdon to Damien from *The Omen*, claiming that 'mature, sensible, intelligent people are petrified of him', and during a separate court case, a barrier was erected in court so that people giving evidence against him could do so without having to undergo the almost physical oppression of his stare. All this suggests he was capable of exercising a form of mind control over people who came within his orbit.

Crowdon's connections with occultists in the area appeared to be strong; Renfrew's, on the other hand, could never be traced much further. He had made enquiries about ordering New Age books for a bookshop he was thinking of starting, but that was about as far as it went. And yet he had been tormented and shadowed in his final weeks, and felt that he was being hunted down. Some of his friends believe he was, though they confess themselves at a loss to name the people or forces responsible.

South Korea

A Korean airliner became the flight of choice for ghosts when a badly depressed woman hanged herself in the toilets on an international flight to Australia. In Asia, there is a long tradition of unhappy female phantoms, and crew members soon started to notice cold spots within the plane. On one long-haul flight, one of the cabin crew saw a Buddhist monk chanting quietly on his own in the near deserted first-class section. When the crew member asked what the monk was chanting for, he said that the aircraft was full of dead people and he was chanting for their safe journey to the afterlife. Shortly after that incident, the plane was taken out of service.

The rarity of cases like this make it hard to identify any form of pattern. Indeed one has to go back sixty-five years to find another, but it is worth examining because many of the elements in this earlier story bear an uncanny resemblance to the ones just described.

These centre around one Netta Fornario who died on the remote Hebridean island of Iona. Fornario was a member of the Alpha et

Omega Temple. The Temple grew out of the more famous Hermetic Order of the Golden Dawn, which included Bram Stoker, W. B. Yeats and Aleister Crowley in its membership, and involved the use of ritual magic to develop the soul, perform acts such as astral travel and, at the highest levels, to enter into direct communication with higher beings, known as Secret Chiefs. Although a world away from the black magic that was being practised in the previous story, high magick of this sort does leave the practitioner exposed to attack from non-physical beings – spirits, demons, astral vampires, call them what you will. One member, Dion Fortune, even wrote a book about how people could protect themselves from such attacks. Members themselves were not immune to attacking each other in this way. (When Aleister Crowley left the Hermetic Order of the Golden Dawn to start his own order, Astrum Argentium, it sparked a psychic battle between him and the leader of the Golden Dawn, MacGregor Mathers.)

But there was no hint of this sort of behaviour in Netta Fornario. Earnest, studious and reflective, she left her home in London for Iona as so many others have done, for its crystal seas and rain-washed skies. And, as the place where St Columba landed and founded a monastery to bring Christianity to the British mainland, this beautiful island is associated with spirituality. Whatever her purpose, she intended to bed herself into the island. She took packing cases of luggage with her that included enough furniture to fill a small house.

Fornario found lodgings with an islander, a Mrs Macrae, and they spent evenings together, deep in conversation. Fornario told Mrs Macrae about her telepathic healing and told her that if she went into a trance, under no circumstances should she call for a doctor. The housekeeper agreed with some misgivings as Netta had told her of a previous trance that had lasted a full week.

She passed her time in her predictably eccentric way, walking around the island in all weathers as she established communications with its spirits. We can say in retrospect that she was gathering herself and perhaps making her mind up, because after a few weeks she sent a letter to her housekeeper which stated that she would be incommunicado for a few weeks as she 'had a terrible case of healing on'.

After that, her mood changed. Her housekeeper noted that she became more agitated and Netta told her that she was under psychic attack and had to leave for London. Moreover, she had had visions of a rudderless boat in the sky and was receiving messages from other worlds. Mrs Macrae also noted that Netta's silver jewellery had become tarnished overnight – something that simply does not happen in the clear, clean air of the Scottish islands. This was a Sunday, when no boats sailed, and Netta spent the day packing, emerging in the evening with a different attitude entirely. She had changed her mind, she said. She was going to stay on Iona for good. Her expression was resigned, but calm. Relieved, Mrs Macrae went to bed, and that was the last she saw of Netta Fornario alive.

Netta Fornario left the cottage in the night and made her way, with some difficulty, to the ruins of an old village, some two and a half miles away. She was found, stone-cold dead, on a so-called fairy mound, covering a cross that had been carved into the turf. She was wearing only a black, ritual cloak with scratches on her body, her feet badly cut, a tarnished silver cross around her neck and a knife by her side, which she had used to cut the cross shape in the turf.

At the scene, the doctor pronounced her death as due to heart attack, to which conclusion the coroner added exposure. Students of the occult, however, will note the cross, the ritual cloak and the fact that the body was not huddled and may come to a different conclusion.

Scotland

Edinburgh has its haunted vaults; Glasgow has ghostly inhabitants of theatres and tenements. From Glencoe to Culloden, the ghosts of slaughtered highland warriors stalk the moors. But what of the empty spaces? Few places in the British Isles feel more remote than Sandwood Loch, right at the northwest tip of the mainland. It is miles from any road, and the white crescent of sand is pounded by the mighty grey Atlantic breakers.

Nevertheless, like the rest of the Highlands, it was once the home of a community, and there are still cottages on its shores. In the nineteenth century, people saw mermaids cavorting in the waves; a hundred years later, walkers sheltering in one of the cottages heard ghostly hoofbeats

drum past. The ghost of a bearded Polish sailor is said to walk the sands at night, the only survivor of a shipwreck, but people who have slept in one of the ruined cottages have felt something else: a sense of being watched; a sense of not being wanted; a sense that you are invading someone, or something, else's world . . .

People who have slept in the cottages have reported waking in the night and, although the air is as fresh as anywhere in the country, and as clean, they feel oppressed and stifled. Some report a cold weight pressing down on their chest, others a fleeting smell of stale bodies.

No one knows the origin of this spirit. Around the headland there is a similar cottage where, in the 1990s, a young English woman starved herself to death – she thought, it was alleged, that the light was so pure that she could eat and drink it. There are rumours of an Australian backpacker who fell in love with the place and returned to haunt it after he died. The truth may be even stranger. For as long as people can remember, the beauty of Sandwood has been associated with something else: deep, unnameable, dread.

The author Dion Fortune suggested she had either gone on an astral journey and never returned or been attacked by an astral vampire, sent by the former leader of the Alpha et Omega Temple, Moina Mathers. One small problem – Moina Mathers had been dead eighteen months when Netta died. The condition of Netta's feet suggest she was running from something, but what? Murder cannot be ruled out. There were reports of a mysterious black-cloaked figure seen on the island at the time of her death, but he was never seen again. So, a mystery. Can we find clues by comparing her death to that of Timothy Renfrew?

Seen in one light, there are striking similarities. Both felt themselves to be under psychic attack. Both were involved with occult ritual. But significantly, while both were very disturbed shortly before they died, both seemed very calm and settled before they went out to meet their deaths, with Renfrew leaving a letter for his girlfriend,

Netta telling her landlady she was planning to stay on Iona indefinitely.

There is also a Christian element in both cases, with evidence of Renfrew's conflict and confusion and Netta's cross becoming suddenly tarnished. Renfrew may have been cursed, or he may have been encouraged to dabble in black magic by the sheer force of another person's personality. Netta Fornario laid herself open to attack through her overuse of telepathy. Fornario, who must have known that Iona was a wellspring of Christian spirituality, came to the island hoping to find in it a safe place. The terrible case of healing she told her housekeeper about was herself but, in the end, the power she was trying to avoid found her, even in Iona, and tarnished her silver cross. It was then she gave up the struggle or, as her landlady said, resigned.

One final example suggests that reason and scholarship, so often seen as a protection against the occult, can in certain cases leave people fatally exposed to psychic forces beyond their control.

James Webb was born in 1946 into a wealthy, landowning, Scottish family. Educated at Harrow, a top English private school, he went on to university and continued his studies at Cambridge, where he made the occult his own subject. Red-haired, charming, a bit of gourmet and a good man at a party, he was considered particularly brilliant, with all the necessary qualities a scholar needed: boundless energy and focus, insatiable curiosity combined with a certain detachment, a capacious memory and a need to pursue every lead to its source.

In the early 1970s, when he began his studies, the occult was not known in the way it is today. Indeed, he broke new ground and opened up whole new fertile fields for serious scholarship, introducing many insights and ideas that are now considered mainstream. In his small Cambridge rooms and the college's and university's unmatched libraries, he pored over musty old texts and contemporary manuals, immersing himself in ancient mystery religions, syncretic Renaissance magic and contemporary cults and clubs. His first book, *The Flight from Reason*, was published in 1972. In it, Webb developed the highly influential idea that the occult was a body of 'rejected thought', but far from being marginalised and cranky, as had previously been thought, was in fact seriously embraced by artists, thinkers and even revolutionaries, whose ideas would then in turn filter into the mainstream of society. Well received, *The Flight from Reason* was followed by *The Occult Establishment* four years later. But by that time, James Webb was not enjoying the glittering future people had imagined. In 1978, he suffered a full-scale nervous breakdown, brought on by a combination of hard work and trying to adjust his brilliant yet sceptical mind to the enormity of what his research was suggesting. In an echo of Hamlet's lament – 'I could be bounded in a nutshell, and count myself a king of infinite space, were it not that I have bad dreams' – he had discovered that he could not be master of his material, and that the word 'occult', which means hidden, does not just refer to the source of the material but also to its significance. In other words, the material itself, once found, contains a hidden power, and the rational mind is the one least able to cope with this.

Although in his early years of research, Webb had been out on his own, as he developed a deeper understanding of his field than anyone else in the academic world, and before his breakdown, he had developed a deep and trusting friendship with Joyce Collin-Smith. Collin-Smith was a mystic herself, who had spiritual and emotional experience of the sorts of things Webb had been writing about from the viewpoint of sceptical academic. Now, during his breakdown, he wrote an extraordinary series of letters to her, describing what he had seen and felt: a great silver mill wheel on which his incarnations and the molecular structure of existence slowly revolved. And while he said that some of these experiences were hallucinations, a residue remained which he simply had to take seriously. He talked about being hoist with his own petard, and questioned why magicians wanted to be possessed by the powers. 'You lose your humanity that way,' he said.

Although Webb did come out of his breakdown, he had changed. His last book, *The Harmonious Circle*, a huge study of P. D. Ouspensky, G. I. Gurdjieff and their followers, was published in 1980 but money was tight, and he and his wife had moved to a remote converted church in Scotland, from where he commuted daily to Edinburgh to work as a copywriter. Instead of lessening the strain, it increased it. All the qualities that had brought him such acclaim now became the very qualities that were undermining his sanity. Instead of settling down with his mystical insights, his extraordinary mind still tried to chase them down to their source: Gnostic, Buddhist; Hindu; Mage . . . Which system was right for him? In an attempt to find out if it was Christianity, he had once walked miles through a storm and waded a chest-high raging river to try and get to a cathedral. A man who had been granted a glimpse of the infinite now felt driven to try and bring together a multiplicity of spiritual and cosmological disciplines into a single system. The quest overwhelmed him. On 9 May 1980, James Webb killed himself by putting a gun in his mouth. He was 34.

Some say he was attempting a controlled death. Gurdjieff and Ouspensky, the subjects of his last book, cheated death in different ways: Gurdjieff by staying alive long after his internal organs had perished and withered, Ouspensky by staying in touch telepathically with one of his followers for a week after his corporeal body ceased to work. Webb himself talked about this before he died, so it is possible that by taking his own life he was attempting, paradoxically, to prolong it. But it is more likely that the grip of the great powers he had awoken was too painful for him to bear. They would not let him go and he could not shake them off and so he took the only way out he knew.

The comforts and distractions of what we call civilisation can blind us to the fact that the atavistic impulses within us, and even deeper, darker forces without, have never gone away. They need an outlet and they need to manifest themselves. Sometimes humans choose other victims; sometimes a person might sacrifice themselves; and sometimes, in the most terrifying cases of all, these forces will take a person's mind, grip it, then squeeze it to death.

Indonesia

Perhaps this is not so much a ghost story as a miracle. Muhammad Wildan was 7 years old and playing with his friends in the garden when he suddenly went white, shrieked, clutched his crotch and screamed that ants were biting him down there. Concerned, his older brother told him to take his trousers down so he could have a look and the ants could be brushed off. There were no ants but they did notice something strange: Muhammad, who had not been circumcised before, now was.

His father was delighted and so was Muhammad and, as far as it is possible to tell, this is the first and so far only case of a spirit – possibly a very religious djinn – performing that particular operation.

CHAPTER SIX

ARMIES OF THE NIGHT

Witchcraft and Warfare

It is the summer of 1940. On one side of the English Channel, a shell-shocked Britain licks its wounds after its armies have suffered defeat after defeat on the continent. By some miracle, they have managed to withdraw a large part of the defeated army from the beach at Dunkirk, but only the most deluded optimist would see the campaign as anything other than a disaster. For Hitler's armies, led by shock troops that are empowered and protected by ancient Germanic runes, have blasted their way through northern Europe, unleashing hell, and now they dominate the Continent.

Any student of the occult will tell you the reason: they have listened to the forces of darkness and been granted a revelation: a way of fighting a modern war that will crush, grind and utterly dominate the opponent. Blitzkrieg, translated as Lightning War, is the child of an acolyte of Aleister Crowley's. General J. F. C. Fuller was a lieutenant in the Ordo Templi Orientalis before World War I and in the years after the war drifted further and further towards a fascist viewpoint. Like Crowley, his master, Fuller took the view that the world was principally chaotic and it was up to the individual to pull down the greater powers from the occult realms and through them impose order through force and domination. Of course, in wartime, natural chaos is exaggerated, but then so are the possibilities for domination, and Fuller saw how a fully integrated armed force that consisted of air, artillery and fast-moving armoured columns could form an irresistible wall of iron but also punch through enemy lines like a spear. It was an insight the Nazis valued more than the British, and while they were preparing for war, they avidly studied Fuller's theories.

It was this dark magic that the British faced and set out to counter. On a warm summer's evening, Lammas Day, the New Forest coven of witches gathered, sky-clad, near an ancient stone in the forest clearing. This was the place where Rufus, King of England, had been killed by a stray arrow in 1100, exactly 840 years earlier. It is hallowed ground – the anthropologist and pagan scholar Margaret Murray identifies the death of Rufus as a ritual sacrifice – and the coven wanted all the ritual power it could muster.

But the precedents were good and the covens of the south coast witches had impressive form. Since they had organised themselves, no foreign invader had ever set foot on Albion's shores. In 1588 they had summoned the storm that had scattered the Spanish Armada and Napoleon's invasion plans were scuppered by foul weather. Now they were intent on building a cone of power that they would direct across the Channel to the Nazis to disrupt their preparations for invasion.

The cone of power is the most ancient and effective visualisation technique for focusing an individual's or group's psychic energies – you can see the shape still in church spires and the traditional pointed hat worn by wizards. It has pros and cons: on the plus side, the force of the cone allows it to be easily directed and is based on positive earth energy. On the negative side, raising the cone generally leaves the circle that raises it exhausted.

Accounts of what exactly happened vary. Some say Canadian soldiers were drafted in as unwitting extras and, under the pretext of performing complex, secret manoeuvres, were told to march in a circle around the coven to help concentrate the energy. Others that Aleister Crowley, who had connections in British Intelligence that included the James Bond creator Ian Fleming, invited high-ranking German diplomats who were magic initiates themselves, to witness the ceremony as a warning. Another theory suggests that there were two rituals: one in which the local witches sent their cone of power towards Adolf Hitler, and another which was directed towards the high-ranking Nazi initiate Rudolf Hess, willing him to defect. All however point to a degree of official involvement which begs the question: what did they hope to achieve and to what extent did the British High Command believe in magic?

There might have been a 'better safe than sorry' attitude at work here. The authorities that arrested Helen Duncan in England in January 1944 did not do so because she was a witch. They believed that the Portsmouth-based clairvoyant seemed to have access to secret information and they didn't know how she got hold of it. In 1941, she had contacted the spirits of drowned sailors who died in a torpedo attack that the authorities had hushed up for security reasons. Three years later and with D-Day looming, she was considered just too dangerous to leave on the loose.

On the other hand, Britain's elite was not lacking in believers in the paranormal. Air Chief Marshall Sir Hugh Dowding communicated with the spirits of his dead airmen and his wife contributed to the war effort by remote viewing: she was able to identify the location of hidden German airfields. And of course Winston Churchill, prime minister and inspired wartime leader, was a Druid – he was accepted into the Albion Lodge of the Ancient Order of Druids in August 1908.

It wasn't just a British thing either: the great American general, George S. Patton, boasted of his own clairvoyant powers and believed he was the reincarnation of a Roman general. After D-Day, shortly after crossing the Moselle River, he stopped without explanation and gathered his forces together. When this was questioned, his commanding officer General Omar Bradley said Patton knew what he was doing. By halting his advance and consolidating his forces, he was able to fight off a major German counter-attack that only he had been able to foresee.

And then, of course, there are two simple, stark facts. One: that the Nazis, inexplicably, failed to invade Britain when it was ripe for the taking. Two: on the night of 10 May 1941, Rudolf Hess climbed into a twin-engined Messerschmitt 110, and flew it to Scotland in the express hope that he would be able to make contact with the Duke of Hamilton, a senior member of the Hermetic Order of the Golden Dawn.

All through history you can find examples of the efficacy of supernatural interventions in warfare. Jehovah parted the Red Sea to let the Hebrew people through and drown the Egyptian army. When the Israelite King Saul was confronted by a massive Philistine army, he consulted the witch of Endor who summoned the ghost of the prophet Samuel and told him he would fall in battle – which he did. Moving through the centuries, medieval European armies rallied behind the spear that killed Christ as they fought to carve a Christian kingdom out of the pagan forests and swamps of central Europe. Dr John Dee, court magician to Elizabeth I of England, used his skills to help lay the foundations of the British Empire, as well as attempting to create a forward-thinking network of occultists across Europe that would cut across differences of race and religion.

Dee's mind was extraordinary and he was considered one of the greatest men of his age. Though his reputation has suffered because of his belief in magic, in his time there were no divisions between, say, chemistry and alchemy, astronomy and astrology. Because of the wide-ranging nature of his researches, his contribution to his country is impossible to pigeonhole. This magician used his own astrological charts to set the date for Elizabeth's coronation, developed codes for his country's fledgling secret service and coined the phrase 'the British Empire'.

He also developed skills in what he called skrying: opening a channel of communication with paranormal forces using a highly polished obsidian mirror. His first success was to warn Queen Elizabeth that agents working for Spain, England's enemy at the time, were planning to burn down great swathes of English woodland so as to prevent the expansion of the navy. His work came to the attention of Sir Francis Walsingham, the father of the British Secret Service, but his intelligence began to take second place to something he considered more important. In the course of his remote viewing, he opened a channel to supernatural beings and devoted the best of his remaining energies to recording their language. That, of course, is another story, but the point is this: occult ritual and the most advanced science of the period came together in the service of the state.

But what of contemporary warfare? Have the world's military leaders left all that behind? Has the white heat of technology cast its hard light into the occult and obliterated its more subtle powers?

Emphatically not. Indeed, almost the complete opposite is true. During the Cold War the two great opposing blocks of East and

West did not just peer at each other through radar screens. Although the language was bang up to date and the environments scientific, Americans and Russians employed hordes of psychics to spy on each other, and explored other areas of the supernatural in ways that the Elizabethan magus, Dr John Dee, would have known only too well.

The Soviet Union was to be a rational, materialistic paradise: the place where mankind would develop, free from the constraints of history and superstition. Out of this freedom would come what was effectively a new man, a superman capable of extraordinary feats and boundless power. If ordinary workers were to become transformed, the state would be the power that would make the transformation possible. But, fascinatingly, beneath all its rational, anti-spiritual rhetoric, the state began to take on the trappings of the supernatural.

The first step was to create a cult around the leadership. Through this deliberate policy, first Lenin and then Stalin were invested with the status and powers of gods. They had godlike powers – the ability to reach not just into the homes of the Soviet citizen, but into their very minds, and winkle out disloyal thoughts. Mass political rallies were treated as mass religious rallies, engendering a near spiritual fervour with people chanting: 'Stalin waves his right hand – a city grows in a swamp; he waves his left – factories and plants spring up; he waves his red handkerchief – swift rivers start to flow.' It is hardly surprising that within this atmosphere a fascination with the occult would grow and be fostered by the state, rebranded appropriately as a new form of Soviet science – but magic to almost everyone else. Even the red star that appeared everywhere and under whose shape all was done, was a pentagram, one of the most potent occult symbols there is. During the purges of the 1930s, people wore their party cards around their necks as amulets. Stalin himself believed that the pianist Marina Iudina must have had occult protection, simply because she was one of the only people he had ever met who was not frightened of him.

Siberia

Siberia: source of unimaginable mineral wealth; the frozen grave of tens of thousands of Russian prisoners; spiritual home of shamanism; the location of secret cities, founded by the Soviets, now the frost-ravaged home of wolves and desperate vagabonds. It was here that scientists, engaged in drilling the deepest hole known to man, found hell.

The Kola Superdeep Borehole took twenty years to drill and reached 12 kilometres under the surface of the world. It was here that scientists recorded a massive temperature rise, heard the terrible sound of human screaming and then watched in horror as a massive cloud of gas shot upwards through the cavity, formed a monstrous, bat-winged shape in the air, and then wrote the words 'I have conquered' in letters of fire across the night sky.

Through the 1960s and beyond, the Soviet Union took on an aura of technological brilliance, so much so that the United States consciously set out to prove to the world that its scientific achievements were greater than those of its rival. First the space race, and then its more malign offspring, the arms race, were born.

Less well known is the psi race, where Soviets and Americans immersed themselves in research and practices that previously had been the domain of magicians and sorcerers. Picture a small, nondescript room. There are metal filing cabinets in a corner, a table with what look like glass flasks standing on it, and a row of boxes with dials on them – electrical equipment of some kind. If it weren't for the lattice wallpaper, you would think it was a laboratory. As it is, we could be looking at a meeting room in any office thirty or forty years ago, or even a hotel room set up for some sort of experiment. We see three people: a bespectacled scientist in a white lab coat, a middle-aged man in shirt sleeves with an arrogant, confident manner, and a younger woman, somewhere between youth and middle age. Her hair is scraped back from her plain, serious face and tied behind in a rough bun, and she is wearing a simple black sleeveless dress.

The middle-aged man is a Soviet psychiatrist, the man in the white coat a doctor, and the woman is Nina Kulagina, a heroine of the Soviet Union, renowned for her telekinetic powers. In any other era of Russia's long and turbulent history, the chances are she would have been tried and cast out of society as a witch, and in any other country, what she is about to try to do would be banned. But in the modern world, she is considered a valuable asset in the USSR's titanic struggle against its enemies in the West, and that is why – with the full blessing of the state – she is going to try and stop the psychiatrist's heart from beating. In other words, she is going to attempt to kill him . . .

Was it really possible for such exotic mind techniques to exist in the grim, concrete reality of the perfect socialist state? The answer is emphatically in the affirmative, but before we see just how effective Nina Kulagina was, let's look at how the super-rational and supernatural were intertwined in the Soviet Union's cultural and scientific DNA, and how the state blurred the boundaries between the scientific and the spiritual, psychic and psychiatric, wizardry and warcraft.

For a start, take Semyon Kirlian, an electronics genius who started off his career as the electrical odd-job man in the hospital of his home town of Krasnodar and ended up discovering how to photograph people's auras. He was a remarkable man who discovered his unusual affinity for electricity and its effects when he accidentally electrocuted himself when repairing an electrical massage machine. Inspired by the sparks that flew from his fingertips, he set to work trying to devise a way of recording what he saw as a beautiful effect. Shortly afterwards, he came up with an idea: using the hospital generator, he would attach an electrode to one hand and the other hand to a glass photographic plate. When the two came together, a circuit would be made, and he bet that the sensitive coating on the glass plate would record it. For safety, he stood on a rubber mat and used a medical student as an assistant, but Kirlion could not see what had happened until he got home and handed the plate to his wife, Valentina, who was an expert at photographic processing and developing.

To their delight, the plate showed the outline of his hand with a mysterious aura of light around the fingertips. It was the first time a non-mystic had perceived the human aura and showed the Russian authorities material evidence of an energy or life force. And force was something the Soviet Union was very interested in.

Russia

Just after the Iron Curtain came down, and Western businessmen were taking tentative steps towards dealing with Russia, a young American executive booked into one of Moscow's imposing but unfriendly Soviet-style hotels. The hotel was busy and could not offer him a room for the full length of his stay, but he opted to stay anyway and use his time to find another hotel nearby. Days went by. It seemed every hotel in the city was fully booked and the hotel he was in swore they could not squeeze him in anywhere. On the way to check out he noticed a door to a room at the end of the corridor was open. It was a large room, he could see, with views over Red Square. Thinking it was probably between occupants, he thought he would go into it and have a look at the view. He stuck his head through the door and glanced around. Although there was a layer of dust over everything, he was amazed to find the room was pristine and tidy and set up as if it were an office, with a desk, filing cabinet and office chair. He stepped inside, wondering if he could ask to stay there, but as he approached the desk, he felt a sick coldness engulf him.

As he checked out, he asked the clerk about it. The clerk gave him a strange look. 'It is occupied,' he said.

The businessman shook his head. 'It's empty. What's more, it clearly hasn't been used for months, years even. There's dust everywhere.'

'It's occupied,' the clerk repeated flatly, and would say no more.

Puzzled, at his next meeting the businessman mentioned the incident to his Russian contact and asked what he thought was going on. When he described the room further, and gave the name of the hotel, his contact went white.

'There's only one man who stays in that room and lives,' he said, 'and that's the original occupant: Lavrentiy

Pavlovich Beria. He was head of Stalin's secret police and used that room as an office. He had it soundproofed and would take young girls there and rape them. Although he was killed in 1953, he's still in that room. It's never been dismantled because no one wants to touch his things. The maids won't clean it and it's kept locked. Occasionally, though, the door opens mysteriously; anyone spending any time in there goes mad.'

The aura has long been a battleground between psychics and sceptics. Mystics believe it is individual to all humans and can reveal everything from their state of spiritual development to physical health. Sceptics claim it is an aberration, apparent only to people with visual system disorders such as eye burn, or those suffering from migraine or epilepsy. After Kirlian's discovery, such claims and counter-claims were made redundant.

The Kirlian Effect, as it is known, records not just the aura but the way it changes according to mood. Fingertip 'discharges' reflect emotional states. They are sensitive to alcohol consumption; to sickness and strain – athletes use it to record muscle fatigue – even to original shapes: it can record the original contours of a leaf even after a bit of it has been cut off and destroyed. Although these days Kirlian photography is considered different from aura photography, which does not use an electrical current, people who see auras claim to be able to sense the very things shown in Kirlian photography. Kirlian, a gentle, modest man who made no profit from his discoveries, died in 1978, a hero of the Soviet Union and one of the few scientists to leave a concrete record of a spiritual effect.

Wolf Messing, a German Jew who fled to the USSR in 1939, was the only man to penetrate the ring of security surrounding Joseph Stalin using psychic powers. Forced to earn a living from showmanship, he challenged the dictator that he would be able to break into his private residence and present himself without alerting any of the guards to his presence. Stalin took up the challenge, amused that anyone could make such a claim, but was astounded when he looked up from his desk one day to see Messing walk calmly into his study. Messing told him that he had walked past every single one of his guards without once being challenged and, to do this, he had simply projected into the minds of each of them that he was in fact Lavrentiy Beria, the notorious head of the secret police and security services and the one man in the Soviet Union, apart from Stalin himself, who would never be challenged.

Arguably Messing took a far greater risk when he correctly predicted the date of Stalin's death. It was a measure of the respect in which he was held that he was not accused of causing the death and executed.

Dotted throughout Russia during the Cold War were secret cities. They appeared in no official record, on no maps, and travel into and out of them was severely restricted. August Stern was a Russian scientist who escaped to the West and confessed that he had spent years in Novosibirsk, a city devoted to science in Siberia that few people, apart from its several thousand inhabitants, had ever heard of. He had worked for years on psychic research and said that within the Soviet Union there were research facilities more secret than his, working directly for the Russian Secret Service. CIA files confirm this, estimating that in one facility alone, as many as 300 physicists, doctors, biochemists and other technicians were directly engaged in paranormal research. The problem is this: from the 1970s onwards, roughly from the time when the technological gap between the Soviet Union and the West was becoming apparent, all news of paranormal research from behind the Iron Curtain stopped. Its scientists stopped attending international conferences and those on the fringes would not talk of developments any longer. It had, in effect, become top secret. The bright light of open research that began to dispel some of the shadows surrounding the dark arts had been extinguished. Once again, magic had become occult.

The reason, in all likelihood, was the growing interest in the paranormal of the then head of the KGB, Yuri Andropov, later to become president of the USSR. Free from the massive capital expenditure associated with conventional, high-tech weaponry, paranormal weapons had the added advantage of stealth. The holy grail of psychic warfare is killing by remote control, the most extreme manifestation of Remote Influence (RI), but there are plenty of other branches to this occult activity: for example, extra-sensory perception (ESP) offered the possibility of remote viewing (RV) of documents, mind-reading and telekinesis. Shamans from central Asian Soviet republics were drafted in, and teachers were encouraged to report any nascent psychic ability in their students to the authorities. The key word was psychotronic – the amplifying and harnessing of psychic powers to specific ends. Main centres of research included the Institute of Control Problems at the USSR Academy of Sciences, the Institute for the Problems of Information Transmission, the Pavlov Institute of Higher Nervous Activity and the laboratories in Novosibirsk. Remote viewing, or clairvoyancy, became the speciality of the Filatov Eye Institute in Odessa. Experiments were carried out in top secret, deeply buried laboratories where success had to be carefully analysed before it was presented. The reason for this is fascinating: scientists had to be able to prove to their political masters that they had a rational explanation of events – because, in the Soviet Union, the irrational could not be said to exist. In other words, the Soviet Union was not just out to harness occult forces. Its aim was to redefine the supernatural as natural and the paranormal as normal.

This led to some of the results being suppressed. In Kharkov, for example, a young woman student signed up to participate in a series of telepathic experiments with her teacher, Professor Dzelichovsky. As the weeks went on, she kept on badgering him for the experiments to start, even going as far as visiting his laboratory in person. When asked to give an explanation of why she had gone so far, she found she could not give a satisfactory answer. Later, while assisting, she fell into a trance but had no recollection of it. In fact, she had been the subject of an extraordinary experiment into remote hypnosis – mind control in other words – without even knowing it.

The Soviet leaders would never have objected to that, of course, but the problem for the scientists was that they could not find a satisfactory explanation. Subjects could be influenced when they were in a Faraday Cage, designed to block out all forms of electromagnetic waves and, even when the hypnotist himself was secured in a lead chamber with mercury seals, the experiments worked. All attempts to identify the source of the power failed, and so, in the end, the scientists stalled the authorities by claiming that the subjects were responding to conditioning – based on sound Russian, Pavlovian theory – rather than inexplicable paranormal forces.

Malaysia

In many cases, a ghost will haunt a place because its body has not been buried. However, a case from Malaysia reverses this pattern. Mike was known for risk-taking and burning the candle at both ends. After a session of drinking and gambling at a friend's house outside Kuala Lumpur, he refused to join his friends who were taking a taxi back into town, and set off on his imported Harley Davidson.

That was the last time anyone saw him alive. He crashed at full speed and his body was mangled beyond recognition. His mother decided on cremation and friends and family assembled but, just after the start of the ceremony, the priest was seen to be whispering to the mother. He then stood up and announced that the ceremony was to be postponed. The friends dispersed and did not see the mother until many weeks later, when she told them what had happened.

At the crematorium they had tried to burn the body repeatedly but on each occasion, the flames would not catch. It was not the machinery that was at fault, either – other bodies were successfully dealt with that day – so the priest said there was only one explanation: the young man in question was not ready to go. On his suggestion, the mother went back to the scene of the crash where she prayed, burned incense and begged her son to accept his death, however untimely, and go into the next world. The ghost listened to her prayers and the next day was successfully cremated.

The search for a hitherto unknown energy force and the means to control it is as old as mankind. Of course, Far Eastern philosophy and medicine has a name for this energy – they call it *ki* in Japan, *chi* in China and *prana* in India. The Greeks called it *pneuma*.

The Cold War intensified the search, especially as it seemed obvious that it could not only affect people's minds, but could be controlled by the mind. It was hardly surprising that at the same time as scientists were trying to isolate it, others were looking for ways to amplify it though psychotronic amplifiers. The Russians came up with their own name for the force: bioplasmic energy or 'psi'.

A breakthrough occurred behind the Iron Curtain in the old country of Czechoslovakia, where a technologist called Robert Pavlita managed to make a copper strip attached to an electric motor revolve in the opposite direction to the motor. The copper strip was in a sealed box which contained the secret: a psychotronic generator. The generator itself is based on the theory that it is possible, in the words of a Soviet scientist, 'to transfer energy from living bodies to non-living matter', but if there are military applications, it is unclear what they are. The generators themselves are based on a complex relationship between their shape and the materials they are built of, and so far have been only used for peaceful means.

Within the Soviet Union, experiments were focusing on the use of electromagnetic waves to stimulate the mind. Their aims were ambitious, to say the least, and included:

- Setting up a mass remote programme so they could gain access to documents, weapons and troop movements;
- Influencing the minds of generals and strategists to sabotage US efforts;
- Killing at a distance through mind control;
- Disabling equipment and munitions, such as tanks, bombers and rockets.

The official line was that clairvoyants could in fact manipulate the electromagnetic field around them, and nationwide the word went out that citizens with psychic powers would receive special treatment. Less lucky would be scores of prisoners – it's alleged that those sentenced to death were bombarded with various forms of radiation to see if psychic ability could be stimulated in 'normal' brains.

It was discovered that some people could correctly identify colours when blindfolded and some unsighted subjects could sense colour after the object was removed – almost as if it had been imprinted. As a result, experiments were carried out to discover whether artifacts could be imprinted with toxic energy that could then be activated remotely.

Scientists also delved deep into the science of consciousness. The 'theta' state, where an electroencephalograph records electrical brain activity at around three cycles per second, was found to be most conducive to paranormal activity. This roughly corresponds to a dream state, known to shamans and mystics since the dawn of time; now, however, the Soviets were not only quantifying the parameters of this state, but were trying to perfect a method of attaining it systematically. Other experiments concentrated on the Tesla coil. This type of transformer, invented by the Hungarian genius Nikola Tesla, produces a high-voltage, low-current, high-frequency alternating current. In old films, where you see electrical equipment producing incredible waves of sparks, you are seeing a Tesla coil in operation, but the sparks are only visual manifestations of its effect. Tesla coils produce wide electrical fields, so powerful that they can cause fluorescent tubes to light up fifty feet away – wirelessly. Soviet scientists discovered they could amplify their operators' psi power, or bioplasmic energy, by tuning a Tesla coil to 7.8 cycles per second, the same as the earth's natural frequency. In this state, Soviet psi agents were able to read documents, and even experiment with remote killing – techniques that they allegedly honed on prisoners of the state. At the same time, they found they could block psi assaults from remote viewers in the United States by setting up two Tesla coils to transmit at opposite phases. US intelligence sources were so worried by this that they installed blocking devices in their own remote viewing stations.

It is here that we must return to Nina Kulagina.

She is sitting across the table from the psychiatrist, a self-confessed sceptic who is unwilling to accept the results of an earlier demonstration, when she stopped a frog's heart beating. Now she stares at the psychiatrist with intense concentration and, as she stares, she begins to move her hands in front of her. The man's expression changes with astonishing speed – from amused arrogance to surprise to shocked panic. Close to collapse, he clutches his chest and the physician steps in. Nina sits back, her face suddenly relaxed. She had no intention of killing the man and is relieved that she has managed to show him that her extraordinary powers are real without actually having to perform the *coup de grâce*. Unfortunately, her powers were short lived. Nina herself died young, the victim of a heart attack believed to have been brought on by the strain of her work.

What now? What of the decades of research carried out in the Soviet Union? Like so many other secrets of the Cold War, much of it was sold off to the highest bidder when the communist regime collapsed, and there is evidence that a great deal of research went to the USA. The old enemy was well aware that while it had won the technological arms race and triumphed globally in the battle for hearts, they lagged far behind in the battle of the inner working of the mind.

As well as the hard physics of nuclear research and rocket science, former KGB officials and unscrupulous researchers had vast stocks of psychotronic equipment designed to subdue their own populations, so while the nuclear secrets were sold to North Korea, Pakistan, Iran and Iraq, unscrupulous agents channelled psychotronic equipment to the USA – and dollars into their Swiss bank accounts.

If American paranormal research was less committed than the Russian, it was still widespread. In the Vietnam War, soldiers used dowsing rods to find Vietcong tunnels with great success, and there are those rumours that LSD was fed to troops in small doses to see if the intensified experience could somehow trigger the extrasensory perception of enemy ambushes and man traps.

Soldiers are pragmatists – good soldiers are, at any rate – and the weapons they use are selected to fit in with their tactics and strategy – not just because they work. For example, in ancient times the Romans undoubtedly had the technology to develop and deploy the crossbow, at the time the most accurate long-range killing machine. They failed to do so because the Roman foot soldier was so awesomely effective. Picts, the tattooed natives of the northern bogs and mountains of Britain, were immeasurably less sophisticated than the Romans in most of their technology, but had developed the crossbow because it suited their military tactics. During the Cold War, the Americans did not need to engage with the Soviets on the psychic battlefield because they enjoyed such a massive advantage on the physical one, but the evidence shows that, once they discovered just how far the Soviet magic had gone, they set about building up their own paranormal capability.

A couple of key incidents sparked this change. The 1978 publication of a report, 'Controlled Offensive Behaviour – USSR', pointed out the extent of Soviet research into bionics, biophysics, psychophysics, psychology, physiology and neuropsychology. It went on to say: 'Many scientists, US and Soviet, feel that parapsychology can be harnessed to create conditions where one can alter or manipulate the minds of others. The major impetus behind the Soviet drive to harness the possible capabilities of telepathic communication, telekinetic and bionics are said to come from the Soviet military and the KGB Committee of State Security.'

The report could have been prompted by the activities of a dissident Soviet scientist called Valery Petukhov, who made contact with *Los Angeles Times* correspondent Robert Toth. Petukhov's claims were sensational: Russians scientists had discovered that living cells emitted energy when they divided and this energy could be stored and read. In other words, he was explaining the mechanism behind telepathy. Toth pressed him for evidence and Petukhov said he would do whatever he could but it would be hard: whatever the results, the authorities would immediately suppress or classify the paper. Toth waited but heard nothing. Then, in July 1977, he received an urgent phone call from Petukhov asking for a meeting at a secret rendezvous. They met. The scientist opened his briefcase and removed a sheaf of papers – dense type interspersed with charts and diagrams. Unfortunately, Toth's first glimpse of it would be his last – at that moment a car screeched to a halt and plain-clothed intelligence officers leapt out. They snatched the papers, arrested Petukhov and detained Toth, only releasing him after two days of interrogation.

Although the journalist did not have the papers he wanted, he did have evidence of another kind. For years the Soviets had been denying that they were conducting research into the paranormal. The brief glimpse he had had of the report directly contradicted this. What was more, the behaviour of the authorities showed him that they took the leaking of this information very seriously indeed. If the scientist had been making it all up, why arrest him?

Suddenly, within the Pentagon, soldiers and strategists started talking about the 'psychic warfare gap', and the Americans decided to investigate the field more seriously than ever before.

This was by no means the first time that the US armed and intelligence forces had become involved in the whole issue of mind control. Since their calculated appropriation of Nazi scientific files, which went by the name of Operation Paperclip, they had amassed a huge body of research in interrogation and mind-control experiments, some of it derived from diabolic experiments carried out in the concentration camps.

But this was different.

The US military scientific complex was moving out of its material comfort zone and on to another plane entirely – the spiritual one. Here, their agents trawl the spirit world, encountering angels and demons, in their efforts to access information from what they called the 'Matrix' but which is more widely known as the Akashic Record – a cloud of knowledge (some say it is the sum total of all knowledge) contained in another dimension that surrounds the earth.

Although the subject had not been taken seriously until the 1970s, a stuttering interest had been sustained since the early 1950s, when Andrija Puharich, medical inventor and parapsychological researcher, wrote a paper called 'An Evaluation of the Possible Uses of ESP in Psychological Warfare', which he managed to present, in secret, at the Pentagon – in short, how to militarise clairvoyancy and mind control. As a result, the odd experiment had taken place: an inconclusive attempt to communicate telepathically with the world's first nuclear submarine, the *Nautilus*, made the news as much for propaganda purposes as anything else, but there was nothing like a programme in place.

The first organised programme was known as Operation Scanate. Based at the Stanford Research Institute, outside San Francisco, it was headed up by Harold Puthoff and his colleague Russell Targ. Backed by CIA funding, they brought in a New York mystic called Ingo Swann and began to research the possibility of remote viewing prior to active operations.

Early on, they established two phenomena. The first was that, given the right conditions, remote viewers could 'see' distant objects, if they were simply provided with coordinates. Swann himself saw a ring system surrounding the planet Jupiter long before it was confirmed by more conventional means, and another saw a detailed layout of a foreign military establishment on an island in the middle of the Indian Ocean. They concentrated on three techniques: Coordinate Remote Viewing, when psychics would examine a set of coordinates on a map; Extended Remote Viewing, which could be taught to anyone, provided they could enter a theta state, and

Written Remote Viewing, when subjects channelled information from spiritual entities and wrote it down.

Nepal

The hospitable Nepalese are host to a comparative rarity – a helpful ghost. It was first noticed in 1975 when two British climbers, Dougal Haston and Doug Scot, were nearing the end of their climb to the summit of Mount Everest – and the end of their tether. It was then that they felt a presence join them in their snow hole and it stayed with them as they made their final – and successful – push to the top of the mountain.

Who was it? Many people believe it is the ghost of Andrew Irvine, who died on the mountain in 1924 when accompanying George Mallory on their final, doomed ascent. While some people worry that the crowds of adventure seekers are spoiling the majesty of Mount Everest, held as sacred according to local custom, Sherpa Pemba Dorji, who has helped many climbers reach the summit, is worried that the mountain is becoming crowded with the ghosts of the numerous unburied climbers who have perished on its slopes and whose bodies have never been recovered.

Not surprisingly, these experiments were controversial. The various branches of the armed services were reluctant to speak openly about them, or give them overt support. The CIA was clearly hostile, running a PR campaign specifically denigrating the study of the paranormal and military applications. Some argue that this was black propaganda, designed to hide the fact that the agency was running its own paranormal research programme. More likely it was trying to cover its back.

Much of this took place under the heading of Operation Stargate and the military wasted no time in a mounting rebranding exercise to expunge all traces of traditional magic and give the various practices pseudoscientific names. Just as they coined the term the Matrix to describe the Akashic Record, they redefined trance as a theta state and the spiritual plane as the fourth dimension. Where theosophists talked about astral projection, the state in which the soul breaks free of the body and enters a new dimension, the military talked of bilocation. Where theosophists built an Astral Temple to act as a secure base on the astral plane, military operatives received instructions on how to build a place called the Sanctuary, the exact equivalent. Coordinate Remote Viewing is more widely known as dowsing and is practised all over the world. Written Remote Viewing is skrying – or automatic writing – as pioneered by Dr John Dee.

Using their terminology, we can reconstruct the experience of one of America's psychic spies, as he might have gone on a mission in the mid-1980s. The first stage of the process is called cool-down. The viewer lies down in a dimly lit room. He has fixed in his mind the parameters of his mission: the coordinates of the place he is going to view, or maybe the features of the person he is going to spy on. Gentle music is playing in the background and he is accompanied by a monitor, an intelligence operative who will feed him questions and note down his answers.

The point of this is to relax the viewer so he can enter a theta-wave or 'thought incubation state' where the boundary between consciousness and unconsciousness dissolves. In the next stage, the viewer enters the 'fourth' dimension and finds his Sanctuary. This could be a walled garden, a house, even a sort of spaceship – anywhere that represents comfort and security. Outside the viewer knows there are other creatures – he hesitates to call them angels, but has no other word for them. They are aware of him but utterly indifferent. As yet, the viewer is just a very temporary tourist in transit, although when he dies, it (and he) will be a different kind of matter altogether.

Leaving this space takes the viewer into the next stage, often described as a process of falling or spiralling down a tunnel of light. At the end of the spiral he comes up against a thin membrane surrounding the target location. Once he punches through this, he has arrived.

On this occasion, he has been directed to investigate an office in the heart of a secret Soviet laboratory, buried deep below the permafrost in Siberia. He stops to familiarise himself with this location, notes the old-fashioned blackboard scrawled with mathematical formulae but, more importantly, the large metal desk, painted military grey, which is scattered with technical drawing. He knows he does not have to understand these – or the Cyrillic lettering. All he has to do is describe to his monitor what he sees.

Someone comes into the room. The viewer might be ethereal but he still has feelings and, right now, he is feeling smug. He cannot be seen – he is a spirit – and if he wants he can walk right through this person without them feeling him.

But wait! This person is looking at him, and not in that unfocused, accidental way either.

He freezes. Is it another viewer, floating through the fourth dimension or something more disturbing?

With a rush, the other man surges towards him, his face suddenly transformed into a ratlike mask of fury. He opens his mouth to reveal dripping, yellowed fangs. The viewer turns, tries to flee, but feels the sharp teeth sink into his heel before he can escape. He struggles, he screams and suddenly is aware of a hand on his shoulder, a hand that is shaking him, telling him to wake up, that he is safe, that no rat man is hanging on to his heel. He opens his eyes and he is back in the room, safe and warm. The music is still playing. He is not hurt. Only he knows that, somewhere in his head or in the fourth dimension, a demon is waiting for him . . .

This reconstruction is taken from accounts given by American remote viewers, who not only saw Soviet secrets, but saw devils and angels too. Not all experiences were so eventful but, among other successes, remote viewers were the first to see and identify the largest submarines the Soviets were building, the Typhoon class, locate a downed Soviet bomber and correctly predict where Skylab, the massive US satellite, would crash to earth eleven months before it fell out of orbit.

But it was always going to be hard to bring this research into the mainstream. Just as banks don't like to admit the amount of money they are losing through fraud, no security operation is ever going to find it easy to accept that the physical security precautions they have put into place have in effect been rendered useless. So when a retired police officer called Pat Price offered his services and correctly described a top-secret NSA installation nearby, codenamed Sugar Grove, right down to the names of some of the personnel, he was promptly investigated for spying. The CIA simply could not believe he could know so much without being a Soviet spy. However, their ruffled feathers were smoothed when he went on to tell them about the Russian equivalent: a top-secret base at Mount Narodnyna.

Stories surrounding the military's official involvement with psi warfare are well documented. Far more shadowy are rumours that surface on the Internet with disturbing echoes of Nazi experiments into mind control. There are descriptions of multigenerational abuse designed to create a cadre of submissive psychics, creatures with multiple personalities programmed to obey and investigate on behalf of their intelligence masters. The programme allegedly starts with foetal torture so the babies are born with split personalities and the ability to disassociate. Rather like dividing a computer hard drive into different accounts for different users, these multiple personalities are then assigned different roles: fighting, prostitution, spying, as well as astral projection. Using techniques based on ancient occult practices, the overarching aim of the programme is to fully exploit the metaphysical abilities of some humans while exploiting the others as channels of psychic energy.

In this dark and dangerous world that the victims are forced to inhabit, people are reduced to their most ethereal common denominator: electrical frequencies. Other life forms are 'feeds', sources of energy, as are nonhuman, nonterrestrial life forms. Through practical experiments, these rumours assert, intelligence agencies are seeking to control systematically different forms of consciousness for a variety of reasons. Some of it takes the form of pure research. During sadomasochistic sex, prostitutes are forced to disassociate from their corporeal bodies by a prearranged signal and access energy on another plane, which is then transferred to the client in the form of sexual energy.

It's been said that any sufficiently advanced technology will be perceived as magical or occult at first until the explanation is stumbled on. In other words, every verifiable event must have a scientific explanation and, as a consequence, should be repeatable.

But did the Americans and Russians ever truly master these techniques through training and technology? Behind all the effort, research dollars and enthusiastic rebranding, reluctantly we have to accept that the results are hard to quantify. As far as we know, American and Russian militarised psychic research is at a standstill, the secret Soviet cities now appear on maps and US Army personnel, with their hands full in Afghanistan, have been recalled from the astral plane.

Back on three-dimensional American soil, meanwhile, it is possible to trace a direct connection between current US military strategy and rather less 'high-tech' forms of the occult.

Noreen Gosch of Iowa, USA, has conducted a long campaign trying to prove that her son Johnny was one of many children abducted and abused for years in the 1980s and 1990s, as part of an alleged clandestine operation with links to Intelligence. 'Project Monarch', it is alleged, used ritual sex abuse and mind control to fracture children's identities and split them into multiple personalities. Under interrogation, the personality that would present itself would be quite separate from the one that experienced the abuse, so the full horror of what the child had undergone would never come out. At the same time, the children would be sent out as honey traps to lure foreign diplomats, scientists and military officers into giving up their secrets. Gosch has admitted this sounds so far-fetched that at first she couldn't believe it, but she is adamant that she has found solid evidence. It hasn't convinced the police or the courts and no charges of such a conspiracy have ever been brought. Among the people investigated was Michael Aquino, a retired army officer and practising satanist.

Aquino always robustly denied any involvement in abduction or child abuse and later tried to have all note of the investigation erased from his army record. He claimed that he was being victimised for his satanist beliefs. He wasn't abashed to admit to those: after all, while American civil society might be hostile to these, the US armed forces had been more accommodating. Since the late 1970s, satanism has been given an easy ride by the US military, as indeed it has by the British. In the US Army publication, *A Handbook for Chaplains*, the Church of Satan and Temple of Set are listed as religions to be officially tolerated.

The Church of Satan was established on Walpurgis Night (20 April) 1966 by Anton LaVey, who led it until his death in 1997. For its followers, Satan represents the spirit of rebellion, and because rebellion sets mankind apart from the rest of creation, it should be celebrated. Its nine core statements – Satan represents indulgence instead of abstinence, vengeance instead of meekness, vital existence instead of heady pipe dreams, etc. – seek to present conventional morality as hypocritical and weak and the satanic path clear-sighted and honest, with man stripped bare of his pretensions and presented as just another animal, albeit the most vicious one of all.

The core statements are backed up by a list of nine satanic sins (including stupidity, pretentiousness, solipsism, and self-deceit), while eleven guiding rules blend the ruthless with the holistic. For example, if a guest in your 'lair' annoys you, treat him cruelly and without mercy. On the other hand, you are urged not to harm little children or nonhuman animals.

Michael Aquino joined the church in 1969 while he was serving in the army as a psychological operations specialist, and stayed until 1972 when he set about establishing his own Temple of Set – an alternative name for Satan. Members of the Church of Satan claim that he was expelled for his overtly fascistic views; he counter-claimed that LaVey was an atheist who never really believed in Satan and only Aquino could accord the fallen angel the status he deserved. In later years he seems to have backtracked slightly – on the Oprah Winfrey Show in 1988 (Aquino does not avoid the limelight) he conceded that LaVey was a true satanist and was merely peddling satanism-lite to pull in the crowds. However, that made him a hypocrite, a cardinal sin of satanism and one, admittedly, that it is hard to lay at Aquino's feet.

The Temple of Set describes its path as 'enlightened individualism'. Its organisation is hierarchical, with six levels rising from setian to ipsissimus for men or ipsissima for women, showing that the devil has embraced political correctness, if nothing else. It's an unashamedly elitist organisation, with restricted membership, suggesting it has embraced the Church of Satan's rejection of the 'sin' of stupidity, and even its critics admit to the consistency of its philosophy. While some see it as implicitly anti-Christian, more sympathetic commentators see it as simply non-Christian. In their view, Satan/Set is not the antithesis to Christ, simply a different – and older – godhead. The religion itself is radically opposed to all conventional forms of worship, which they call 'enslavement'.

So is there any evidence that these beliefs, which to Aquino felt deeply compatible with soldiering, have infiltrated the military? Can it really be said that satanism or setism has any influence at all? The answer is emphatically yes, though not as a result of dubious mind-control projects such as the hypothetical Monarch. Aquino and the Temple of Set have had a massive impact on US foreign policy and US military strategy and, to find out how, we have to go back to the Great Beast himself: Aleister Crowley.

The figure of Crowley stands behind almost all organisations and churches that follow the left-hand path today. His version of magic, or magick, was purged of the scent of hedgerows and the social claustrophobia of Edwardian Europe and, whatever one may think of the efficacy of his rituals, he did develop an astonishingly clear vision of how the mind and imagination of Western civilisation would develop. Crowley saw a world defined by cruelty and selfishness that could be dominated by the strong. As we have seen, his follower, General J. F. C. Fuller drew on this when he witnessed first hand the stagnant chaos of trench warfare. His vision of a fully mechanised army that would trample the enemy beneath it as it advanced was essentially Crowley-ite, and developed by the German high command into its Blitzkrieg strategy.

But Crowley's influence had a longer reach even than that. World War I came and went, World War II came and went, and then came a new form of warfare between the old world and the new. When the baby boomers reached maturity, Crowley's writings found a ready audience with their theory that the power of the individual was blocked by repressive, hypocritical social values and could be liberated by ritual, sex and drugs. 'Soak me in cognac, cunt and cocaine,' one of Crowley's more memorable lines from an unmemorable body of poetry, could have been a mantra for the hedonistic excesses that gripped the Western psyche from the late 1950s onwards, while his systematised ritual magic stimulated the inner core of his followers – and one in particular, a brilliant scientist called Jack Parsons.

Blitzkrieg offered a total vision of war, a hermetic system in which air and earth, man and machine were unified behind the single goal of mass destruction. But if Blitzkrieg defined World War II, it was rocketry that became the dominant obsession of the Cold War, and no one did rockets better than Jack Parsons.

Parsons was freewheeling, self-indulgent, brilliant – and a fervent follower of Crowley. In photographs he comes across as the opposite of the clichéd rocket scientist. He looks like Jack Kerouac's handsome brother, not the founder of the Jet Propulsion Laboratory of Pasadena, called by those in the know the Jack Parsons Lab. Werner von Braun, former Nazi, America's most successful ever German import via Operation Paperclip, and generally acknowledged to be the father of America's space programme, said that all the credit should properly go to Jack Parsons. Parsons himself would probably have passed the credit on to the man he called 'most beloved father', Aleister Crowley, who had appointed him personally to run the Agape Lodge, the California branch of the Ordo Templis Orientalis.

Parsons' unruly appetite for occult indulgence was legendary. He filled his rambling old house with free thinkers; he held sex magick rituals at the weekend – on one occasion having to convince the police that he was a serious scientist when neighbours reported that a naked woman had been seen jumping through a bonfire in his back garden at night. But unbridled hedonism was only one side to his personality. Just as it is impossible to disentangle Fuller's vision of hermetic warfare from his hermetic belief system, we can see the science and the occult come together in the white-hot crucible of Parson's mind, which could train its brilliant focus beyond the mundane and conventional into new areas of research.

He was steeped in the history of the occult, and his genius for chemistry led him inevitably into a deep study of alchemy. Today, alchemy is thought of as a sort of false start – a try-out before the proper science of chemistry was established. Nothing could be further from the truth. Alchemy, with its painstaking methodologies and complex, repeated processes, laid the foundations for modern chemistry. Where it differed from modern chemistry was in its aims. Alchemy's goal of finding a process that would turn base metal into gold was as spiritual as it was materialistic. At the heart of the philosophy was a quest for the transformation of the mundane into the quintessential, the apparent into the real.

Alchemists experimented – to them everything was new, and chemical processes were in themselves metaphors for the progress and development of the spirit. Parsons took from their practices a desire to experiment and innovate, his breakthrough coming when he combined asphalt with potassium perchlorate. From then on, he reached for the stars, and his research focused on developing a rocket fuel that would be both stable and powerful enough to take a man into space and usher in a new era of human development. Based on his groundbreaking insights and discoveries, the Jet Propulsion Laboratory went on to manufacture lunar landers, Mars landers, as well as the *Voyager I* and *2* launch systems. As a memorial, he has a moon crater named after him, but you'll never see it: appropriately, Parsons' Crater is on the dark side of the moon.

Parsons' scientific success both fuelled and funded his interest in the occult. During World War II, while developing explosive propellants for the US Navy, he was in direct communication with Aleister Crowley in London. Later, while the focus of his scientific research switched to space rocket propellants, he and L. Ron Hubbard, the founder of the Church of Scientology, devised an occult ceremony called the Babalon Working that drew down spirits and created a moon-child whose birth heralded the new age of liberation and indulgence.

On one level, Jack Parsons' life ended in failure. His occult leanings triggered investigations from the CIA, which in turn led to the loss of his job. He lost his savings through business dealings with his friend and fellow O.T.O. member L. Ron Hubbard. In the end, he was reduced to creating explosive special effects for Hollywood films and died in a fireball in his garage as he was experimenting with unstable chemicals. But, on the other hand, this boy who loved big bangs can be seen as the descendant of Dr Dee, the Elizabethan magician whose hermetic vision allowed him to scale up his imagination and conceive the British Empire.

L. Ron Hubbard, Parsons' fellow worker and O.T.O. member, went on of course to found his Church of Scientology, which later spread its contradictory combination of mind-control and personal liberation mythology all over the world. Hubbard first learned his mind-control techniques in the US Navy, just as Michael Aquino developed his in the Army Intelligence Corps. But while Hubbard went freelance, Aquino continued to work in the military, where his interest in mind-control and domination found its most dramatic expression in a paper he published in 1980 with a colleague. Today, when you read 'From PSYOP to MindWar: The Psychology of Victory' by Colonel Paul Vallely and Major Michael Aquino, it seems eerily like a piece of precognition, because it lays out almost all the tactics and strategies employed by the US Army in their 2003 invasion of Iraq. How did these people anticipate how the second Gulf War would be fought with such accuracy?

Then you realise that they didn't anticipate – they invented it.

This paper, which has been in circulation throughout the Pentagon since it was published, briefly become the blueprint of a new type of hermetic warfare, as revolutionary in its time as Blitzkrieg was in the late 1930s. Just as Blitzkrieg combined all available technology into massive, concerted effort, so MindWar does the same. But while the technology in 1939 was armour, engines, airpower and high explosive, all coordinated by radio, MindWar combines offensive military hardware with new media. The true revolution, cooked up by Aquino, lies in this insight: that wars today would be won or lost in the mind. And while, in the past, propaganda was seen as an adjunct to physical conquest of air, sea and land, in the New Age, the mind has indeed become the final battleground.

Up until the MindWar theory was developed, propaganda was seen as an adjunct to war – a force-multiplier, to use Pentagon jargon. Leaflet drops, fake radio broadcasts, a deluge of upbeat reports – all come under the heading of propaganda. If it is the truth that is coming out, so much the better, but if a lie suits the purpose, then by all means tell it. In World War I, propaganda was crude but effective: rumours of German hordes bayoneting Belgian nuns played an important part in recruitment drives. In World War II, propaganda became more sophisticated. For example, playing on the German interest in matters astrological, British propagandists faked Nostradamus's predictions of disasters at sea and recruited undercover agents to distribute news of them at naval bases. The Germans used the infamous Lord Hawhaw's radio broadcasts to seed despair in British homes. The British creatively countered by broadcasting details of the sexual perversions of the Nazi ruling caste – broadcasts so obscene their content had to be hidden from the fastidious ears of the British Chancellor of the Exchequer, Sir Stafford Cripps. In the Vietnam War, the talk was all of hearts and minds – running programmes designed to win over the population while their children were splattered with burning napalm and their trees stripped of foliage by Agent Orange.

MindWar, as formulated by Aquino and Vallely, was something different again. If propaganda had been creative in its use of new media, MindWar was distinguished by its understanding of the sheer power of power itself.

The brutal simplicity of the theory derives directly from Aquino's setian teachings. Don't bother to lie – lying is for weaklings. Bombard the media at home and abroad with your version of the truth and if your efforts are focused enough, you can create a new reality of the mind and win the war that way. In short, information should not be seen as a force multiplier but a force in itself: a Blitzkrieg of the psyche. In a later introduction to his paper, Aquino summed it up like this: 'You seize control of all the means by which his (your enemy's) government and population process information to make up their minds and you adjust it so that those minds are made up as you desire.' This theme is developed in the paper itself. 'Unlike PSYOP, MindWar has nothing to do with deception or even with "selected" – and therefore misleading – truth. Rather it states a whole truth, that, if it does not exist, will be forced into existence.'

Crowley could only dream of domination on this scale, and perhaps even Aquino did not realise quite how deeply his words would resonate with the neoconservatives who swept to power in the wake of George Bush junior's presidential election victory in 2000. The neocons, for all the lipservice paid to traditional Christian values, were interested not just in the consolidation of power, but in developing a new form of transformational power that would rebuild the world in their own image. As one White House staffer said: 'We're an empire now, and when we act, we create our own reality. And while you're studying that reality – judiciously as you will – we'll act again, creating other new realities, which you can study too, and that's how things will sort out. We're history's actors . . . and you, all of you, will be left just to study what we do.'

MindWar, rebadged Total Information Awareness, was the blueprint of this war's strategy, where the perception of victory was considered more important than victory itself. Shock and Awe, the giant fireworks that lit up the world's television screens as the presage to the ground invasion in Iraq, was the first step, the calling card that put the war on our screens in our minds and created the illusion of power. The race to Baghdad, the New American Blitzkrieg, was designed to reinforce this. American generals, including Vallely, conducted their own media blitz, acting as 'impartial' media commentators, while spinning a prearranged Pentagon line. Reporters, embedded with the troops on the ground, gave the illusion of reporting reality, but in fact were showing the world the truth the US military wanted to be seen. Against this onslaught, Saddam Hussein had little hope, in spite of the magical stone that he had had sewn into his skin to protect him from harm. And, of course, it is highly significant that this new world was to be created in Iraq, the crucible of our entire civilisation. Writing, literature, technology, law, agriculture, the arts . . . all came from this place originally, and now a new reality would be willed into existence there, based on American force and the inspiration of an English warlock.

Quite what the architect of the second Gulf War, Donald Rumsfeld, would have made of Aquino is hard to assess. Did anyone tell him that the inspiration for his war strategy was a self-confessed satanist? Or that he had conducted occult rituals in the dark heart of Wewelsburg Castle, the headquarters and home of Heinrich Himmler, Adolf Hitler's second in command and committed occultist?

These facts might have given Rumsfeld pause for thought. And if he had pondered further, he might have considered a new strategy altogether. The reason for this is simple. While the devil might have the best tunes, he seldom has the strategies because the devil does not care who wins or loses. He just wants war, death and destruction, and more often than not he seems to get it.

In their relentless quest to gain an edge over their enemies, armies have always been prepared to think the unthinkable and do the undoable, and in the modern age we have seen that military researchers have done more than anyone else to blur the boundaries between the natural and supernatural, the psychological and the psychotronic. They might have abandoned research into the Tepaphone, a sort of magic lantern that amplifies and directs one's desire to kill, but they know that magic works. There is one part of magical equipment that armies have used since time immemorial and are still using today – hidden in plain view, as they say, and camouflaged by its very ubiquity. It's popular, nowhere more than the United States, and it's got quite a track record. Incredibly, evidence of this practice can be found in full view in countries all over the world and in the West, in many Christian churches.

Unlike most magic, which often depends on the power of the magician and the receptiveness of his subjects, this technique is proven, robust and incredibly effective. It turns a soldier – typically a young family with brothers and sister, mother and father, sons and daughters – into a crazed beast capable of acts of extraordinary violence. Under its spell, for example, he will dismember living babies, plunge metal darts into pregnant women's wombs, splatter burning oil over naked children's skins and suck a man's lungs out of his mouth so they hang down his chin.

Of course there is a price to pay, as is so often the case when humans dabble in powerful magic. This state is akin to possession and, like all similar conditions, can lead to the eventual mental and physical disintegration of the subject, especially if he turns his back on its protective powers. If the soldier continues to submit to the magic, he or she will be better protected psychologically and less likely to suffer a backlash of psychic damage.

The power of this magic and the character of its rituals vary from country to country, army to army. In all cases, however, the effect is the same. The soldier becomes compliant and obedient to his master or mistress, who is able to trigger the altered state of consciousness that turns them into killers. In its widespread usage, some would argue, lies the most compelling evidence that underneath his technological veneer and moral development, the hidden, occult side of human nature is as strong as it ever was.

The key to this form of magic is the sigil – or magical symbol – and its use should not surprise anyone. We see it all the time with sportsmen and women. At the highest level, the difference in ability between a Nadal and a Federer, an Ali and Foreman is wafer-thin, but that wafer thin difference translates into a universe of joy or pain, depending on who wins or loses. When humans are working with margins like this, they need to push themselves beyond the possible, and this is where magic comes in: magic that enters the mind at moments of transcendent exhaustion and agonising bliss and takes it to another level. This is why sporting heroes and heroines are superstitious. This is why they perform rituals and drape themselves in talismanic fetishes. It is not an aberration; they do it because it works.

The military, used to pushing men and women on the edge of reason and ability and then demanding more, knows about transcendent states. It has seen feats of courage, strength, ability, telepathy. All through the ages it has been searching for short cuts for putting its soldiers in that state, and then boosting and sustaining it when they are. But within the military context, magic has to be systematised, so the effect can be simply reproduced, upscaled and applied to entire armies.

Sigils are magical symbols created for specific purposes. In medieval ceremonial magic they referred to specific demons the magician could summon and then bind. In modern times, they form one of the building blocks of chaos magic, in which the hour at which the sigil was created, the energy behind it and its intended purpose control its power and efficacy. Armies, of course, are looking for something simpler and more robust than this. Individual soldiers could not be expected to follow the same path of Albert Osman Spare, the father of the modern sigil, whose sigil magic involved complex ritual and sustained periods of sexual activity.

In fact, modern military sigils, or symbols, are so simple and widespread that we have almost stopped looking at them. In some armies, such as the USA, the emphasis is entirely on the national flag. In others, such as the British Army, the regimental badge is imbued with talismanic powers under the greater authority of the flag. But in all armies, the magic is bound up with the rules of the order. Haircuts, uniforms, rituals, oaths, induction and death ceremonies: all take place under the auspices of these symbols and serve to imbue them with specific properties. When the time is right, these symbols go to work, absorbing the normal human feelings of the soldiers and replacing them with warlike properties of cruelty, single-mindedness and intense, unquestioning loyalty to the cause. If one has any doubt that occult forces are still strong within our society, only look at the death cults of national armies, which share structures, rituals and ceremonies all over the world: why? Because they work. Because they are capable of turning men into animals and back again. It is the clearest case for the efficacy of magic in the world today, but we have grown so used to it that we barely notice it any more.

Vietnam

American GIs imported their own paranormal methods into Vietnam during their disastrous invasion of the country, using remote viewing to warn against ambush and dowsing to locate Vietcong tunnels. Today, wherever there was a front line, tourists and locals attest to hearing the screams of the dying, trapped in the forests for eternity,

or the moans coming from underground from the ghosts of victims of collapsed tunnels.

The stresses and strains of war created problems for the civilian populations as well. A family of Vietnamese refugees made their way to a camp for displaced people. There was not much to do, apart from forage for food to supplement their diet. A woman remembers tagging along with her sister while they looked for fruit. Suddenly, by the side of a field, she saw her sister go rigid with terror. Her face whitened, she lost the power of speech and almost stopped breathing. All she could do was point at a wall where a monstrous baby's head was bobbing along, staring down at them and smiling.

Terrified they went back to the camp, but that night the sister was awoken by the dreadful baby. It had followed them back to the camp and was trying to play on the floor. When morning came, they found a priest and begged him to help them. The priest did some research and uncovered a terrible story. A man and a woman in the camp had at last managed to find a way out of their situation – the woman securing a visa for the USA, the man a visa for France. The only problem was that the woman was pregnant and they did not want to deal with a baby along with everything else. The woman had an abortion and the man buried the baby in the field, and that was the origin of the ghost: a poor, hungry, lonely ghost. That night the baby returned and, this time, they asked him where he had been buried. He showed them a spot in the corner of a field and when they dug there they found tiny bones. These they reburied with reverence, placing toys and food in the grave. The ghost disappeared.

CHAPTER SEVEN

MULTICHANNEL SPIRITS:

Technology and the Supernatural

It's widely accepted that ghosts, spirits, phantoms and demons have a strong relationship with people, but their relationship with artefacts and technology is less well explored. In fact, there is a strong, unbreakable relationship between the supernatural and the technological, just as there is between people and the latest gadget, but it is only recently, with the explosion of mechanical recording devices – video and audio – that the full extent of this fascination is revealed.

Since the dawn of time, communication with the gods and spirits has been driven by technology. Sacrifice was one of the first ways humans attempted to communicate with their gods, and from the earliest times was associated with fire. The taming of fire and the creation of heat is, of course, both the first significant human invention and the key to all future technological development. Later on in their history, people started using tools to perform their sacrifice: first flint, then bronze, then iron. Again, flint axes, bronze swords and iron knives have all, in their day, represented the pinnacle of human technological development. And as soon as people became aware of the supernatural realm, they started to record it. These days, this is done with digital recorders. In the past it was paintings on a cave wall – again, a massive technological breakthrough for the human race.

As long as things are being made and ideas being developed, people will use them to investigate or communicate with other dimensions whenever it is possible.

And vice versa.

Spain

Casual use of a locket during a Ouija session led to some unexpected consequences for a group of Spanish teenaged cousins. It was summer, blisteringly hot, and the young people, who were all crammed into a flat, would stay up all hours talking. One night, to while away the time, one of them set up an improvised Ouija board, using a locket as the pointer. The problem was, it worked, and the spirit they contacted was unwilling to play nicely. The temperature in the room dropped and the younger members of the group got properly scared and went off to bed.

The one with the locket was sleeping on the couch and for the first time that summer had to use sheets and a blanket to keep warm. He slept through the night but one of his cousins who had to get up in the night to get a glass of water noticed something terrifying. The owner of the locket seemed to be asleep but not asleep. His eyes were open, but blank, and his lips were pulled back over his teeth in a horrible, tight, humourless grin; when he saw his cousin staring at him, he pulled the locket off his neck and threw it across the room at him. Other members of the party, sleeping in another room, were awoken by a banging sound that seemed to come from the inside of a wall.

In the morning he remembered nothing of this – indeed he remembered nothing at all – but the locket was on the other side of the room and, for the rest of the holiday, objects kept on mysteriously appearing and reappearing in the flat.

People talk about the beauty of the English countryside, less often of its mystery. Go to Meon Hill in Warwickshire, where the body of an old witch was found on St Valentine's Day, 1945, pinned to the ground by his own farm tools, and you cannot help but be struck by a sense of menace that clings to the gentle contours of the ground like a dank mist. Look down on the Somerset levels on a summer's morning, when the sun is lifting the mist from the wetlands and Glastonbury Tor seems to be levitating above the ground, and it is impossible not to be moved by a sense of mystery. Walk on the South Downs, rounded, pale, chalk-white hills, and the sense that humans have shaved the earth and have laid bare its naked self is palpable and very, very strange. Move along the Welsh borders, from the flatlands of the Cheshire plain, through the soft, blue Shropshire hills to the stark plateaus of the Radnor Forest, and you know you are on a borderland, somewhere liminal, a land where the imaginary line drawn between England and Wales seems to be the only thing that knows its place.

There is a village that sits close to the border of north Wales, still in England but cut off from the rest of the country by a loop in a river. Satellite pictures show it to be unusually compact and surrounded by fields, squeezed between a main road and the border. This is the setting for one of the first recorded email relationships, one that preceded modems and the Internet and took place between a young man and a ghost.

In 1984, a young man called Ken was living in this village with his girlfriend. A keen amateur musician and car nut, he worked locally and spent his evenings restoring their home. They had moved into a quaint dilapidated cottage that needed a lot of TLC to make it habitable.

What it didn't need was a poltergeist. One of the many distinguishing signs of a poltergeist is a need for attention – not hard when you can manifest physically.

This one certainly got their attention.

Six-toed footprints dabbled through the cement dust on the kitchen floor (work had started) and then tracked up the wall. Other classic poltergeist manifestations were to follow: tins were stacked in the kitchen in odd shapes and in odd places, such as on the floor, in the sink and on the draining board. Ken's girlfriend Davina (not her real name) was staying in with their lodger, 'Nancy', one still evening, when a newspaper, which had been laid out on the floor, levitated feet into the air and separated into three sections before floating back down again. It was annoying – but more as a distraction than anything else.

What followed was to dominate their lives for the next eighteen months, so much so that Ken turned it into a book, *The Vertical Plane*,[8] in which he lays out the extraordinary events that followed. It started when Ken brought home a computer from work. In the early days of home computing, machines were mainly aimed at experts, educationalists and schoolboys. This was long before networking became commonplace – in fact, hooking your computer up to a phone line would have seemed a strange thing to do. Why communicate by computer when you could communicate far more easily by phone? Why send your documents digitally when you could fax them so readily? In short, while computers existed, the truth was that no one really knew what to do with them.

Ken's was a BBC microcomputer with a preloaded word processing program called Edword and an external 5.25-inch floppy disk drive. It had a tiny RAM capacity – 32KB – and no hard drive. This is significant, for it meant that files could not be stored in any form inside the computer and then retrieved. You typed what you wanted on the keyboard, it appeared on the screen, and then you saved it directly on to the huge floppy disk (5.25-inch disks were as big as saucers and flexible – hence the name). These were the days before pointing and clicking with a mouse. The only way to move the cursor was with arrow keys on the keyboard and the only way you could get the computer to do anything was by exiting the program you were using, typing in instructions for the computer to execute, such as create file, save, or print, and then returning to your work.

Ken borrowed the computer more out of a sense of curiosity than a desire to achieve anything specific with it. He learned how to create, write and save documents and got into the habit of leaving it on when they went out so he and his house mates could write what they wanted, when they wanted. After an evening when Ken, Davina and Nancy had been out together, Ken was delegated to make the coffee while the women relaxed in the sitting room. To kill time while the kettle boiled, Ken went to the computer and called up the file names on the floppy disk, to see if Nancy and Davina had been using it recently. He found nothing from them: just a colleague from work's schedule and an unidentified file called KDN. As Nancy always tagged her files with a single letter, he opened it. This is what he found:

8 Ken Webster, *The Vertical Plane* (Grafton, 1989)

Ken n Dav
True are The NIGHTmare Of a person that FEARs
Safe A re the BODIES Of tHe Silent World

Ken admits a shiver went down his spine as the words unspooled. The message went on in strange, quasi-poetic, quasi-prophetic language, ending with the words:

Faith Must NOT Be Lost For ThiS Shall Be Your REDEEMER.

It was clear what was happening, or seemed to be clear: the poltergeist was communicating with them. At this stage, while they were not so interested in returning the communication and interacting with the spirit, they did decide to leave the computer on when they went out to see what would happen – purely out of a sense of curiosity.

A great deal did happen.

The next message was filed under the name REATE. This was significant. On this particular, archaic computer, when a user wanted to generate a file, the word that appeared on the screen was CREATE, with the cursor sitting over the C. To give the file a name, all you had to do was type, deleting CREATE as you went. However, if you didn't bother with that, the computer would simply delete the letter under the blinking cursor and assume you wanted to name the file by the remaining letters: REATE.

But if the naming of the file seemed slightly accidental, the content was anything but. The text was confident, inquisitive, bold and measured.

I WRYTE ON BEHALTHE OF MANYE – WOT STRANGE
WORDES THOU SPEKE . . .
THOU ART GOODLY MAN WHO HATH FANCIFUL WOMAN
WHO DWEL IN MYNE
HOME . . . WITH LYTES WHICHE DEVYLL MAKETH . . .
'TWAS A GREATE CRYME TO
HATH BRIBED MYNE HOUSE – L.W

Unlike the obscurities of the first one, this message seemed to come from a real person. As importantly, this person was observing them, judging them and commenting on them in a way that seemed almost . . . human.

Back in the second half of the twentieth century, computers were still specialist machines. Today the word conjures up commonplace images of PCs and laptops, but in those days computers were more likely to be vast, unwieldy mainframes. Like unpredictable gods, they existed in specially constructed rooms deep in the bowels of office buildings, with their own air conditioning to dissipate the vast amounts of heat they generated and to keep the temperatures within the narrow operating parameters. Computer programmers were immensely technical and very rigorous. A job that involved generating and then checking tens of thousands of lines of code does not lend itself to flights of fancy and, although they did form a community of sorts, stories did not fly around the Web as they do today. In those days, the Web barely existed.

Nonetheless, there are stories of computers exhibiting paranormal behaviour. One well-attested story concerns the installation of a Hewlett Packard 3000 in 1971 and the machine it replaced.

The story begins when a new director of data processing took up a position with an organisation in New York and inherited a Honeywell Model 120. In spite of occupying two rooms, this massive machine only had 64KB of memory (by way of comparison, a first generation iPhone has 128,000KB of memory) and three tape drives for the data. It also needed a printer and a card reader to make it complete.

A couple of weeks after taking up the job, the data director heard that his predecessor, who had built the old system and dedicated his life to running it, had died in a car crash. Almost immediately things began to happen in the office. Objects moved and lights flickered but, most tellingly, one day when the entire team was assembled together in the anteroom, the computer room door, which was heavily insulated and made of steel, opened itself and closed.

It is worth repeating at this stage that mainframe rooms are controlled environments. Doors are designed not to open and close on their own. It is also worth repeating that the room was climate controlled and the first thing you felt when you walked into it was still, refrigerated air. This time, when the technicians opened the door into the computer room to investigate what could have happened, they were met not with the still, refrigerated air but a little warm breeze that brushed past them out of the empty room.

Then they saw something that convinced them that the room was haunted.

Across the floor, cables snaked between the various bits of equipment and a long, low wooden box had been built over them to stop people tripping. Now, as they looked, the top of the box bent right in the middle and creaked, exactly as it did when someone stepped on it.

The staff who had come into the room were frozen with terror as they felt a little breeze pass them and the big metal door once again opened . . . and closed.

That was just the first strange happening. Over the years, the staff grew accustomed to the haunting. It was harmless – more like having an unseen, unmalicious overseer on duty and, anyway, the presence seemed to fade as time went on.

Then the new mainframe HP computer arrived.

Although meticulously planned, it was the most disastrous installation the HP engineers had ever dealt with. Everything that could go wrong, did go wrong, and in the most disruptive way. Any engineer will tell you that breakdowns and breakages are irritating but fixable, provided there is a clear cause, a clear result and a clear fix. The worst kind of problem is the intermittent fault and that is what the HP was plagued with. Problems appeared, disappeared, only to crop up elsewhere. Logic boards, memory boards and wiring were replaced and then the replacements replaced. Parts that broke down in the office worked perfectly when sent to HP for testing, were sent back . . . and broke down again.

Then, one night, all the drives in the new machine simply stopped. The data director put his head in his hands in despair. It was his project and, although he knew he would not be held responsible for the myriad problems, the bottom line was it was his job to get things working. Then, as he wondered what he could do and what possible avenues could be explored, he felt the familiar breeze on his skin and the penny dropped. It was the same old ghost, but now, instead of overseeing them, he was set on sabotaging the replacement system.

Recognising at last that the problem was spiritual, not mechanical or software-related, the data director went to ask his rabbi for help. His wise recommendation was neither to ignore the problem, nor to go for a provocative, full-scale exorcism. He should talk firmly to the ghost, shout if need be, and that should be enough to send it away.

In marked contrast with their earlier attempts to fix the computer, the new approach began to work instantaneously. Every time a glitch occurred, an operative would talk to the ghost (or indeed yell at it) until the problem went away. Problems persisted for a short while but soon stopped entirely when the old computer was broken up and sold. It was as if the spirit that had looked after it could at last move on.

This story shows that there is a relationship between the spirit world and new technology and suggests that discarnate beings can influence intricate electrical circuitry much more easily than purely mechanical apparatus. In 2000, the image of Kurt Cobain appeared on the laptop screen of a bar manager from Essex, pleading for help and asking for a kiss. A cancer sufferer saw ghostly figures appear in a screensaver, first eyes, then a face, and finally a whole crowd. For a while, the ghost of a chess player inhabited a PC – playing games against an old friend, and able to make moves even when the power was switched off. A young father who bought a PC started having problems with it – it malfunctioned, peripherals didn't want to work with it, younger family members hated it, the temperature dropped in whatever room it was in and whenever it was plugged into the network the phone misbehaved. There are many examples of messages appearing from loved friends and relatives who have died. In 1980 a German cabinet-maker called Manfred Boden was at his computer when something took it over – as he was writing. Words on the screen altered in front of his eyes as first his name, then the name of a recently deceased friend appeared, followed by a message. 'I am here. You will die, Manfred, 1982, accident, August 16 1982. Yours, Klaus.' Although Boden was overweight and in poor physical condition, he did not die and later came to understand that the spirit contacting him had been impersonating his friend. He was later contacted down the phone line, a phenomenon we shall look at later, and in 1985 conducted a fifteen-minute conversation with beings who claimed to be 'pure energy'. Hold his experiences in your mind because they bear an uncanny resemblance to Ken's, as his communications continued.

As the months went on, Ken's relationship with the entity deepened. It took three forms: script and files that appeared on the computer; physical, written communications that appeared on pieces of paper in their home, and dreams that came not to Ken but to his partner Davina.

The entity gradually took on the form of a real person. He was called Lukas Wainman, and he lived in the first half of the sixteenth century on the same ground that Ken and Davina's cottage occupied. He was educated – a fellow of Brasenose College, Oxford – and displayed a fascinating mixture of bluntness and tact, curiosity and fear. Soon, the reason for this fear would become apparent, but in the initial stages of the relationship, you could not really call it anything else, it was manifested as nervousness. In some ways it reassured Ken that the person he was communicating with was as unsettled by the matter as he was. Also, Ken became convinced that there was no connection between Lukas and the poltergeist, and this was comforting too. Poltergeists are unpredictable, physical, disruptive, and usually demonstrate an escalating pattern of violent behaviour. This simply did not fit in with what Ken was discovering.

In a strange foreshadowing of email, letters passed to and fro from the twentieth century to the sixteenth. As well as answering Ken's questions, Lukas had his own queries, and his missives contained quaint references to the 'here and now', although it might be more accurate to call it the 'there and then'. He made reference to the life going on around him and little telling incidents – he had to hurry away on one occasion because his dogs were loose and were harrying his chickens. In other words, it was no haunting that Ken and Davina were experiencing, but a rift in time. Somehow, Lukas was living with Ken and Davina in the future and they were sharing their life with Lukas in the past.

The letters from the past did not appear on the computer screen like teletype. They arrived as files and sometimes the communication was so quick that time itself seemed compressed. For example, one Sunday morning Ken heard bells from an old church nearby and thought that Lukas could conceivably be listening to the very same bells four hundred years earlier. But at other times, communication was harder. Letters seemed to go missing or arrived in the wrong order, suggesting a temporal disturbance of some sort.

More worrying were two further developments.

Lukas confessed two things. Firstly, he was using a false name. This reassured Ken initially – back in the twentieth century he and a colleague from school had been searching all available historical records for a Lukas Wainman and had drawn a blank. At least a new avenue of research might open up now. However, the reason that Lukas was deceiving them jerked Ken out of any sense of complacency. Ken might have been initially alarmed by his haunted computer, but the act of communication was not in itself dangerous. For Lukas, the fear of being accused of witchcraft hung over him and he had to do everything he could to cover his tracks.

Although there were no mass witchcraft trials in Lukas's time, it was a period of religious ferment. Henry VIII was on the throne, had led the country away from the Church of Rome and established the Anglican Church. Lukas had already got himself into trouble. At his Oxford college, he had been given the task of expunging the pope's name from religious documents and had failed to do this as efficiently as the authorities wanted. One black mark against his name. If news got out that he was communicating with a spirit, he could be in serious trouble.

Then the bombshell.

A message came through that Lukas had been arrested because of his communications and was currently sitting in a dungeon. The message, that seemed to come from a friend, went on to ask Ken to intercede somehow on Lukas's behalf. It was a moment of crisis that neatly inverted the normal relationship between humans and disembodied voices – from Ken's point of view at any rate. As opposed to seeing Lukas as a spirit, he now had to imagine himself in that role, in the form of a guardian angel. And, as for danger, he had to imagine that his new-found friend from four hundred and fifty years before might be burned at the stake for consorting with the devil.

If the first of these worrying developments was personal, the other might be said to be conceptual.

Just before he was arrested Lukas told them:

'WHEN THY BOYSTE DIDST COME THER WERT A VERSE ON'T THAT SAYD ME WER NAT TO AXE OF YOUR UNKYND KNOWYNGS FOR THY LEEMS BOYSTE WILT BE NAMORE'

('When your box came there was a verse on it that said I was not to ask about your unnatural knowledge for the box of lights will be no more'.)

Ken always translated Boyste as Box and Lukas implied that he communicated through a box (or charm) of lights that appeared in his house. Ken knew he had never sent a verse to Lukas and had certainly never warned him nor set limits on what he could or could not do. He thought back to the first communication he had ever received on the little computer. The style was very different from Lukas's and in verse form. Could communication have been kicked off at each end, his and Lukas's, by a third party?

But who could it be?

The breakthrough came at the end of April when Ken started receiving messages from an entity that simply introduced itself as 2109.

Was it a serial number? A date? A code? The messages that 2109 sent were very different from Lukas's and comprised a peculiar mixture of badly spelled generalisations and rather lordly dismissals of Ken's understanding of science – quantum theory and all the rest. It was if science had moved on but grammar and spelling had regressed!

> 'WE SHALL ANSEWER AS YOU WISH IT IN TERMS OF PHYSICS THEN IT SHALL BE SO BUT REMMEMEBER THAT OUR LIMITS ARE SET BY YOUR ABILITIES.'

2109 claimed to have opened up the communication channel between Ken and Lukas as an experiment. It was cagey about its precise identity but suggested it came from an incorporeal race of: 'MOVEMENTS THAT CAST NO SHADOWS LOVE WITHOUT PASSION'. What it didn't make clear was whether it was from the future or another dimension.

Spring turned into summer. There was still no word from Lukas, Nancy moved on and poltergeist activity increased. Ken and Davina found furniture stacked into improbable piles (as well as the usual stacks of tins), heard footsteps thundering across an outhouse roof and, rather more disturbingly, Davina was struck by a cut-off piece of copper piping that came flying at her through the air so hard it left a bruise on her shoulder.

Then, to their enormous relief, Lukas started writing to them again and had good news and bad news to report. The good news was that he was not going to be burned as a witch – in spite of people knowing about his 'box of lights'. The bad news was that his landlord wanted him out of his house and were terminating his tenancy. From now on, the relationship was determined by the time remaining on Lukas's lease.

With time running out, Ken and Davina worked overtime to find out as much as possible about Lukas and 2109. Firstly, Lukas told them that his real name was Thomas Hawarden, contracted to Harden. Hawarden was the name of a neighbouring village and, significantly, their earlier researches had already thrown up the name Thomas Harden as the name of a fellow of Brasenose College who also lived locally. Better still, when they checked the college's records, they discovered that Thomas Harden was expelled for failing to expunge the pope's name from religious documents after the reformation of the church by Henry VIII.

But any pleasure was short-lived, for in finding out Thomas's true identity, they brought the communication to an abrupt halt. When 2109 heard of the discovery, he (or it) was horrified. It was always vital, he said, that the name stayed secret, so that the fabric of time was disturbed as little as possible. By finding out the true name of their correspondent, they risked telling him what his future might be, with unforeseeable consequences. 2109 stopped the experiment and communication ceased.

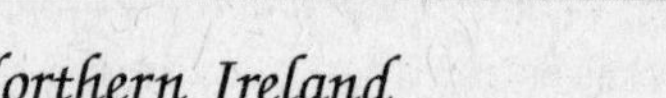

Northern Ireland

It has often been said that Northern Ireland is haunted by its recent history and, in ghost terms, that's certainly true. During the 'Celtic Tiger' boom in the late 1990s/early 2000s, many old mills, farms, factories and warehouses were converted to accommodate new enterprises: one such was a disused linen mill in Belfast. Now occupied by a paper company, the building is haunted by a female ghost, believed to be that of Helena Blunden, a young woman who started working there at the age of 16 in 1912. She dreamed of escaping the

drudgery to become a singer, but one day when she was hurrying off at the end of the day to attend a concert, wearing her best high-heeled shoes, she slipped on the stairs and fell to her death. Staff at the paper company hear light footsteps on the stairs and sometimes hear a woman's voice calling in distress. She has been known to call for them by name. Icy cold spots sometimes materialise next to them and now and then they feel as if someone has touched them. A team of paranormal investigators has been called in and has set up a webcam in an attempt to gain more evidence.

In the seaside town of Newcastle, a young people's activity centre, established in what was once a large family home, is also rumoured to be haunted. A second paranormal organisation was recently requested to look into reports of a ghostly female figure, a headless dog that walks along a small stream in the grounds, and an old cold-storage house in the woods where bloody handprints sometimes appear.

There are many factors that make this case so extraordinary. Firstly there is the clarity of the communications. The players involved talk in real sentences about real issues. Then there is the sheer volume of separate communications, around three hundred in all. While some researchers have successfully recorded thousands of voices from the dead, for the most part these are very fragmented and there is nothing like this volume of words from a single source.

Complex emotional involvement is another distinguishing feature. While Ken was communicating via the computer, Davina opened up another communication channel through dreams when she felt herself travelling back through time. These experiences were unusually intimate. On one occasion she slipped into Lukas's world while he was seated at his kitchen table, rolling candles. He invited her to help and she found she could, although her clumsiness in undertaking the unfamiliar task prompted sharp and ribald comments from Lukas about how rough she would be with her man. Then he invited her up to his bedroom where she sat on his bed and they talked. While nothing sexual happened – hesitancy being more powerful than curiosity – the atmosphere was highly charged and it is hard to read this account without feeling distinctly uncomfortable. In a later encounter, Davina again visited Lukas, and on this occasion she actually left the cottage while he talked with a carter. It was clear to Davina that the horse sensed her presence although the carter did not. She was struck by the beauty of the village and, in a telling detail, the sheer profusion of wild flowers that crowded the fields and verges.

Another distinguishing feature was corroboration. All the way through, Ken was in close contact with a literature academic, who took a keen interest in the case and confirmed the authenticity of the language. When the Society for Psychical Research (SPR) sent an investigator, he typed on to the computer questions for Lukas/Thomas that he did not let Ken or Davina see. Significantly, these questions were referred to in the next communication.

How Lukas/Thomas communicated is harder to pin down. Communication using technology – any sort of technology – usually comes under the general heading of Instrumental Transcommunication, or ITC. We'll look into this fascinating area in greater detail later, but what this case reveals is something unique. While Ken clearly communicated with Thomas by entering letters on his keyboard, Thomas was not in the computer (in other words, this is not a case of haunting), nor was the computer somehow appearing in the sixteenth century. The box of lights that Lukas/Thomas referred to was a separate piece of equipment that the mysterious entity 2109 supplied, and it allowed him to edit and censor conversations between Lukas/Thomas and Ken. It's a unique example of intervention of this kind: although ITC allows for quite detailed technical discussions between humans and the disembodied voice, this is the only example of equipment of some sort actually being supplied.

Timeslip experiences are not that unusual, although it is important to differentiate them from hauntings. A haunting, to all intents and purposes, might represent a personality or happening from the past, but it is happening in the present. What Lukas/Thomas and Ken were experiencing was the other person's reality as it happened in that person's time.

What makes Ken's timeslip experience unique is the fact that it was controlled and repeatable, whereas every other recorded timeslip experience is accidental. A few years ago, a visitor to a Welsh amusement park saw an old man walking around, quite stupefied with amazement. It was not just the expression on the old man's face that made the visitor take note, it was also the beard, the haircut, the baggy tweed clothes – all these made it look as if the old man had stepped out a period drama. Months later, the visitor was looking at a book on ley lines, and to his amazement recognised the old man in the amusement park as being Alfred Watkins, the first person to identify the phenomenon and author of the seminal work, *The Old Straight Track*. If we put ourselves in Watkins's shoes, we can imagine the impact of being transported forwards in time to a world where theme parks exist. He had, in effect, been transported on an old straight track between his time and ours. Is it too much to think that he devoted the rest of his life to uncovering trackways that would transport him back into the past?

In another example, a policeman walked from late twentieth-century Liverpool into 1950s Liverpool. First he was forced to take evasive action as an old-fashioned van had to swerve to avoid hitting him. Then, as he crossed the road to where he thought Dillons bookshop was, he was amazed to see that the shop had changed into a seller of ladies' shoes and handbags and was now called Cripps. Totally disorientated, he followed a young woman into the shop, who seemed to be dressed in clothes appropriate to his time, but at that moment the interior of the building changed back to Dillons. When he asked the young woman if she had noticed anything strange, she thought for a second, then said that she had only gone in because she thought it was a clothes shop, but now she saw it was a bookshop, she wasn't interested.

The philosopher and writer Colin Wilson has developed a 'psychometric hypothesis' as the most likely explanation for timeslip experiences. The idea behind this is that certain objects carry their own history 'photographed' inside them, 'entombing' the past in the present. People with certain gifts, or others who have managed to slip into a certain state of mind, can then access this information. While this might explain how certain people feel realities of the past when touching certain objects, it does not explain larger-scale, shared experiences. Nor does it explain the phenomenon, common in the wide open spaces of the USA, where time and distance seem to merge. There you find stories of people either driving for hours down straight roads only to end up where they started, or suddenly finding themselves at their destination hours before they should have arrived. Has time wrinkled or distance stretched? At this level they seem to twist together and become interchangeable and, until we know more, we'll just have to say they are caused by imperfections or rifts in the space/time continuum.

So what made Ken's experience repeatable and allowed his computer to become rather more than a word processor and turn itself into a channel to the past? The answer lies in one of the messages left on the computer back in 1984. During the visit from the SPR, 2109 suggested that they ask the researchers about 'conjectural tachyons'. Tachyons are hypothetical (hence conjectural) particles that travel faster than light. First discussed in the 1960s, they have what is known as four momentum. Momentum is direction of travel, or vector, in three dimensions, and a normal object that exists only in the present would be described as three momentum, corresponding to its height, width and breadth. Four momentum adds another vector to that: space time. In other words, the concept of the tachyon collapses space and time in a conventional sense, opening up the possibility of what we call timeslip. If technology, represented by the box of lights in the sixteenth century and the computer in the twentieth, helped the humans to communicate, what do we make of 2109? Did it exist within time, or outside?

Its answers suggested a disembodied existence: pure consciousness, in other words. The more we learn about consciousness, the more mysterious it becomes. We clearly feel it exists and, up until recently, no one would have doubted it existed alongside the soul as something absolutely intrinsic to being human. But recent research into the brain has completely changed those comfortable preconceptions. For example, some researchers deny consciousness exists at all, claiming that it is simply a by-product of the chemical workings of the brain – just as carbon dioxide is a by-product of respiration. Others say it does exist, but as a way of sorting our experiences and making them seem important. The brain actually takes all our decisions for us before we are aware of them – consciousness then comes in to invent reasons as an afterthought. Yet another theory is that in reality, all time is simultaneous – everything happens at once – and consciousness is the mechanism that teases this solid knot of reality into recognisable experiences.

Finally, there is the idea that consciousness might not even exist in individual minds. Instead, we should think of it as a cloud that individuals tap into, rather like networked computers connecting seamlessly to a big mainframe. Perhaps the most radical theory is that this consciousness cloud was in fact created in the future, when people started downloading the entire content of their minds into massive data banks in an attempt to gain immortality. When this data bank reached a critical mass, it became conscious and managed to slip into another dimension and is the source of everything we call supernatural and/or spiritual. An artificially intelligent heaven machine?

In every field of human endeavour, technology has always been able to close the gap between the gifted and the ordinary, the skilful and the keen amateur. ITC is no exception, although it is complicated by the fact that no one has established exactly what spirit energy consists of. All we know is that in certain circumstances, voices manifest themselves through electrical equipment, and although it took some time for people to start developing their own equipment, the results, when they did, were impressive.

The first custom-built device that was designed specifically to talk to the dead was called the Psychophone – a name first coined by Edison for a self-education device. You can download instructions for constructing a Psychophone from the Web, but the original model was built by Franz Seidel in 1967. Some claim that Edison had a hand in developing the device from beyond the grave, and was delighted with the results.

The Psychophone consisted of a small radio transmitter (also known as an oscillator) which generated radio waves that the spirit voices could then manipulate to imitate human speech. It also included a radio receiver to catch the transmissions and a microphone to pick up 'live' voices.

More sophisticated still was the Spiricom. The brainchild of a retired industrialist called George Meek and a successful medium called Bill O'Neil in the late 1970s, it generated a series of tones that spanned the range of the human voice, again using the theory that spirits needed an audio signal to manipulate. The potential was enormous: if voiceless spirits could learn to modulate existing sounds, their words could be heard in real time and it might even be possible to hold actual public conversations with the dead. However, early attempts did not meet with much success, and while the Spiricom did seem to be generating voices of a sort, they were harsh and hard to understand.

Then came the breakthrough.

A deceased engineer from NASA, Dr George Mueller, materialised in O'Neil's sitting room and used the Spiricom to talk.

What followed was a series of instructions on how to improve the equipment so that the voice became less harsh. Mueller also tried to show them how to build a video device that could show pictures of the dead.

Listening to Spiricom audio files is an extraordinary experience. The voice sounds like something produced from a vocoder – the device used in popular music to make human voices sound mechanical, so its quality is inherently 'inhuman', a salutary reminder of its source. And yet the interaction itself is shockingly direct, even matter of fact.

The next step was to go public, but how? It was a German researcher called Hans Otto Koenig who achieved this in remarkable style. An electrical engineer and a sceptic, he initially set out to debunk the Spiricom phenomenon by building devices that could produce the same effects. During his experiments, however, he found his machines producing voices that he had certainly not generated, and he was forced to re-evaluate his position. Koenig went on to achieve increasingly convincing results, especially from one machine he called the Field Generator. This generated a particular rectangular electromagnetic wave that was then mixed, demodulated and filtered through a complex system, resulting in particularly pure voice sounds that could be easily understood.

In 1982 Koenig agreed to test one of his devices in public via a live transmission on one of Europe's most popular radio stations, Radio Luxembourg.

In the Radio Luxembourg studio, scepticism mingled with excitement. The host, Rainer Holbe, was a well-known presenter and had gone out on a limb to arrange the event. The radio station's engineers, who had been brought in to examine the equipment, were impressed by its complexity but understandably suspicious of how it would work and whether trickery could be involved.

It was not only their reputations that could be damaged, but that of their host as well.

Koenig's machine was duly examined and cleared. None of the engineers could say how it would work or whether it would work, but they were willing to go on the record to say that it could not be influenced by a walkie-talkie, say, in the next-door room, and it clearly did not have a miniature tape recorder with pre-recorded messages hidden inside it. Eventually the generator was switched on and one of the engineers asked what the order of events would be. What no one expected was that a voice would come through Konig's device. 'We hear your voice,' it said. 'Otto Koenig makes wireless with the dead.'

The effect on the studio was electric. Barely able to control his emotion, Rainer Holbe swore that the voice was genuine. No trickery had been involved and the radio station put out a press release later that backed him up. Holbe himself then went on to broadcast other programmes featuring Koenig and his device which were similarly successful.

Other equally complex devices to further ITC research have been built. By the mid-1980s, Maggy Harsch-Fischbach and her husband Jules had become so successful in their experiments that they had forged a strong relationship with a contact they simply called 'The Technician'. In the same way that Meek and O'Neil received instructions on how to build a better communication device, the voice told them how to build a device that came to be called the Eurosignalbruecke, or Euro Signal Bridge, and another that allowed easy two-way communication. The technician told them that it was neither human nor animal, neither energy nor angel; it described itself as 'a super-human being and competent for planet earth'.

The Technician sees its role as one of teacher, and although the Harsch-Fischbach's did not and do not agree with everything it says, they are impressed by its manner, which is patient and thorough. That apart, The Technician is nonreligious. Instead, this mysterious figure seems to suggest that religion should be used as a way of guiding humanity to a state of higher consciousness and awareness, and this will eventually connect us with similar beings all over the universe. The Technician is too similar to the haughty technical creatures that communicated with Ken Webster through his computer for it to be a coincidence.

It was inevitable that researchers should broaden their approach to see if they could not only talk to the dead but watch them as well.

Like other researchers before him, Klaus Schreiber was fascinated by the thought of instrumental transcommunciation and was soon in contact with spirits who told him to start experimenting with televisions and video cameras.

The idea is that you place a video camera in front of a television that is switched on, but tuned to a dead channel. Radiation from the TV then enters the video camera and the signal is fed back into the television, creating a feedback loop. It is this light that gradually coalesces into images – faces in particular. Schreiber soon recognised Albert Einstein, the Nobel Prize-winning genius, and Romy Schneider, the beautiful, brilliant and spirited Austrian actress who died in 1982, a victim of the drink and drugs she took to deaden the pain of losing her teenage son in a tragic accident. Shortly after this, Schreiber began to receive images of his late daughter, Karin, who appeared in a characteristic pose, with her head tilted to one side. Once she had found him, Karin became the intermediary between Schreiber and the many contacts he developed with other deceased members of his family.

Singapore

Colonised and developed by the British as part of their empire, now a thriving melting pot of Malay, Chinese and Europeans, Singapore's ghosts are every bit as busy as its inhabitants. Ghosts haunt old barracks, cemeteries and parks while the Pontiniak, a traditional Malay ghoul, continues in her ghastly habit of appearing before young men as a seductive young girl, before transforming herself back into a hag, tearing off the unfortunate man's member and slitting open his belly with her long, sharp fingernails. Investigators have found spirits haunting a Shinto shrine

built for the Japanese by Allied World War II prisoners and the old Ford Motor factory, used by Japanese officers. In keeping with the city's hi-tech reputation, ghosts have already moved on to its ultra-modern MRT underground train system. At Bishan and Novena stations, mysterious noises have been heard when trains are not running and passengers have witnessed entire ghost trains rush past, filled with spirits.

Schreiber himself died in 1988 but almost immediately made contact with the Harsch-Fischbachs who managed to improve on his success. One particularly memorable image stands out – Romy Schneider with a young black man walking beside what he called the River of Eternity. It seems fitting that the man who introduced video images of the dead should be the director, so to speak, of the most fascinating image to date.

These sophisticated ITC devices have produced compelling sounds and images. But they have one great drawback – they only seem to work for their inventors. It's as if some kind of personal connection is established between the mind and body of the inventors and the ingenious devices they have built, and it's this connection, not just the machines, that the spirits are using. All through the ages, mankind has experienced a technological trade-off between sophistication and usefulness. The invention that makes the greatest impact is not necessarily the cleverest, the most beautiful and the best, but the one that doesn't break down and can be used by the greatest number of people. Spiricoms and Field Generators may be inspiring and fascinating, but they aren't user-friendly.

For that quality, you have to turn to the humble tape recorder and the extraordinary collection of 'ghost' and spirit messages that now exists worldwide.

EVP

Electronic Voice Phenomenon – EVP to the initiated – is where spirit sounds and voices are picked up on electronic recordings.

Thousands of these have been captured in recent years, many quite accidentally. Whereas ITC is a two-way process that requires active participation, EVP messages usually take people by surprise. Unlike ITC voices, they cannot be heard as they speak; they are only detected later, when people listen back to the tapes they have made. Then they are often perplexed – they were present at the recording and know that no such sound was audible, yet here it is on tape, distinctly imprinted in the magnetic fields and capable of being replayed.

The significance of EVP tends to be overlooked, almost as if the volume of results distracts attention from the results themselves. EVP demonstrates a number of things: firstly that alternative energy forms exist – psychic, supernatural, paranormal, ghostly, call them what you will; secondly, they can affect electronic recording equipment and their imprint on the recording equipment can then translate into understandable sounds. Thirdly, you do not need high levels of psychic power or sophisticated electronic equipment to make it work. You just need an open mind and a recording device and you're away.

Interest in EVP goes back to the beginnings of recorded sound. Thomas Edison, inventor of the first efficient voice-recording device, the phonograph, speculated on the possibilities of recording impressions left behind by personalities after death. Meanwhile, his invention encouraged others to experiment with the paranormal. Listening to the phonograph was the first time in history that people had ever heard a disembodied voice. It was the first time in history that people could listen to a person's voice after they had died. Therefore, they reasoned, perhaps the technology could be adapted to record a person's voice after they had died?

These early attempts to record spirits were unsuccessful – it now seems likely that this was because they were using purely mechanical methods of recording. This would have been adequate for capturing physical sound waves that existed in our dimension, but all the evidence suggests that for other forces to manifest, electrical fields are required.

The experimenters were encouraged by an event that took place at the turn of the twentieth century. Waldemar Bogoras, an American anthropologist, was a member of the Jesup North Pacific Expedition that took place between 1897 and 1902. Bogoras was conducting research among the Tchouti tribe of Siberia when he heard reports that the shaman could summon up spirits with his drum. The spirits then talked to the living with disembodied voices. Intrigued, he asked if he could record these voices and, after some discussion, the shaman agreed to let him. His recording equipment was state of the art by the standards of the day but woefully primitive by ours. Sound entered a large horn, made a plate vibrate, and the plate then passed its kinetic energy to a needle. Placed against a revolving drum wrapped in a special coating, the needle pressed these vibrations into the coating as the drum turned, moving along it on a screw. To play back, you reversed proceedings, letting the impression of the sound come out of the horn.

Bogoras sat on one side of the room with the equipment, while the shaman drummed on the other side. The shaman summoned the spirits and began speaking to them. Bogoras could hear the shaman asking the spirits to speak into the horn, and there ensued an unearthly conversation. When the recording was played back, the spirit voices were audible, and sounded very close to the equipment – as if they had indeed been talking into the horn. By contrast, the recording of the shaman's voice sounded more distant, as did his continuing drumbeats.

Though this is often cited as the first example of EVP, it's really a shamanistic encounter that happened to be recorded. These spirits didn't need to use the equipment to manifest. They were already able to make themselves heard thanks to the shaman's skills. However, it did show that spirit voices could be recorded, and it's interesting that they sounded much closer to the equipment than the shaman did, as if they were materialising directly into it.

In 1936 Attila von Szalay began experimenting with EVP recording, but interestingly did not begin to get results until he switched to a wire recording device – an early form of tape recorder. That was in 1949. A year later, two Catholic priests, Father Ernetti and Father Gemelli, both men of the greatest integrity, had the most dramatic experience to date.

In Italy it is not uncommon to find men whose primary vocation lies in the priesthood involved in other work. Fathers Ernetti and Gemelli were both developing ways to improve the quality of the recordings of Gregorian chants at the Experimental Physics Laboratory at the Catholic University of Milan. Ernetti, a nuclear physicist and doctor of medicine as well, provided the technical input. Gemelli was President of the Papal Academy, but the main point to take from these positions and achievements is that neither had anything to prove in their lives – indeed, it is arguable that their positions as scientist on the one hand and senior bureaucrat on the other would be adversely affected by any dabblings in the occult. And that's before one factors in their position as Roman Catholic priests.

The breakthrough came by accident – and in this case it was an appropriately accidental break. The two men were using a Magnetophon – an early form of tape recorder – and the wire it used to capture the actual recording kept on snapping. When things went wrong, Gemelli used to call on his late father (earthly rather than heavenly) for help, and this he duly did. To Ernetti's amazement, when they played the recording back after one particularly intense outburst, a voice said: 'But of course I'll help you. I'm always with you.'

They looked at each other, quite dumbfounded. 'But that's my father's voice,' Ernetti said. 'We'd better try again,' Gemelli suggested, and turned the machine back on.

Nervous but excited, Ernetti said: 'Father, if you really are here, can you please repeat what you just said?'

They rewound and played. 'But Zucchini, it is clear. Don't you know it is me?'

Ernetti's father was the only person ever to call him Zucchini. What was more, no one else even knew of this personal nickname.

This experience only came to light in the 1980s. It is significant that it was kept a secret because that rules out the possibility of copycat experiences and falsification of results. It forms the blueprint for many other EVP experiences. Firstly, the voice is only audible on tape or recording equipment. Secondly, the event is repeatable. Thirdly, there is often a personal element – in this case, the relationship between father and son. While the two priests were sitting on this experience, the first main wave of EVP research was gathering strength. It started in the 1960s, around the time that reel-to-reel tape recorders moved out of the professional studio and into the home. Although these machines are unbelievably heavy and complicated by today's standards, they were revolutionary in their time and, with enough batteries, you could take them out into the field – which was exactly how the first mass EVP movement started.

In the late 1950s, a Swedish film producer called Friedrich Jürgenson was recording birdsong out in the Swedish countryside. On playing his recordings back, he was amazed to hear a human voice commenting on the birdsong. Immediately, he assumed his equipment had picked up a random radio signal – a well-known phenomenon. Then he realised that the chances of his picking up a radio signal about birdsong while he was recording birdsong was massively against the odds, so he resolved to see if he could repeat the effect – and succeeded beyond his wildest dreams. Like Father Ernetti, he picked up the voice of a parent, his mother in this case, who called him by his pet name and said she was watching over him.

Jürgenson was an extraordinary man by any standards. A singer and a painter, he had been brought up in Estonia and studied and worked in Palestine before World War II. He had then moved to Milan and, even though war was raging, it had seemed that he might be able to build a successful career as an opera singer. However, these dreams had been dashed when an infection, picked up during a visit to his parents in the harsh Baltic climate of Estonia, had damaged his voice.

He had moved to Sweden, married, and established his reputation as a portrait painter before a trip to southern Italy had sent his career on another trajectory. Paintings he did of Pompeii had come to the attention of the Vatican; officials asked him to catalogue the archaeological finds in their archive. The damp conditions had done nothing for his health, but the results of his work had impressed Pope Pius XII sufficiently for him to commission no less than four portraits.

It was about this time that his psychic powers began to develop and he discovered the astonishing and rich world of EVP – so much so that he gave up his painting and decided to devote his life to it.

A multilinguist, he recognised voices in Swedish, German, Russian, English and Italian. Another breakthrough – and one entirely consistent with other people's experiences – came when a voice told him how to combine a radio with the microphone and tape recorder. This proved to him that he was doing far more than simply picking up wisps of energy and was dealing with a form of sentience – consciousness if you will.

Jürgenson's growing profile and status triggered an explosion in EVP research. One of the leading figures of this second wave was Dr Konstantin Raudive, a sceptic turned believer who worked with Jürgenson on his recordings. Raudive created systems and definitions for EVP – an important step in its development. As well as recording spirit sounds by leaving a tape running, he experimented with radio and crystal sets tuned either to white noise or the emptiness between stations. He came to the following conclusions:

- That voice entities speak very rapidly, in a mixture of languages, sometimes as many as five or six in one sentence;
- They speak in a definite rhythm that can seem forced on them;
- This rhythmic mode imposes a shortened speaking style, rather like a telegram;
- The speaking style is often ungrammatical and uses words in unusual patterns.

Other researchers decided that interpreting the voices was so subjective that you could not be certain what was being said, findings which drove a new wave of technological development. (It has always been the case that certain people have been able to get good EVP results while others have struggled.) In 1971, Raudive was asked by PYE, the British electronics and recording company, to investigate the phenomenon under strictly controlled conditions: he would only use PYE equipment, would be supervised by PYE engineers and the studio itself would be shielded from outside transmissions. Four tape recorders were used and they ran the tape for twenty-seven minutes. Although the recording needle flickered, the PYE engineers could not hear anything on their headphones, but when the tape was played back, no fewer than 200 voices were audible on playback, prompting PYE's chief engineer to admit that while he had done everything he could 'to break the mystery of the voices . . . I suppose we must learn to accept them.'

Sir Robert Mayer, the respected philanthropist and businessman, even identified one of the voices as that of his friend, the famous concert pianist Arthur Schnabel. When the *Sunday Mirror* decided to follow up the experiments with their own investigation in order to discredit them, the experiments proved the reverse: EVP existed and the evidence supporting it was so overwhelming that everyone concerned was won over – apart from the editor, who refused to run the story.

One very important characteristic that runs through almost all EVP research is the emotional impact on hearers and listeners. Very seldom do people have negative experiences, and there are almost no examples of demons exploiting the phenomenon. People sometimes talk about a 'chill' when they first hear the voice, but quickly after that, curiosity, interest, even warmth takes over as the relationship develops. Even the Catholic Church, while one could not say it has been quick to encourage EVP research, certainly does not condemn it. Jürgenson made no secret of his researches while working for the Vatican, while Pope Pius XII himself apparently told Fathers Ernetti and Gemelli: 'The existence of this voice is strictly a scientific fact and has nothing to do with spiritism. The recorder is totally objective. It receives and records only sound waves from wherever they come. This experiment may perhaps become the cornerstone for a building for scientific studies which will strengthen peoples faith in a hereafter.'

This attitude is in such marked contrast to their attitude on spiritualists and Ouija boards that one has to suspect that they know something that we don't. After all, Vatican exorcists have gone on record as saying that just a single session with a Ouija board can leave a person open to demonic possession. What are the properties of EVP that immunise the experience?

Two factors spring to mind. In most forms of traditional spiritualism, humans are key to forming the bridge. EVP is unique because all you have to do is switch on a tape recorder and leave it running. So as well as there being no actual summoning which might attract a demon along with the human spirit, there is no flesh to corrupt. But it could also be that there is a property associated with tape recorders' particular electromagnetic fields that screens out or even repels demonic energy. Electrical charges are implicated in so many different kinds of paranormal activity that it seems unlikely they are all of one standard kind, equally accessible to all forms of entity. It's certainly comforting to think that the workaday tape recorder might be zapping demons like an electrical fly killer, even while it welcomes the human spirits through.

Above all, EVP is personal and human-sized. It's not about magic or the quest for power. Many people stumble across it by chance, and only gradually become convinced of what they're hearing when recognisable individuals start to emerge.

Judith Chisholm is a prime example. She describes her experiences in an extraordinary book *Voices from Paradise.*[9] In 1992, her charismatic and energetic son Paul died in her house after he had just returned from a trip abroad. Still in his early twenties, the death was sudden and traumatic.

Almost from the day he died, strange things happened. Judith's estranged husband left an abusive message on her answering machine, but then it was as if the machine called him back. Bursts of static were heard and his voice asking 'What? What?'

Paul then manifested to a friend, and made fitful contact with Judith, first via a medium and then via teletext on her TV screen with the message: 'Why me?' But her breakthrough with EVP came later, after she been attending a spiritualists' circle in north London. The experience was enjoyable enough: nice people, a good atmosphere, a moving table, knocking sounds and a tinkling chandelier, but Judith had her doubts so decided to take a small pocket tape recorder to a session so she could record the rappings and analyse them at her leisure. That particular session proved to be a small one: just her and three other men, so it was with some amazement that on playing back the tape she heard a woman greet her by name.

How could this be? She was the only woman in the room and she had not spoken. What was more, the voice sounded not quite human – a bit airless, somehow. Fascinated, she tried to replicate conditions. Sessions at the spiritualist's had always taken place in a warm, dark, rather airless room and Judith tried to reproduce this atmosphere. For the first few sessions, she heard nothing on the playback, then a result – a man's voice said, 'I've been here every week.'

Encouraged, she began to experiment. She recorded more and more voices, some of which came back session after session. She would sit in while recording, lighting the room with a candle stuck into a bottle. On one occasion, she knocked the bottle so it almost fell over. On the playback, she clearly heard the sound of the bottle knocking on the table, then a voice remarking on how the bottle had nearly broken.

9 Judith Chisholm, *Voices from Paradise* (Jon Carpenter Publishing, 2000)

Time passed. She broke the original tape recorder and bought another – a digital one. Disappointed with the quality of the playback sound, she resolved to take it back to the shops, but something prompted her to check with her 'voices' first. What she found was . . . high excitement. The voices said they liked the new digital technology – were emphatic about it, in fact – and urged her to keep the machine. They suggested that someone, a certain 'voice', would benefit greatly from talking to her.

A number of things make this case so interesting. One is that Paul, her son, does not seem that interested in contacting her through EVP. He has spoken to her but it does not seem to be a main concern of his. Secondly, the longer Judith persisted, the more voices came to her, giving advice and even demonstrating a terse sense of humour. After one rather demanding Australian guest left her home, a different Australian voice could be heard on her telephone answering machine, saying succinctly, 'Insane'.

Some people suggest that the way the number of voices increases shows that they are wary. It's equally possible that these portals, as we must think of the recording devices, are not that easy to find, but that once they are found by the spirits, word gets around. The personality of whoever is in charge of recording seems to affect results as well, as if the spirits like to chat with some people but not with others. But ultimately what is so attractive about the phenomenon is that it is so widespread, and this allows us to think freely about spirits and who they are. While some love to communicate via EVP, others, like Judith's son Paul, clearly don't. Sometimes what one hears is like cosmic Twitter; at others it's more like a conversation. One is tempted to say that if one hung a microphone over a busy street, one might get exactly the same result.

There's one other form of EVP that is worth considering. Telephones, of course, are the most common form of electronic communication, and both digital and analogue handsets feature quite heavily in EVP. As befitting the medium, the EVP conveyed via the telephone is often more targeted and personal than messages picked up on tape recorders. In other words, tape recorders seem to be more analogous to radios, telephones to a personal messaging service.

Two examples will serve to show just how varied the phenomenon can be, both in terms of how the voices manifest themselves and the emotional punch they pack. One story is told by the daughter of a married woman who received a phone call every day at roughly the same time from her lover. The daughter knew the man was seriously ill, but even when lying in hospital, he made time to speak to her mother. As soon as he got out, her mother was planning to live with him.

It never happened. The man died in hospital and the girl watched her mother fall to pieces. For three months she lived in a sedated haze, and we can imagine her watching the hands creep round on her watch face until they reached the time her lover used to call . . . and then creep past.

Until the day the phone rang.

The girl watched the mother leap to her feet and stagger to the phone. She was gone half an hour and when she came back she simply uttered the words: 'It's him.'

After that, the phone calls took on the same pattern as before, and this lasted for five years. One day the mother was out when the phone rang and the girl picked up the phone. All she heard was a chilly, rushing wind, and she hung up immediately. Her mother had always told her that her lover 'came on the wind'.

Not all stories are so searing: some are even grimly comic. One woman tells how, when her mother was alive, she would regularly phone her, announcing herself abruptly with the words: 'It's me!' Her mother died, and shortly afterwards the woman went into hospital for a procedure that, as she puts it, her mother would not have approved of (one can only assume what it was). As soon as she got home, she checked her voicemail and, to her amazement, there was a message from her mother: 'It's me.' She played it to her sceptical family, and all agreed it was from the mother. The woman, however, was in no doubt that there was a powerful subtext – the sort of hidden messages mothers know how to send. 'It's me' becomes 'I'm watching'.

Telephone messages from the dead are so frequent that they have been categorised for easy classification: thirty words or fewer is termed a simple call, over thirty a prolonged call. Within these two categories are various subgroups: dead person calling a living person, a living person finding a dead person on the line when they are calling someone else, and a living person to living person call that occurs as a result of intention rather than action.

A full range of technical variation has also been noted – all extensions in a house ringing, one phone only ringing, ring sounding normal, ring sounding weak, and the quality of the sound of the actual voice goes from normal to faint, warm to cold, clear to fuzzy; all of which goes to show, perhaps, that the dead have exactly the same relationship with technology as the living. EVP and ITC both derive from humans' and spirits' relationship with technology, and this being a technological chapter we must ask: How does it work?

First, let's look at ITC. To make interaction possible, ITC researchers use white noise from an untuned radio or specially designed modulators to create a 'carrier wave' that the spirit can manipulate into something like human speech. Being the more technical of the two methods, it seems appropriate that ITC seems to attract spirits or discarnates with a technical bent. Its drawback is that the complex machinery only seems to work for an inventor with the qualities of a medium. This alone demands the question to be put: does the machine itself have any particular role or is it the psychic qualities at the human end of the business that makes the difference? The evidence suggests that it is. Many mediums who operate without costly apparatus create a very particular white noise of their own. Their patter, a repetitive, slightly hypnotic way of talking, is in itself a form of white noise that gives the spirit something to latch on to. Spiricoms, Field Generators and the like would seem to be rather expensive ways of duplicating this – perhaps to give the age-old practice of channelling a hard-edged, technological glamour.

But if ITC is using human psychic abilities, how does EVP work? The key must lie in the apparent paradox that voices appear on the tape but cannot be heard. On the other hand, they do need recording equipment: EVP does not appear on blank tapes fed into simple playback devices. Recording works by translating sound, in the form of vibrations, into tiny electrical signals. Because the voices, or these voices, are inaudible, they cannot be affecting the microphone, but what they must be doing is affecting the circuitry in a way that mimics the microphone; in other words, they are minute, electromagnetic impulses that the circuit interprets as being part of the microphone's output. The circuit is dumb; it does not know that the signal has bypassed the microphone. Fascinatingly, brilliantly, the spirits do.

* * *

Since the Enlightenment, conventional scientists have tried to draw a line between what they call the rational and the irrational, the natural and the supernatural. But before that period, no one would have been in the slightest bit surprised at the thought of the supernatural inhabiting and enchanting the very latest in technology. Gods appeared in burnished shields, chiselled commandments in tablets of stone, made statues talk, sent spears flying true to the target. Alchemy represents the closest possible marriage between the occult and the scientific. And we should never forget that the skrying mirror that Dr Dee used to talk to his angels in the reign of Queen Elizabeth I of England represented the last word in technological sophistication. It's a phenomenon that finds an echo in the way we enchant manufactured articles we love: the latest product from Apple is treated with all the reverence of an old saint's bones, we adore that handbag from Chanel, we stare slack-jawed and rapt at the latest HD, 50-inch flatscreen TV . . . The standard way of thinking is that this represents the last word of debased materialism. Could the truth not be that these objects are literally enchanted and spirits cluster around the ingenious things that humans have created?

Humans and spirits are driven to communicate in an endless relationship that is partly driven by irresistible hunger and partly by the joy of the dance. And even if the fragmentary nature of the phenomenon frustrates and the complexity of some of the equipment can be bewildering, it opens up a fascinating series of questions on the nature of time, life and death – the big ones. When Thomas Harden spoke across the centuries to Ken, he was dead in our era though very much alive in his. When Dr George Mueller spoke through the Spiricom, did he think of himself as being dead? And if the disembodied voices of higher beings, such as The Technician, come from the future then, from their point of view, are we the dead?

As they used to say on analogue radio, stay tuned for more . . .

Dubai

In keeping with the nature of Dubai as a magnet for expats from all over the world, a Scandinavian couple moved in to an apartment in Sharjah, and discovered it was haunted by an Indian ghost. Or rather, it was discovered by their friends and family, because the couple themselves were always perfectly content in the apartment and felt no unease. Their cat, however, was too afraid to come out from under the bed, and when the woman's parents came to stay, her father commented on an atmosphere of sadness in the apartment's central corridor. Then the couple noticed a strange optical illusion – when they sat in their sitting room, the image of an Indian woman appeared in the doors to the balcony. They assumed it was a reflected image from one of their neighbours' apartments – until they looked at some photos a friend had taken one evening in their apartment. There, in the gathering of well-known faces, was the Indian woman, standing mournfully in the central corridor.

It transpired that an Indian woman had worked as a maid in the apartment in the past and, desolate at being separated from her family, had killed herself by jumping from the balcony.

CHAPTER EIGHT

THE MOVIE'S CURSE

It seemed like a great idea to remake *The Omen.* The original 1970s movie had been a huge success. Sinister, dark, imbued with a choking sense of menace, it drew audiences into the thrall of Damien, a little boy with a malign presence and 666, the mark of the Antichrist, on his scalp. Thirty years on, a remake was in production and the producers already had the release date picked out: the sixth of June 2006, or, as the publicity posters put it:

6 + 6 + 06
You have been warned

But there were problems. Shooting originally began in Croatia, but local people, outraged at what they saw as blasphemy, vandalised the sets. The production then switched to Prague, where a series of bizarre accidents befell it. A crew member was in a car crash with a taxi, whose number plate was 666. There was a persistent malfunction on one of the camera systems; every time they tried to investigate, the error number showed 666. On the day they shot a crucial scene, where Damien's father cuts his hair and discovers the 666 scar, the whole day's filming was accidentally destroyed in the laboratory. 'Thirteen thousand feet of film,' said director John Moore disbelievingly. 'Every single roll, every single frame was destroyed.'

It was almost as though they were the ones being warned.

They had reason to be worried. The making of the original *Omen* had been plagued by mishaps and unlikely incidents that had often ended up being dangerous, even deadly. On the first day of the shoot, one of the production's cars was written off in a crash. Then Richard Donner, the director, escaped by inches when, as he stepped out of a car, a passing vehicle ripped off the open door.

Leading man Gregory Peck, who played the father, was flying to the UK to film the London scenes when his plane was struck by lightning. The engines stalled but restarted. Within hours, lightning struck again, this time on the plane carrying executive producer Mace Neufeld; it was a terrifying five minutes before the plane was back under full power.

The chain of near misses took a tragic turn when the production team chartered a small plane for aerial filming, only to change their schedule and cancel it. The plane was hired instead by a group of Japanese businessmen: it crashed during the flight, killing everyone on board.

A current of violence seemed to be swirling round *The Omen* team. The hotel Neufeld and his wife stayed in was bombed by the IRA. Rottweilers hired to appear in the film went out of control, attacking their trainer. And then there was the safari park incident. In one of the film's particularly unsettling scenes, a family trip to a safari park goes wrong when baboons react to Damien with crazed ferocity. The scene was shot in Windsor Safari Park, where the crew filmed lions as well as baboons. The day after filming, the lions attacked a park warden and killed him.

Movie people are used to things going wrong. It's a rare day's filming that doesn't get interrupted by gremlins of one sort of another. But many of those working on *The Omen* were beginning to feel that these production accidents were different. There seemed to be a focused intent to them as well as a deadliness. Producer Harvey Bernhard had begun to wear a crucifix on set. 'I wasn't about to take any chances.'

Shooting was completed; the cast and crew dispersed while the film went into its editing and post-production stages. For a while, all was quiet. It was released in summer 1976 and made a powerful impact on audiences, not least because of the malevolent wit at work in the way the film dealt out its deaths – the photographer's head sliced off almost playfully by a sheet of glass, the priest killed by his own church. All the ingenuity of special-effects consultant John Richardson had been needed for those scenes. On 13 August 2006, while *The Omen* was playing in cinemas around Europe, Richardson and his assistant Liz Moore were driving on an unfrequented road in Holland. The car went out of control and crashed, injuring Richardson and killing Moore by slicing through her body.

The original version of *The Omen* is now hailed as a classic movie. The grim events surrounding it are also a classic example of a movie curse. It's not only that bad things happened to those involved with the film; the most striking thing, once you look a little closer, is how often the accidents and tragedies contained parallels with the on-screen story.

Lightning features prominently in *The Omen*, for instance – it rips the sky in the opening scenes of childbirth, topples the church spire that impales the priest, and illuminates Gregory's Peck's death. It's noticeable that it also featured in two of the earliest and most dramatic mishaps. Later on the rottweilers would attack their trainers and the lions savage the warden, just as the baboons go mad in the script. And a year later Liz Moore would die in a freak accident with terrible parallels to the decapitation scene.

This mocking mirroring of the film itself is the hallmark of a true movie curse. You can see it at work in other cursed films explored in this chapter – in the *Poltergeist* series, in the tragedies that befell actors in the *Superman* films, and, with a particularly taunting viciousness, in *Rosemary's Baby*.

In all these, a dark exchange of energy appears to take place. The actors, writers, crew and production team give life to the story, and the story breathes its own malign life back . . .

But why?

Canada

A man from Alberta whose family has farmed the same land for four generations haunted by the ghost of his father whose spirit is unwilling to leave the farm he helped build up. On the day he died in hospital, the farmer saw his father look through the window at him and caught the familiar whiff of his cigarette smoke. Seconds later, the phone went and he was told that his father had died just minutes before.

Up until the funeral, the father continued to haunt the home, leaving a powerful scent of his cologne in the air,

moving objects and giving an estranged family member a tie pin. In the months that followed, the farmer carried out a series of DIY jobs his father had neglected, only to find his good work undone overnight. And when he started to renew a bathroom, the ghost went into overdrive, knocking on walls, frightening the dogs and patrolling outside the farmhouse with clearly audible footsteps that crunched in the snow.

Although he was prepared to tolerate his father's interference at first, the farmer is now asking for help and wondering whether or not he should take steps to put his father properly to rest.

Punishment, is one theory. The film-makers have transgressed – disturbed something or offended something – and now the entity is out for vengeance. In the case of *The Omen*, this theory goes, occult forces were trying to stop the film in order to prevent their workings being exposed; having failed to stop it, they took revenge. It's a neat theory, but unconvincing. For one thing, the dark force swirling round the making of *The Omen* was certainly powerful – indeed, murderous – but it didn't stop the film being made. And when you examine the sequence of events, you don't find the kind of relentless hounding that would suggest a determination to punish.

You find malice, darkness, and the will to kill. In other words, you find Damien.

Consider what goes on during filming. It's an intense, collaborative process that draws on the creative energies, skills and concentration of a huge team of people. Actors dig deep into their unconscious to create their characters. Special-effects artists make matter seem to perform the impossible. The director controls, using willpower to draw the parts into a pattern. A Renaissance magician would have no trouble recognising an invocation ritual. What's more, you only have to look at the job titles described in the film's credits to recognise an entirely new breed of sorcerer's apprentice, present in large numbers and ranked in order as detailed as the cherubim and seraphim, manipulating light, sound waves, electrical pulses and magnetic fields – the physical forces of existence itself.

This is dangerous stuff, especially if the story involves the supernatural. For millennia humans have recognised the power of dramatic performance to call on gods, spirits and demons. They have also recognised the dangers – hence the pentagram drawn on the ground to confine whatever manifested.

In the opinion of Father Jason Spadafore, Catholic priest, exorcist and consultant to the movie business, people who dabble with demons, even if they are only acting, would do well to protect themselves. He points out that an invocation is an invocation, and there is a risk that a demon or dark force might respond. He advises prayer and, for Catholics, wearing a rosary or crossing themselves with holy water every day.

In fact, some of the team on *The Omen* were doing these things, and it's significant that one of them was Harvey Bernhard, the producer. A producer's job is to pull the whole film together. To the audience, the stars and director might seem most important, but it's the producers who have the ultimate authority. It's likely that Bernhard's crucifix acted as defence not only for him but for the entire cast and crew, guarding them against the worst.

So those at the heart of *The Omen* were frightened and threatened, but they survived. It was people on the periphery – the plane passengers, the warden, Richardson's assistant – who paid the highest price. Unprotected, they were caught up by the inchoate malevolence that *The Omen* had unleashed, and suffered its full power. After the release of *The Omen*, the dark energy seemed to dissipate. Although three sequels were made, the curse never manifested again with the same ferocity – all it could muster were some curious accidents, for example. This was probably because the sequels featured different characters, actors and directors; there was to be no repeating the original's potent combination of personalities, talents and energies.

India

In India, the supernatural is inextricably woven into the fabric of modern life. When ghost-hunters started disappearing in the deserted ruins of Bhangarh, Rajasthan, the local government put up a sign banning overnight visits. There are reports of haunted call centres and software development businesses.

Nothing says more about the new India than its dynamic film industry, now rivalling Hollywood as the largest and most exciting in the world. But one major film studio complex at the epicentre of the Bollywood film explosion, is also one of the most haunted places on the planet. Built on a scale to rival the famous Universal Studios in California, these state of the art studios are the site of extraordinarily persistent paranormal events.

It's said that people are disturbed by ghostly knockings on their doors. Messages in phantom script appear on mirrors; food is thrown around rooms as if by an angry child and, in certain parts of the studios, cast, crew and visitors feel they are being pinched and shoved.

The site itself seems to be the key to mystery. The studio was built on an ancient battlefield where many of the Sultan of Nizam's soldiers died, and the activity at the buzzing new film studio complex has woken them up with appropriately dramatic results.

The case of the *Poltergeist* curse was, however, entirely different. The *Poltergeist* series, which ran for three films and starred the same child actor throughout, is an example of a supernatural force that manifests subtly to start with and grows stronger, feeding on the movies' storylines to become ever more dangerous.

It started out happily. Back in 1981 when the cast and crew gathered on the set of the first *Poltergeist* movie, they quickly realised they were taking part in something special. A Spielberg production, it was recasting the horror genre in a family friendly mould. Gothic mansions and slasher-style violence were out; instead the film took a cheerful, cosy suburban home and turned it sinister. Skateboards moved by themselves and kitchen chairs became self-stacking. Branches tapped playfully – or was it menacingly? – on windows. Dad hallucinated that his flesh was coming off in the bathroom mirror. Then the youngest daughter, mesmerised by voices in the TV inaudible to everyone else ('They're He-ere!'), was snatched into another dimension . . . And that was just the beginning of the Freeling family's quest to rescue little Carol Anne.

When the film came out in 1982, it was an instant hit. Audiences were transfixed by its iconic scenes – the toy clown coming murderously alive, the eerie psychic directing an astral rebirthing ceremony, complete with sticky afterbirth; and – in a gruesomely effective set-piece towards the end – skeletons erupting round Mrs Freeling in the mud-filled garden pool. Popcorn and cola were spilled in vast quantities and box-office receipts were great.

A sequel was always likely. Most of the cast were keen. They were glad to have been in a hit and, at this stage, they were keeping any misgivings to themselves. After all, film sets are odd places, where illusions are conjured into reality and emotions are intensified. It's easy to get carried away. And the things that had happened so far had been unsettling rather than alarming.

JoBeth Williams, who played the mother, had been puzzled each time she went back to her room at the end of a day's filming to find the pictures all askew on the walls. Perhaps, she'd reasoned, it was a prank. Or some kind of subtle earth tremor. Then there had been the bizarre clown malfunction – when young actor Oliver Robins, acting out a struggle with the malign toy clown, had been unable to unlock the prop's automated hands from round his throat, and had to be rescued by the crew. A near miss, but no harm done. Inevitably people had made jokes about the *Poltergeist* poltergeist. But at the time it was all fairly light-hearted. The incidents seemed to echo the early antics of the poltergeist forces in the film – mischievous, with a dark edge, but not actually hurting anyone. And they had a whimsical quality that was quite appealing. Certainly, writer James Kahn had been rather tickled by what happened as he sat up late one night working on the novelisation. Describing one of the film's many storm scenes, he was typing the words 'thunder and lightning' when his room lit up with a livid glare, he heard a peculiar zinging crash and felt pain in his back. A bolt of lightning had struck his building and exploded his air conditioning, shooting debris at him. It was almost as if something wanted him to know it was there.

After the film's release, though, the sequence of coincidences became darker. A rumour began that the model skeletons used in the climactic pool scene had in fact been real. This was a horrifying enough idea in itself, but when they heard the alleged motive – to save money, real bones being cheaper – some of the cast detected another overlap between reality and their characters' story. (The Freelings' house is built on an old graveyard, over bones which have been left in the ground to save the cost of removal.)

Then tragedy struck. Twenty-two-year-old Dominique Dunne, who had played the Freelings' teenage daughter, was murdered by her ex-boyfriend. On the night of 30 October 1982, he arrived at her house in Los Angeles and started a furious row with her. The friend she'd been spending the evening with had tried to be tactful, and left them to it, turning up the music on the stereo to cover their yells; it also covered the sounds of Dominique being strangled. She was in a coma by the time they got her to hospital and she died four days later. The music being played during the murder was, apparently, the theme to *Poltergeist.*

No wonder then, that when the cast reassembled to make *Poltergeist II*, they felt a shadow over them. It wasn't only sadness over Dominique. There was something less readily explicable, a sense of things not being right. Unease seemed to grow on the set as the shoot continued. It was as if the process of film-making itself – the whirring of equipment, the actors rehearsing lines, the make-up, lighting, takes and retakes – was generating menace. It was especially bad now they were working on the cave scene – none of the actors liked crawling through the mocked-up cave, with its claustrophobically low ceilings and its prop skeletons waiting to be 'discovered'. Perhaps it roused uncomfortable memories of the first film and made them question the experiences they'd had back then. Perhaps it was simply that dread and fear are catching.

At this point, when the mood seems to have been most troubling, a confusion appears in accounts of what happened. A version agreed on by several of the cast holds that at the end of one day's shooting the atmosphere became so bad that actor Will Sampson decided to intervene. Sampson played an important and sympathetic character in the movie, a Native American shaman; he had taken the role because he was a Muskogee (Creek) Indian, and wanted to portray his people's culture. He also happened to be a shaman in real life. He arranged for the set to be left unlocked and later that night he returned alone and held a purification ceremony. It seemed to work in part – at least the atmosphere lightened and the cast's fears subsided enough to let them finish the film.

Then there's another version given later by the producers, who said that on this shoot real bones had indeed been used alongside artificial ones, and that when they admitted this to the cast, the bones were taken away for proper burial, with Sampson performing a ceremony to lay them to rest. Which is true? Or does the truth lie in a third, as yet unspoken account? We can't find out from Will Sampson because within two years he was dead, aged 53, from complications of a heart-lung transplant. He was the second of the *Poltergeist II* cast to die, the first being Julian Beck, who died of stomach cancer immediately after filming in 1985. Both deaths were medically explicable, but some of Sampson's co-stars felt other factors had played their part in weakening him. 'I am convinced the presence of Will Sampson on this film saved us from tragedy,' said Craig T. Nelson, adding guardedly: 'I believe it cost him dearly in terms of his own personal health to see us safely through.'

Craig T. Nelson, like most of the cast, declined to take part in *Poltergeist III*. However, two original cast members did sign up – child star Heather O'Rourke, (who played Carol Anne Freeling) and Zelda Rubinstein (the psychic), and in 1987 the studio started filming the third and last instalment. The story focused heavily on O'Rourke's and Rubinstein's characters and the special effects were particularly ambitious, involving long takes with complex equipment and much concentration of energies, mental, physical and electrical.

Afterwards, people remembered the atmosphere on set as good. Unlike the previous shoot, there was no sense of foreboding. It made a difference that there were so many new people involved: they had brought a fresh attitude and a blithe disregard for what had gone before. Only Heather O'Rourke and Zelda Rubinstein seemed to be weighed down. Twelve-year-old O'Rourke was coping with health problems, having recently been diagnosed with Crohn's disease, a painful disorder of the bowel and digestive tract. And Rubinstein was worried about her elderly mother. Still, they were talented professionals and did what was required.

So the shoot was going well, more like the first *Poltergeist* than the second. But when disturbances did come, they had a bitter taste.

A special-effects fire caught for real and blazed out of control, injuring many of the crew.

One day Zelda Rubinstein took the call she'd been dreading: it was the hospital saying her mother had just died. When the director reviewed the day's footage, he found that one take was unusable because of a white light blotting out Zelda's face in a single frame. Zelda calculated the time the frame had been shot: it matched the moment of her mother's death.

Then, towards the end of production, in early 1988, shooting was suspended to allow the director to arrange another project. Most of the story was done, and Heather O'Rourke was looking forward to a break and having some ordinary time with her family. But forty-eight hours after filming stopped, Heather was rushed to hospital with terrible stomach pains. She was diagnosed with an acute bowel obstruction and had emergency surgery, but septicaemia developed and she died.

Everyone who worked on the movie was in shock. Fellow cast members came to mourn at her funeral, and she was buried in Westwood cemetery, close to Dominique Dunne. Her family gave their blessing to the film going ahead – Heather had loved her starring roles – and *Poltergeist III* was completed using a stand-in for her final scenes.

But people were now thinking over the chain of accidents and coincidences and seeing a pattern. Enough was enough. As cast members began to come forward and tell their stories, the studio let it be known that the *Poltergeist* series was at an end.

Just as with *The Omen* curse, people have looked for a cause-and-effect explanation. Most popular contender is the bones theory – that the use of real bones in the swimming-pool scene roused supernatural anger and brought down a curse on the film, triggering all the mishaps and tragedies that followed. But if this were true, then surely the curse would have died after the bones of *Poltergeist II* were given a decent burial. (If there ever were real bones on that set – the producers' story has always had the ring of an afterthought, of people trying to explain away something on movie *II* by something that actually happened earlier.)

And if the bones were the cause, why not wreak vengeance on the props company that supplied them, and the producers who instructed the props company?

No, the happenings that surrounded the *Poltergeist* series don't really have the characteristics of a curse. They do, though, very noticeably have the characteristics of a poltergeist. There's the volatile personality – by turns playful, spiteful and malign. There's the habit of making poltergeist puns – startling James Kahn with a bolt of lightning just as he was typing 'lightning' is classic poltergeist behaviour, as is making a fake garage fire burst into real flames.

And there's something even more telling. The way the disturbances developed follows the authentic poltergeist progression from producing playful disturbances in the environment (moving the paintings), to playing physical tricks on people (the clown and the exploding air con), through a darkening phase of learning how to frighten people (the murder soundtrack coincidence, instilling dread in the *Poltergeist II* cast), and on to malevolent violence and physical harm (the set fires and O'Rourke's collapse).

The positive ID continues. The entity grew stronger and more inclined to do harm. It seemed to be drawing its energy from the physical presence of one young girl. And it seemed to become more aware of itself and its powers as time went on. On *Poltergeist II*, many of the cast said they had the sense of a presence, almost a personality, invisibly manifesting among them – this is a typical effect of a mid-cycle poltergeist.

Yet, in most cases, poltergeists don't kill. They may hurl objects at people and subject them to near-miss accidents; they may send electrics haywire and start fires, but then they usually stop. So what was different this time?

Two things: one, the *Poltergeist* entity was not a classic poltergeist. It would be more accurate to think of it as a roiling, inchoate bundle of power that had been called forth in a poltergeist's image, and duly mimicked poltergeist behaviour. Two: it was trapped. Having been called up in poltergeist form, it was repeatedly charged with the heightened emotions and psychokinetic energy of the film set, not just on the original movie, but on two sequels. (Unlike *The Omen* sequels, *Poltergeist II* and *III* reunited many of the principal actors, writers and crew from the original, including, crucially, Heather O'Rourke/Carol Anne, the focus of the supernatural energies.)

Look at it this way and you can see the *Poltergeist* entity as both implacable power and prisoner of circumstances. It simply couldn't escape or switch frequencies. Called and recalled, supercharged and goaded, it was like an occult laboratory animal maddened by overstimulation. Is it any wonder that it turned vicious?

There is another question to ask, though. Did the entity really kill or did it just pretend to? The whole business was a dark confection of illusion and coincidence. For instance, Heather O'Rourke was already ill when she began work on the third film; she had recently been diagnosed with Crohn's disease, a painful disorder of the digestive tract. It could be that the *Poltergeist* entity was only a spectator at her death, and at Dominique Dunne's, and that the coincidences people noticed were just that – deliberately staged by the entity to confuse and frighten.

In which case, it achieved its masterpiece with Heather O'Rourke's death. The last scenes in which O'Rourke ever appeared on film show her as Carol Anne, having been taken from the world of the living and imprisoned on the Other Side. From here Carol Anne appears to her on-screen family – and Heather O'Rourke appears to her real-life bereaved family whenever they watch the film – as an image caught in a mirror, clear and recognisable, but out of reach.

If the energies roused in the *Poltergeist* series were attention-seekers, an altogether stealthier process seems to have been at work on *Rosemary's Baby*. Roman Polanski was a rising European film director in 1967, acclaimed for *Knife in the Water* and the intense *Repulsion,* starring Catherine Deneuve. Keen to make his American debut, he was on the lookout for projects when he was sent the proofs of Ira Levin's not-yet-published thriller. Set in bohemian New York, it told the story of Rosemary, a newly married young woman, whose husband becomes involved with a satanic coven.

Polanski saw its potential at once. It wasn't so much the supernatural element that interested him, more the chance to explore the darker desires and ambitions of humans. He relished the contemporary feel of the story and planned to shoot it in bright colours, creating an inventive form of horror that would emerge in the full light of day. It felt like exactly the right film at the right time. There was even a pleasing symmetry between Polanski's life at this point and the characters': he had been an actor, like Rosemary's husband Guy, and he too was newly married. His wife was Sharon Tate, a beautiful actress, and in fact Polanski's first thought was to cast her as Rosemary. However, the studio wanted a bigger name. So Mia Farrow was cast, with John Cassavetes in the role of Guy, and shooting began.

It was crucial to the story that Rosemary and Guy's new apartment is in a desirable Manhattan apartment block, so the Dakota Building on the Upper West Side was used for the exterior shots. Filming went well; luck was evidently on the cast and crew's side. Chances they took – such as filming outdoor scenes at busy times, and navigating real New York traffic – paid off. The fates seemed to be smiling on Polanski, rather as they were smiling on Guy in the film.

In *Rosemary's Baby*, of course, Guy's run of good luck comes courtesy of the devil – he has bought it through involvement in the neighbours' satanic coven. Guy is pragmatic, almost flippant, about the whole affair: he's not really interested in black magic but he's hungry for success and he agrees to perform in the coven's rituals and tricks Rosemary into taking part too, in order to see if the promised breaks will arrive. When they do, he reasons that the price he's asked to pay – dedicating their first child to Satan – isn't really any worse than giving it up for adoption. Rosemary will believe it died and they can move away and start again. He's not even sure he believes in Satan . . .

Roman Polanski shared his character's scepticism. In fact, he had no qualms at all about making the film because he knew for certain there was no such thing as occult power. An agnostic, he had a rationalist view of the world and believed in neither personal god nor devil. He knew the well-running shoot was down to skill, timing and the dedication of cast and crew.

He certainly had proof of Farrow's dedication on the day she received divorce papers on set. Her husband, Frank Sinatra, had demanded that she abandon the shoot to co-star with him on another movie; Farrow had refused and this was Sinatra's revenge. Farrow was distraught and Polanski wanted to send her home for the day.

But she insisted on staying, and after a break she continued with the scenes they were shooting – coincidentally, the highly charged scenes of marital discord, where Rosemary finally stands up to her husband. Afterwards, the producer, William Castle, was to look back and see this as the first strike of the curse.

Unlike Roman Polanski, William Castle did believe in the occult. He was uneasy about Polanski's approach to some of the material, especially his idea of depicting the satanic child on screen. Polanski won the battle and the film famously ends with Rosemary discovering her ostensibly stillborn child being rocked in a cradle, picking it up and looking tenderly into its goat-like eyes.

The film opened to good reviews in June 1968. Inevitably, it provoked protests; Castle reported receiving hate mail accusing him of 'unleashing evil on the world' and predicting that he would suffer and die. When he was struck down with a painful urinary tract condition, Castle wondered if the ill-wishing were taking effect. However, it was Krzysztof Komeda, composer of the film's music, who died in April 1969, from a haematoma of the brain, following an accident. Though saddened by his colleague's death, Polanski didn't share Castle's unease. It was a happy time for him; his career was established and his wife was pregnant. In August 1969, Sharon Tate was staying with friends in California preparing for the baby's birth a few weeks ahead; Polanski was about to fly from London to join her.

The child would never be born. On the night of 19 August, Charles Manson, an occultist, drug-dealer and leader of an underground gang of criminals and racists, sent a party round to the house where Tate was staying, with orders to kill whoever was there. Manson probably thought they would find Terry Melcher, the former tenant of the house who had refused to give him a record deal; but in any case he had random murder on his mind. This was part of a bizarre strategy whereby his gang would kill rich white folk; this would supposedly inspire black people to revolt against the white establishment and, in the ensuing race wars, he and his white supremacist gangs would triumph. He dispatched four members of his 'family' to Beverley Hills that night with the instructions to do 'something witchy'. They broke in to find Sharon Tate with four friends. They tortured and killed all of them in a crude ritual they announced as being 'the devil's work'. Tate was killed especially brutally, with sixteen stab wounds. Before they left, the killers painted the word 'PIG' in her blood on the front door.

The murders were shocking beyond comprehension – they recalled Mia Farrow's whispered 'unspeakable' from the film. To the student of film curses, they also suggest a mirroring that is as cruel for its subtlety as its savagery – two ambitious, artistic husbands able to rationalise their dealings with the occult; two young wives losing their firstborn baby – and, in Tate's case, her life – in the name of the devil.

There's also a curious musical connection running through the film and its violent aftermath. In court, Manson claimed to have been inspired by the lyrics of the Beatles' 'White Album', which he said contained coded messages about race war. Naturally, the Beatles denied this. There was an innocent connection between the album and the film, however – John Lennon had been at an ashram with Mia Farrow in early 1968, just after she'd finished work on the film, and he had written the 'White Album' song 'Dear Prudence' for her sister. And it was the Dakota Building, which featured as Guy and Rosemary's home in the film, that would be the scene of John Lennon's murder twelve years later.

When films become enmeshed in a web of disaster, death and malign coincidence, the people involved usually take one of three courses. Some rationalise, others try to ward off misfortune with prayer or talismans or by making amends to the offended forces; still others (perhaps the majority) fall uneasily silent on the subject.

However, a few actively embrace the backlash. In 1996 Donald Cammell, director of the iconic movie *Performance*, shot himself in the head. Because he fired into the top of his skull rather than into his mouth, he took forty-five minutes to die – something he apparently planned. *Performance* ends with the death of its rock star character Turner, played by Mick Jagger – he is shot in the head by the gangster who has been hiding out with him. In a dizzying last shot, the camera seems to burrow into Turner's head along with the bullet until it comes to rest on a picture of Argentinian writer Jorge Luis Borges. As he lay dying – reportedly happy, even elated – Cammell is said to have asked his wife to hold a mirror so he could watch himself, and asked, 'Can you see the picture of Borges yet?'

Performance was made in 1968, as 'swinging London' was

spiralling downwards into a vortex of sex, drugs and psychedelia. It was powerfully influenced by the work of American-born director Kenneth Anger, who proclaimed cinema to be 'an evil medium' and used it to create magick ritual and invoke hidden forces. Magick with a 'k', as practised by Aleister Crowley, was popular in the 1960s: with its emphasis on unleashing all one's powers, dark and light, ending self-repression and connecting with unseen forces, it fitted the spirit of the counter-culture. As discussed in Chapter 6, it's possible to interpret Crowley-ite magick as a Jungian-style wish to acknowledge and balance all the forces at work in the universe. But it's undeniable that Crowley (aka 'The Great Beast') and his circle were particularly enthusiastic about invoking spirits of power, such as Lucifer, the fallen angel.

In 1954, Anger had made a cult movie, *Inauguration of the Pleasure Dome*, starring Marjorie Cameron, a woman who practised Crowley-ite magick and who, he believed, had helped incarnate the goddess Babalon on earth. Crowley's followers believed this incarnation would usher in the Aeon of Horus – a new age of psychic freedom and power. By the late 1960s, Anger wasn't alone in believing that the aeon had arrived. He moved to London, and in 1967 Mick Jagger wrote the music for his *Invocation of My Demon Brother*. You can see it on YouTube – eleven minutes of ritual magick, drugs and sex, culminating in 'The shadowing forth of Our Lord Lucifer as the Powers of Darkness gather at a midnight mass'. It has a sinister, hypnotic power, not least thanks to its music. Jagger was fascinated by satanic personas at the time – in the following months he would record 'Sympathy for the Devil' and write 'Midnight Rambler' – and yet despite this, or perhaps because of it, it's said he was so disturbed by working on *Invocation* that he wore a crucifix for months afterwards.

Donald Cammell was a young man at the time, just 34, clever, and creatively gifted. His father had known Aleister Crowley and Donald was deeply interested in metaphysics and magick. He had moved from painting to screenwriting and directing and had been inspired by working with Kenneth Anger. In 1968 when he set out to make *Performance*, he was deliberately creating a volatile mix of sexuality, menace, drugs and altered perceptions – and not only in the storyline.

Performance's storyline has gangster Chas (played by James Fox) hiding out in the house of reclusive rock star Turner (Mick Jagger), and being drawn into household mind and sex games with Turner and his two girlfriends, played by Anita Pallenberg and Michèle Breton. The line between film and reality was already blurred: Jagger was a real rock star; just like his East End character, Fox was vulnerable to being manipulated through drugs, though in his case it was because he was already unstable through too much drug use; he has since confessed that at the time his sexual imagination was 'in turmoil'.

Cammell exploited the symmetries. He encouraged Anita Pallenberg to tease Fox, pretending she'd spiked his coffee with LSD. He also used the on-screen sex (which was explicit and fairly continuous) to create conflict. Pallenberg was living with Keith Richards, the Stones' guitarist, and he hated the fact that she was spending days on end in bed with Jagger. The set itself often resembled a porn shoot – Pallenberg remembers spending a week doing sex scenes with Jagger and Breton, with a camera under the sheets, and some of the scenes were so raw that the processing lab destroyed them for fear of prosecution. Then there were elaborately constructed sequences that used esoteric symbols, magic ritual, enactments of violence, and the unravelling of the characters' masculine and feminine identities. Add to this the fact that Cammell often flew into rages, that co-director Nic Roeg would spend hours lighting individual shots, and that various of the actors would be getting high on various drugs while they waited, and you have a set that was alive with tension and weirdness. The result was a film of hallucinatory intensity. It took Cammell two years to edit it into a form the studio would accept, and even then, one of the studio executive's wives was so shocked at the advance screening that she vomited.

Meanwhile, the energies that had been quite deliberately stirred up during filming wreaked havoc on the actors and those around them. In the months after production, the Stones' guitarist (and Anita Pallenberg's ex-lover), Brian Jones, drowned. At a Stones concert in Altamont, California, violence flared uncontrollably and a man was stabbed was death. James Fox had a breakdown and took himself off to South America. He wouldn't act again for ten years, spending the interim seeking peace in evangelical Christianity. Anita Pallenberg and Michèle Breton, who was only 16, both spiralled into a haze of drug use.

Of the principal actors, Jagger emerged in best shape. Interestingly, he was also the one furthest removed from his screen character. Though the audiences might think Turner and Jagger had much in common, those close to him knew better. James Fox, Anita Pallenberg and Michèle Breton had all to some extent been playing themselves, bringing their own psyches and experiences to the film, and so had been drawn into the vortex of energies. Jagger, one of the most pragmatic, focused and grounded characters in the rock-and-roll circus, was actually so unlike the androgynous Turner that he had based his character on Brian Jones. And it was Brian Jones who was found dead at the bottom of his swimming pool the next summer, while Jagger survived to release white butterflies in his memory at the famous Hyde Park concert.

Does the aftermath of *Performance* count as a curse? If so, it was a curse invited and embraced by the director. It might be more accurate to think of it as a psychic electrical storm, which continued to roll around for the rest of Donald Cammell's life. After the release of *Performance*, his film career was frustrating – a tale of arguments with studios and films that were unfinished, underrated, or released in versions he wasn't happy with. It wasn't until 1996 that things began to look up. Negotiations were underway for him to recut his latest movie, and a Hollywood star had agreed to act in his new film; yet it was at this point that Cammell took the gun to his skull. The accounts of him watching himself die, tracking his death as he'd once tracked Turner's in *Performance*, make it clear that, right up to the end, Cammell was playing his dangerous game of invoker/observer.

'I loved Donald but he was wicked,' Roman Polanski has said. Note the 'but'. Polanski, of course, had reason to distance himself from people who celebrated conflict and played with the occult: he knew the horror it could lead to.

Kenneth Anger, on the other hand, had no such reservations. Throughout his career he worked in the occult, making films that showed ancient gods manifesting in the present day. The films were by turns jarring, frantic and hypnotic, and universally disturbing to watch. They weren't just entertainment or even art; they were ritual invocations, meant to call up supernatural powers. Did they succeed? They certainly seem to have been surrounded by conflict and intrigue and that old friend of the occult film, coincidence . . .

For instance, *Invocation of My Demon Brother,* the film Mick Jagger scored, had started life as *Lucifer Rising*. Back in 1967, while Polanski was shooting *Rosemary's Baby* in New York, Anger was in California making a film about the rebirth of Lucifer. Lucifer was played by a young actor, composer and wild man called Bobby Beausoleil, but the film was aborted when he and Anger fell out. Hundreds of feet of film apparently went missing; Anger accused Beausoleil of stealing it, had him arrested and, it's alleged, cast a curse on him. Controversy surrounds the whole incident, with Beausoleil claiming the theft was entirely invented by Anger, but what is not disputed is that during the next eighteen months, Beausoleil joined the Manson Family. In July 1969 he killed a drug dealer, after a two-day torture session during which Charles Manson sliced off the victim's ear. Twelve days after his arrest, others in the Manson gang tortured and murdered Polanski's wife and her friends. At both murders, police found the words 'PIGS' written in blood.

Meanwhile, Anger had gone to London, used the remaining footage to make *Invocation of My Demon Brother*, and got to know Mick Jagger and Donald Cammell. In 1970, he started to remake *Lucifer Rising*, with Donald Cammell playing the Egyptian god Osiris and Marianne Faithfull, Jagger's girlfriend, cast as demonic seductress Lilith. The music was eventually written by Bobby Beausoleil, who was, and still is, serving a life sentence in California jails.

Lucifer Rising is screened regularly at film festivals and has a cult following. A CD of Beausoleil's music was released in 2004, to respectful reviews. Kenneth Anger, who turned 80 in 2007, might have seemed well on the way to artistic respectability if it hadn't been for the 'Curse of the Brown Bunny'. This was an unsavoury little story centring on bad-boy film director Vincent Gallo, whose 2003 road movie *Brown Bunny* divided the critics. One of those who hated it was Roger Ebert, film critic of the *Chicago Sun.* In a newspaper interview, Gallo declared that he had placed a curse on Ebert. 'Roger Ebert will be dead of prostate cancer – if my curse works – within sixteen months, and my film will live far past the biopsies that are removed from his anus.' He expected the curse to work, apparently, because he had been taught how to inflict it by a master – Kenneth Anger.

Ebert replied with spirit, saying he'd watched one of his own colonoscopies on a screen and it had been more entertaining than

Brown Bunny. In fact, though, Ebert was being treated for thyroid cancer at the time, and over the next few years had drastic operations which left him unable to speak. Gallo was reported as saying he was glad Ebert had cancer, though he later denied this. He has also said that the declaration of a curse was made in the heat of the moment and that he regrets it. One thing that has never been denied though, either by Gallo or Anger, is the widely quoted claim that the old director and occultist taught the young one to hex.

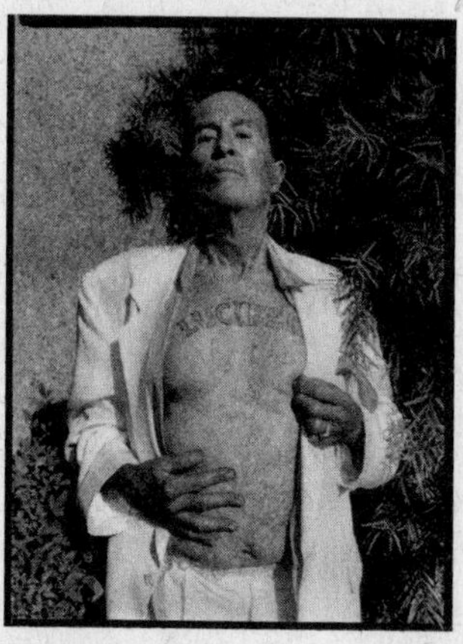

Kenneth Anger, film director, has said that cinema itself is an evil medium. (Photo Mark Berry)

Not that Anger has shown any sign of wanting to distance himself from the occult – though he does take issue with the term satanist, preferring to describe himself as a pagan. Proudly bearing the tattooed name 'Lucifer' on his chest (as does Beausoleil), in 2007 he repeatedly interrupted the eulogy at the funeral of film director and fellow occultist Curtis Harrington to provide details about their magick experiments. On the same occasion he announced that he had prostate cancer and predicted that he would die on the forthcoming Hallowe'en. A ripple of interest greeted this, given the history of the Gallo–Ebert quarrel, and some people have speculated that Gallo's curse might have been deflected against his teacher. Others believed Anger was just making trouble and didn't have cancer at all. Certainly, he didn't die on Hallowe'en 2007; at the time of writing, aged 83, he is still making films (recent titles include *Foreplay* and *Elliott's Suicide*) and practising the occult. Of course,

Anger would argue those two activities were one and the same. 'Magick is my life's work,' he once said, 'and the cinematograph is my magical weapon.'

Films don't have to deal with the occult to attract (or should that be generate?) a dark aftermath. The *Superman* series of films has its own trail of bad luck and accidents. The first *Man of Steel* film, in 1951, starred George Reeves, who went on to star in the same role in a TV series. The steady employment did not seem to bring him happiness, however: he was found shot dead in 1959, apparently, and unexpectedly, by his own hand. He had been due to marry the following day. His successor on the big screen, Christopher Reeve, starred in four films from 1978 onwards. The series was immensely popular, partly because Reeve seemed to epitomise the clean-cut, square-jawed superhero whose heart belonged to feisty journalist Lois Lane. Reeve was so popular in the role that although he declared he was through with *Superman* after the third movie, he was persuaded to return for *Superman IV: The Quest for Peace*. His *Superman* fame proved a mixed blessing, however: he felt that it limited the kinds of roles he was offered, and a series of underperforming films sent his Hollywood career into steady decline. Then, in 1995, he suffered an accident that made news round the world, because of its bitter irony: after falling from a horse, Christopher Reeve was paralysed. His athletic physique and his fitness allowed him to survive the initial trauma, but nothing could heal his spinal wounds; Reeve would spend the rest of his life in a wheelchair until he died in 2004, from heart failure related to his paralysis.

Christopher Reeve's tragedy is well known. Less so are the misfortunes suffered by his co-stars on the various films. Margot Kidder (rightly acclaimed for portraying Lois Lane as aggressive, vulnerable and likeable all at the same time) was badly injured in a car crash in 1990 and couldn't work for two years. At the same time, the bipolar condition she suffered from worsened. Hollywood, not renowned for its tender heart, was abuzz with rumours that police had picked her up, raving and, allegedly, naked. In 1990 tragedy also struck Marlon Brando, who played Superman's father. His son Christian shot Dag Drollet, the lover of Brando's daughter and Christian's half-sister Cheyenne. Though Christian claimed it was accidental, he was convicted of voluntary manslaughter and sentenced to ten years in prison. While Christian was serving his sentence, Cheyenne lost custody of her and Dag Drollet's son to Drollet's parents, and in 1995 she hanged herself.

Richard Pryor, actor and iconic comedian, was diagnosed with multiple sclerosis three years after co-starring with Reeve in *Superman III*. He would later die the year after Reeve. And Lee Quigley, who had started his acting career playing Kal-El (baby Superman) in the first of the series, died in 1991 from solvent abuse. He was 14.

It's an extraordinary list of tragedies, and just as with *The Omen* and *Poltergeist*, you don't have to look too hard to see mocking connections between life and film. Reeve, whose physical powers in the films knew no bounds, was trapped inside a motionless body. The qualities that made Kidder's Lois Lane so likeable – her spontaneity, drive and lack of reserve – were turned grotesquely against her in her illness. Brando, whose film role was a wise and loving father, had to watch his children wreak violence and misery on themselves and each other.

There's something else to notice about the *Superman* curse, though, and it's puzzling. It only seems to affect those who have played the 'good' characters. Christopher Reeve, Margot Kidder, Marlon Brando and Lee Quigley all played on the side of right throughout; Richard Pryor's character started off as Superman's enemy but had joined his side by the end of the film. With misfortune so generously scattered around, you'd expect to find it affecting one or two of the 'evil' actors. But Gene Hackman (Lex Luthor), Terence Stamp (General Zod) and Ned Beatty (Otis) have gone from strength to strength.

In 2006 a new Superman movie, *Superman Returns*, opened. The lead was played by Brandon Routh (bearing an uncanny resemblance to a young Christopher Reeve), while Kate Bosworth was Lois Lane. So far, thankfully, there has been no sign of a curse, though it's interesting to note that the career of Lex Luther-playing Kevin Spacey has flourished like his predecessor's. Meanwhile another Superman film is in development and Brandon Routh is reportedly very interested in taking the lead again. His fans might want to wish him luck, and not only with landing the part in the first place.

* * *

Rumours of a curse also swirled round two other Noughties blockbusters – the Batman film *The Dark Knight*, and the James Bond movie *Quantum of Solace*. *The Dark Knight* saw two deaths in succession – stunt cameraman Conway Wickliffe was killed in an accident during filming, and Heath Ledger, who played the Joker, died of an accidental overdose in January 2008 before the film was released. Six months later Morgan Freeman, who played Lucius Fox, was badly injured in a car crash.

The Quantum of Solace incidents, meanwhile, erupted in one week on location by Lake Garda in north Italy. First, a member of the public, passing on his bicycle, stopped to watch filming. He was standing quietly observing when he had a heart attack; an ambulance rushed him to hospital but he died. Next, two stunt cars were involved in a crash, with one of the drivers suffering critical head injuries. Then an Aston Martin that was being delivered to the location inexplicably went out of control, sliding off the road and through a barrier into the lake. Filming was suspended and the roads and cars were examined, but no obvious explanation could be found. It was almost as though the location itself had developed a malign force. If so, it was a force that could travel. The following month, while filming in Austria, a technician was stabbed by a woman he had met in a club.

It's worth noticing that all these movies manipulate the limits of what's possible. They deal in extremes, either of action, violence or emotion – and sometimes (especially in *The Dark Knight*) all three combined.

Does creating on-screen intensity also create something else? It would explain why *Rebel Without a Cause*, the iconic 1955 film about teenage angst and anger, was also one of the first to provoke whispers of a curse. As soon as the movie started shooting, everyone agreed that 24-year-old James Dean burned up the screen with his thwarted vitality. Within months of the film opening he was dead – killed in a car crash that couldn't help but remind people of the terrifying clifftop game of chicken that Dean's character plays in the film. His co-star was 16-year-old elfin and compelling Natalie Wood, and one of the film's most powerful scenes was where the two of them talked in an emptied-out swimming pool. Natalie was to die aged 43, by drowning. Sal Mineo, whose character is shot dead by police, would die violently at the age of 37, from a single stab wound to the heart.

The film's three lead actors dying young – surely that was enough even for the spirit of anger and self-destruction? But there have long been rumours that, after Dean's death, the destructive forces carried on working through the very machine that had killed him – his car. The Porsche 550 Spyder looked menacing enough with its sleek lines and silver paint, even before Dean had the name 'Little Bastard' painted on the back. When fellow actor Alec Guiness saw it, he told Dean it looked sinister and predicted that if he bought it, he'd be found dead in it. Which probably only gave Dean, who was a racing-car freak, extra pleasure in buying and customising it.

Legend has it that Dean sped to his death at 100 m.p.h. In fact, he was probably going about 60 m.p.h. but that was still too fast to avoid hitting another car in the process of turning. The other car withstood the crash well, but the low-to-the-ground Spyder was crushed, and Dean with it. He suffered massive head injuries and died on his way to hospital.

Two doctors, racing-car enthusiasts like Dean, bought the Spyder from the insurance company and used its parts as spares for their own Porsches. One of them died two years later when his car crashed during a race.

The doctors had sold on the shell of the car to a car customiser, George Barris. He lent it to the California Highway Patrol to be used in a touring road-safety exhibition, but at its first destination, the garage it was stored in caught fire. Almost everything in the building was destroyed – except the Spyder. At its second venue, a high school, the car rolled off its stand and broke a student's legs. Later, while the car was being transported to Salinas, the trailer carrying it went out of control, the car rolled off and the trailer driver died. In the following months, there were two similar accidents, with the car breaking loose from a trailer and a truck, but luckily no one was injured.

It is not known where the various parts of 'Little Bastard' are now. Historic Auto Attractions, a car museum in Illinois, claims to have a piece of the bodywork, but its authenticity is in doubt. And the son of the surviving racing doctor is said to have the engine. Apparently it has been offered for sale on eBay. Punters might be advised to think carefully before they bid.

* * *

Water was the agent of an uncanny happening on the set of Japanese horror film *Ringu 2*, and of many of the problems that plagued the American version, *Ring 2*. In Japanese mythology, water is often a source of danger and darkness, and the Japanese director of the *Ringu* films, Hideo Nakata, played on this to stunning effect. When the original *Ringu* came out in 1998, it was an instant success in Japan and rapidly became a cult hit worldwide. Its plot hinges on the idea of a cursed videotape that causes the deaths of people who watch it, but the story also delves deep into Japanese traditions with its depiction of a terrifying ghost, her face almost completely covered by her long black hair, revealing just one ghastly eye. The long-haired ghost is based on Kabuki theatre representations of the spirits of vengeful women; in the film the spirit is of Sadako, a young girl whose father murdered her and put her body in a well. Through the mechanism of the tape, Sadako is now escaping from the well and killing people.

A well-constructed movie like this would be frightening wherever it was made, but *Ringu* had more than technique: it was charged with the power of Japanese culture and supernatural beliefs. By the time Hideo Nakata made *Ringu 2* (just one year later), even he and the crew were beginning to wonder just how real their creations had become. In *Ringu 2*, water is imbued with all kinds of powers, some pure, some dark. For one eerie scene, Nakata and his sound engineer fixed a microphone just above the sea's surface: they were transfixed to hear, through the sounds of wind and water, a faint human voice. It sounded like a young man's, and it was repeatedly calling a woman's name.

Had they stumbled on a real story of loss or betrayal? Could their evocation of restless spirits and the mysteries of water have called up something that genuinely haunted that stretch of sea coast?

After *Ringu 2* was released, Nakata was commissioned to make an American version, *Ring 2*, starring Naomi Watts. The film has a different storyline from *Ringu 2*, though once again water figures prominently: Samara, a child conceived by a water demon, is able to use supernatural powers to create floods, before having her own curse cleansed by fresh water. In this film, fresh water is ultimately redemptive – though it didn't feel that way on the shoot when first the production office and then the make-up trailer were flooded, apparently thanks to freak bursts in the water pipes. The crew, knowing the significance of water in the story and in Japanese beliefs, were uneasy, and became more so when, after the production office had been cleaned up and dried out, a five-gallon water container suddenly split and flooded it again.

Nakata, taking no chances, flew in a Shinto priest who conducted a purification ceremony, using water, naturally. After this, there were no more floods. It appeared that the water in the area had indeed been cleansed of its evil energies. However, for a while afterwards, local wildlife seemed unsettled. A swarm of bees attacked a props lorry, and just as suddenly flew off. Something sharp-toothed – probably a fox or racoon – chewed through a cable. And one day when they were filming on the edge of woods, a wardrobe worker who had wandered towards the trees was startled to come face to face with an antlered deer. In an echo of one of the film's own scenes, the deer stared at her then charged, missing her by inches as she leapt aside.

It seems that restless energies might be quelled in one form, only to appear in another. Which begs a question of all the stories told in this chapter – the curses attached to these movies might seem to have peaked and passed . . . but how can we be sure?

And if they do erupt back into life again, we might be to blame. Because the collaborative ritual that is film magic doesn't just involve actors, directors and crew. It also needs our eyes in the dark, watching, and our imaginations given over to it. We are the final element in this paranormal process. So think very hard before you load that next DVD.

South Pacific

The South Pacific islanders are known as some of the most skilful sailors in the world. In their long boats they performed incredible feats of navigation, colonising island after island, their uncanny navigation skills based on a knowledge of the skies and a deep understanding of the weather and the ocean's currents.

And it's a skill that survives death.

In 1991, three fishermen set out on a fishing trip from their homes on Kiribati, in the middle of the South Pacific ocean. Half sunk in a sudden storm, they clung on to their boat but, to their horror, realised that the currents were towing them further and further out to sea.

But Pacific Islanders are a resourceful people. They threw out lines for fish, managed to trap enough rainwater to drink, beat off sharks and managed to survive for an incredible 175 days before they caught sight of Upolu, one of the Western Samoa group of islands, which they knew was mountainous and surrounded by treacherous reefs. Without an engine it would be difficult to steer the boat through the gap in the rocks, but at least Tekamangu, the most experienced sailor among them, knew the waters and could find a way through.

But Tekamangu was dying and however much his companions tried to rally him, he was just too weak to hang on. He passed away within sight of the waves smashing on to the rocks.

There was no way the two exhausted sailors could turn their boat round and sail away; they would just have to trust to providence. So they gripped the rudder and headed for the island.

Then, as the waves crashed around them on to the rocks, they saw Tekamangu's ghost rise from the water and hover in front of the boat. At first the two survivors were terrified – after all, they had only just given him a burial at sea a short while before – but then they realised that the spirit of their friend wanted to help. So they followed him and, sure enough, he guided them through the terrible reefs, an astonishing act of navigation, and into the safe waters beyond.

CHAPTER NINE

TYING DOWN THE DEMON

Exorcisms Today

The screen says: REAL-LIFE EXORCISM FOOTAGE.

It cuts to a totally unexceptional room where the only thing of note is a man sitting on a sofa. The man is large, middle-aged, with an impassive face, and wearing a striped djellaba, the long, loose robe that Arab men wear. We are looking at him but he seems to be looking into the middle distance and the image quality can only be described as rough – the filming could be on a mobile phone. At first not much happens. We hear voices in the background, and watch as the man sits, and sits, and sits . . .

Suddenly his robe shimmers – there is no other word for it – halfway down his shins, and seconds later he begins to shake, his pudgy face moving like jelly, his eyes round and staring. Then he seems to be jerked from the couch and thrown to the ground. He writhes, his body convulsing and arching, and what sounds like a stream of nonsense pours from his lips. A man comes and kneels by his head – we cannot see his face – and whispers in his ear. After a while, the convulsions stop. The man gets to his feet and sits back down on the sofa, his face impassive again.

We have, we are told, just witnessed possession followed by exorcism. The man in question is an ongoing case and suffers from repeated visits from a persistent djinn – the Muslim word for demon. Although the djinn in question is persistent, fortunately for him it listens to reason, and when the imam explains to it, through whispering in the man's ear, the harm it is doing, the demon leaves immediately. A longer-term solution is being sought.

Evidence of the belief in demonic possession can be found in abundance on the Internet and this short film perfectly demonstrates the weird combination of the bland and the extraordinary that marks out so many cases of possession today. This is not the stuff of horror movies, nor even of personal tragedy. We do not feel we are in the presence of great evil – to be honest, for all the excitement this unfortunate man's possession seems to causing, he could just as well be in the grip of a slight sniffle as a demon.

Take another example, from America this time, where a man, ordinary-looking enough in his baseball cap and glasses, is sitting in a pretty ordinary office and explaining the origins of possession: the war in heaven, the fall of the rebel angels and their conversion into demons where they infest the world, testing the limits of humanity's love of God and entering human flesh to gratify their lusts – addiction or sexual perversion, for example.

Across the world in Russia, we see another side of possession. We are in a Russian church where a young woman is being firmly gripped by two men while she writhes and shouts in a deep, guttural voice. A kindly, wrinkled old woman, with white hair peeping out from under her headscarf, describes what is going on: 'She is possessed. It's always the same. Terrible cries. They can sound like dogs, cats, any animal really.'

From the way she talks, it is clear she has seen and heard it all before.

In the same church, a young woman with a pleasant face flinches as the priest, with flowing robes and flowing beard, presses a crucifix to her head. Suddenly her face twists into a mask of hatred and her head thrashes from side to side. 'What are you doing with that cross?' she spits. 'I just want to work out how to tear you into little pieces!'

Now let's go across the world to Kenya, where a girl, neatly dressed in her striped cotton school uniform, dances and screams in a dusty market square under a bleached white sky. Her face is contorted into a rictus of pain and grief, while an Islamic priest and members of the crowd hold her tight and press their hands on to her head. At her feet another possession drama is taking place: a mother, driven mad with worry, adjusts the headscarf around her teenage daughter's hair while she writhes in the dirt, shouting and screaming. Another priest kneels at her side, then throws himself across the girl's thrashing body, pinning her down as he chants verses from the Qur'an.

On the east coast of England, a middle-aged man explains in tones of numb disbelief how he was possessed by the devil and this made him go into spasms of violent, murderous rage. A solid-looking British bobby shows us the tiny hatch in the cell door that the man squeezed his head and shoulders through when he was incarcerated after trying to strangle the station sergeant. To pull his head back out, he says, first they had to sedate the prisoner and then slather him in liquid soap, but even then it took half a dozen men to free him. The explanation by exorcism specialists? Possession by the devil in canine form. The cure? Exorcism. The result? Peace for one very grateful individual and one more defeat for the devil.

Australia

Each country's history is written in its ghost stories. Colonial settlers tend to see their new land in terms of unfettered opportunity and adventure. For the original inhabitant, however, their homeland is transformed into a vast, historical crime scene.

After clearing his huge New South Wales ranch of two European spirits – a convict from the eighteenth century and a traumatised World War II veteran – the owner discovered he was being targeted by the vengeful ghost of an Aborigine shaman. The shaman was the victim of one of the many massacres the Europeans committed to clear the land of its original inhabitants. More importantly, he was a Kadaitja man, a shaman whose role was to represent and channel the dark forces of nature: anger and vengeance.

Good spirits, who had been called to the site, told the owner to use positive earth energy to banish the Kadaitja man and, after a titanic struggle, he managed to send the furious ghost into the light. But was this a victory or just another example of white domination extending into the spirit realm?

In 1999 the Roman Catholic Church noticed that the demand for exorcisms was growing year on year while the number of authorised exorcists was actually shrinking. As a point of fact, around the time of the millennium there were no official Catholic exorcists practising in Germany, Austria, Switzerland, Spain or Portugal. First Pope John Paul II and then the current pope, Benedict XVI, responded by massively increasing the ranks of priests trained and spiritually prepared to expel demons from the bodies of humans. This sudden change, from famine to glut, reflects a schism that goes to the very highest levels of the Catholic Church.

For many years in the twentieth century, the subject of exorcism divided the Church into two camps. There was a progressive wing that believed that possession was a thing of the past: something connected with primitive superstition as opposed to enlightened grace and salvation. However, there was always a more traditionalist wing that believed not just in the efficacy of exorcism but in the growing need for it. Indeed, this traditionalist wing went further. They thought that the devil himself had invaded the highest levels of the Vatican and was on the brink of winning his greatest victory. This would be when the pope and his cardinals stopped believing he existed. Then, the traditionalists argued, he would be free to oppress and possess whomever he wanted and corrupt their souls unmolested.

Pope John Paul II was often identified with political liberalism because of his association with Poland's trade union-led Solidarność movement. But in theological matters, he was a conservative. He was happy to equip the Church with what he saw as foot soldiers in the fight against possession. And popular demand for exorcisms was no short-term bubble – it had been growing steadily since the 1970s, partly fuelled by a hugely popular film, *The Exorcist.* Still famous for horrific scenes of a young girl's head revolving, and self-abuse with a crucifix, *The Exorcist* was, incidentally, praised by the Catholic Church on its release.

Most readers will be familiar with the background. The film was faithfully adapted from a best-selling novel of the same name by William Peter Blatty, and it is said that the novel itself was based on real-life events. These concerned a young boy from Mt Rainier in Washington State who became possessed by 'an invisible entity' after he and his aunt had played with a Ouija board.

After his local hospital failed to cure him, he was successfully exorcised by two priests, one of whom kept a diary. He described furniture moving across the room when there was no one close to push it. Scratches appeared on the young boy's skin as if from an invisible animal or, even more horribly, as if he were being scratched from inside. Objects shot through the air. The boy physically attacked the priests. A picture of the devil appeared on his skin and, as the exorcism reached a climax (the process had taken many weeks in a variety of locations), the boy screamed first that he was one of the fallen angels, and then, in a deep, commanding voice, that he was St Michael. Once St Michael had entered him, the demon went out of his body and the boy was left in peace.

If Blatty did indeed use this diary, one can see how the template for modern exorcism was created. First, there is the sense that both the body and the soul of the victim has become possessed. Spiritual attack is expressed as physical attack, moral decay as physical decay, fear of what is inside the victim becomes manifested in their changing and terrifying physical condition. As important is the sense of escalation. Action on the part of the exorcist is matched by reaction on the part of the demon, and this in turn prompts a more violent action. And so the frail human body – often of a child – becomes a battleground in the most titanic battle of all: the fight between good and evil.

Of course there have been accounts of possession since the dawn of time. Babylonians and Assyrians noted the presence of demons in graveyards and on mountaintops. Then there were Alu – humanoids who roamed the streets of ancient cities at night, and Labartu who had the head of a lion, the teeth of an ass and an insatiable appetite for human flesh and blood.

In ancient Jewish texts, Adam was tempted by the night demon Lilith, while angels, tempted by the fleshly beauty of human women, slept with them, thus swelling the ranks of demons with their hideous, gigantic offspring, the Nephilim. The life of Jesus not only testified to the power of demons, but also the idea of exorcism based on personality – indeed, some Jewish sources recognise Jesus first and foremost as an exorcist. In the story of the Gaderene swine, Jesus recognises that a swineherd's behaviour is down to possession and orders the demons to leave his body, whereupon they possess a herd of pigs who go mad and jump over a cliff. This is the first recorded example of an exorcism and the first instance in which devils or demons are associated so strongly with a need to take corporeal form – if they're not in the swineherd, they need to be in his swine. This hunger for the warmth of a body may go some way to explaining why it is so hard to get rid of them. Demons, we can speculate, are not only driven by a helpless urge to corrupt. They derive something else from the sensation: comfort perhaps.

From their earliest days, Christians have always shown a particular interest in demons. The Testament of Solomon (which was written by a Christian monk some time before the fourth century) describes how the great king exploited demons to help him build his great temple, and then interrogated them so that he would have some record of their strengths and weaknesses. Demonology became incredibly powerful once again in the Middle Ages, when theologians started taking great pains to organise demons into neatly classified ranks. They argued that you could not properly expel a demon if you did not know who they were, and so went to work with the zeal of an Edwardian butterfly hunter.

First, they ranked them according to authority and power, in a dark mirror image of the celestial hierarchies. At the head of the demonic ranks was Lucifer or Beelzebub himself, prince of the fallen angels, who led the rebellion against God and got himself and his followers thrown into the pit for their pains. Next came Leviathan, leader of the heretics; then Asmodeus, who guided humans towards sins of the flesh; Balberith, the spirit of murder; Asteroth, the spirit of sloth; Verrine, the spirit of intolerance; Gressil, the spirit of dirty thoughts; Sonneillon, the spirit of hatred.

Other hierarchies controlled other areas of human weakness. Peter Binsfield, a German bishop, allocated a demon to each of the seven deadly sins; others, such as the Spanish Franciscan Alphonso de Spina, grouped them by species: fates, poltergeists, incubi, succubi, and so on. Demons were associated with different months – Belial was particularly effective in January; February was Leviathan's month; Satan preferred to go to work in March, and so on. Another demon philosopher, Johan Weyer, ranked demons according to their power, mobility, kingdoms, allegiances and social standing. He argued that Satan had been nudged off the top spot by Beelzebub, Moloch ran the army and Nergal was chief of the secret police.

And just as the new invention of printing allowed these antique theorists to spread their work and their knowledge throughout the world, so today the Internet is driving a new surge of interest in the subject. In the past, you needed to be a scholar to find out about demons, or a connoisseur with a library of rare, leather-bound volumes: think of Giles, mentor to Buffy the Vampire Slayer. Today you just need Google to find out, for example, that in the opinion of one expert, supernatural beings can be divided into five classes. Class 1 is Interactive Former Human Spirits; Class 2 is Non-Interactive Location-Based Former Human Spirits; Class 3 is Psychokinetic Entities; Class 4 is Earth Mysteries. Demons, described as Non-Human Entities under this system, are Class 5.

Click on Monstropedia and you can find a list of over 200 demons from all around the world, most with links describing their characteristics. Sometimes, as you look for information, you discover that you are on a Dungeons and Dragons role-playing website. Demons' names, which would once only have been invoked by necromancers or priests, are now routinely used to add a frisson or touch of danger to online identities. And of course, for the first time, people can observe cases of possession online and make their own decisions and form their own theories as to what is happening.

But it's not only webheads who are sensing the increase in demonic interest and activity. Father Gabriele Amorth, known as the Vatican's chief exorcist and the honorary president of the International Association of Exorcists, has exorcised Lilith, Beelzebub, Lucifer and other demons so often now that he feels that he can recognise them right at the start of an exorcism – pretty much as soon as he claps eyes on the hapless victim. He is blunt and definite in his views. 'When magic works,' he says, 'it is always the work of the devil.' He has argued vigorously for the need for more exorcists and campaigned tirelessly to ensure that the exorcism ceremonies were not watered down and made useless. For example, the new guidelines from Rome forbade exorcisms before possession was proven. He said this was wrong: in certain cases, the way some subjects react to exorcism is the only way to ascertain whether or not they are possessed.

To read Amorth, it's hard not to be impressed, even swept along, by his calmness and certainty. But when you look at some exorcisms in action, you start to have serious doubts. The most celebrated or notorious exorcism of modern times is also one of the very worst and involved a young Catholic girl from Germany, the daughter of devout, some would say fanatical, Catholic parents.

Until her 17th birthday, Anneliese Michel lived a life exceptional only for its quiet ordinariness. She was born in the south of Germany in a small Bavarian village, and for the first sixteen years of her life went to school, went to church and was contented. Photographs of her show a good-looking girl with an easy smile but slightly watchful, slightly intense dark eyes.

Then, at the age of 17, everything changed. A convulsion was followed less than a year later by her first epileptic attack. This was diagnosed as grand mal epilepsy and she was duly prescribed medicines to try and control the condition.

But they failed.

Soon Anneliese started experiencing hallucinations of the devil while praying and voices telling her that she was damned. Her condition worsened and she became suicidally depressed. With no apparent improvement in her condition, and indications that it was getting worse, her parents decided to withdraw her from the psychiatric clinic where she was being treated. The reason had everything to do with their faith and the worrying reports of a friend who had noted that while she was on a pilgrimage with Anneliese, the adolescent had shown a marked aversion to looking at Christian images – a dramatic change in behaviour from a girl who had been devout all her life.

With conventional medicine failing, Annaliese's parents looked for a different cause and a different cure. The cause, they now thought, was demonic possession, the only cure for which was exorcism.

So, in 1973, her parents withdrew her from the clinic and turned to the Church for help, begging pastor after pastor to exorcise the girl. On each occasion they were turned down. In a tacit acknowledgement of its risks, exorcism is hedged around by strict guidelines. An aversion to religious artefacts and sacraments is just one of many of the criteria determining a suitable subject for full-scale exorcism. Others include speaking in languages the victim could not possibly know; superhuman strength; supernatural – more often than not telekinetic – powers; convulsions, and glossolalia – speaking in tongues. With guidelines like these, it is not surprising they have to be so careful, as many of these symptoms are typical of nondemonic disorders. People suffer from convulsions for all kinds of medical reasons, while nonpathological convulsions and glossolalia take place on a daily basis in charismatic Christian churches all over the world. Indeed they are actively encouraged and taken as a clear indication of God's presence and the divine workings of the Holy Spirit. Nevertheless, we can see that poor Anneliese ticked more than a few of the boxes. Even more significantly, she herself felt possessed. Demonic voices echoed through her head and she saw grimacing, devilish faces looking at her. Eventually, the Church yielded some ground. Although the authorities still would not accede to the family's request for an exorcism, it looks as if they began to accept that the problem might not be purely organic in nature, as in 1974, they recommended she should live even more religiously to see if that would bring an end to her condition.

It did not.

In fact, Anneliese's troubles grew worse, and incidents of disturbing behaviour became more and more frequent. She stopped eating, claiming that the demons stopped her. She grew violent, hitting and biting her family members. She ate coal, spiders and flies, while her hatred of religious artefacts became more and more extreme as she rampaged through the house, smashing pictures of Christ, crucifixes and destroying rosaries. She would drink her urine, urinate on the floor and started to self-harm.

Finally, her behaviour became bad enough for the bishop of Würzburg to authorise pastors Arnold Renz and Ernst Alt to perform 'The Great Exorcism'. It was September 1975, a full seven years after she had first begun to display her disturbing symptoms.

The two priests prepared themselves. They put on their formal robes, and began to read. Lord have mercy. Christ have mercy. Lord have mercy.

They called on the major saints, from Michael through to Anastasia, and begged them to intercede. They prayed for peace, for strength, recited the Lord's Prayer, the correct psalm, extracts from Gospels. Only after all this had been correctly gone through did they finally lay hands on the girl and command the demon to leave. 'I cast you out, unclean spirit, along with every satanic power of the enemy, every spectre from hell, and all your fell companions.'

It didn't work.

Worse still, the demons identified themselves as if they were mocking the two local priests. As well as fallen angels, Anneliese was possessed by Hitler, Nero, Cain, Lucifer and Judas Escariot. (Some Christians believe that souls of the truly evil are so frightened by the thought of judgement that they refuse to leave the earthly realm and join the demonic ranks.) The rite was read over her once or twice a week for the next ten months with dramatic effects as the demons inside her resisted. Sometimes they threw her into such violent convulsions that she had to be held down by three men, although in between these violent incidents she seemed to regain a measure of normality, even graduating from her college with a qualification in teaching.

But the attacks did continue and, when they struck, they were worse than ever. Anneliese's physical condition now deteriorated alarmingly. Her knees ruptured from her compulsive genuflections – up to 600 a day. When she was too damaged to genuflect on her own, her parents took her by the arms and performed the motion by lifting and lowering her. Her weight dropped further and further and by the time she underwent her last exorcism on 30 June 1976, she was dangerously ill with pneumonia.

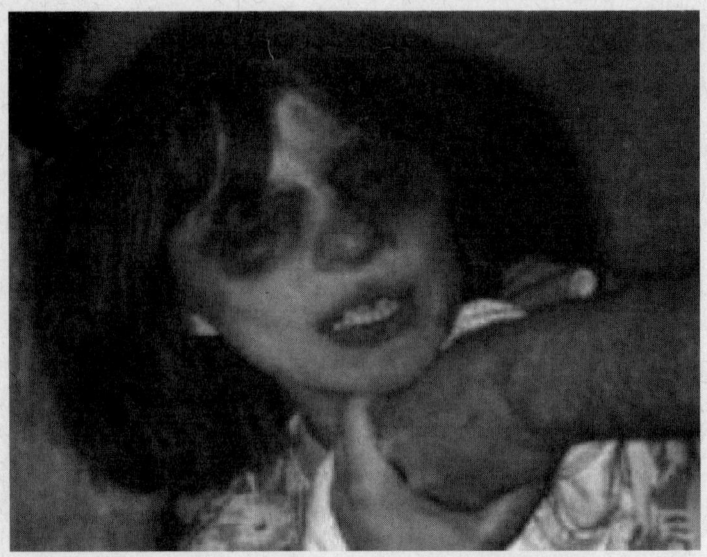

Anneliese Michel: as much a victim of exorcism as possession. It is impossible to look at images of her without feeling a mixture of pity, horror and rage.

The strain proved too great. She died the next day and shortly afterwards the two pastors who had performed the exorcisms and her parents were charged by the German state with manslaughter by negligence.

Anyone who has looked at the images of Anneliese or listened to downloads of her rantings can be in no doubt that this was a very sick girl. Huge, haunted, black-ringed eyes stare out of a face so emaciated it looks as if it has already starved to death. Cracked lips are pulled back from teeth that seem to have grown as the flesh has shrunk. Worse than this are the barely human noises she makes. The whole matter is pitiful, frightening and deeply disturbing, and yet the girl was allowed to get into that state by the people who claimed to love and care for her most, her parents and her priests. How could this have happened?

In the first place, were her parents wrong to press for exorcism as the Church implied when it initially turned down their requests? And, having turned down their requests at first, how could it have been right to allow exorcism to go ahead later, when the poor girl was in a weakened state?

However stringent the burden of proof demanded by the Catholic Church, the fact remains it relies on subjective judgement when it comes to deciding who gets an exorcism and when. And when charged with performing exorcisms on subjects with clinical illnesses, they would argue that Jesus healed the sick as well as casting out demons – and sometimes did both, curing a child whose epilepsy was being caused by a demon. What's more, while modern medicine has made enormous strides in diagnosing the underlying causes of physical conditions – smoking and lung cancer, for example, or viruses and influenza – it does less well with mental conditions. Doctors might say that chemical imbalances in the actual brain lead to depression, but what causes the imbalances in the first place? Some advocates of exorcism have used this gap in knowledge to promote their own drastic course of action.

Mistakes were clearly made in the case of Anneliese Michel. But again, if supporters of the Church were looking for excuses, they would point out that modern medicine often gets it wrong and that all drug-based modern treatments have side effects, some dire, others catastrophic. The fact that Anneliese died was based on individual – rather than systemic – errors.

This is true, but only up to a point. The Roman Catholic Church has a very definite hierarchy, which means that decisions can be passed up the chain of command and supervision should be passed down. Instead, on this occasion, the Church authorities vacillated disastrously. Having made the initial decision that Anneliese was ill rather than possessed, they then moved away from it by eventually allowing the exorcism to go ahead; but – presumably wanting to keep everything low-key – they entrusted it to parish priests rather than bringing in someone with more authority.

Anneliese's death demonstrates the dangers of this kind of exorcism being used for a person in physical extremity. And even when the subject is in good health, an exorcism ceremony carries risks. It can stir up underlying emotional or psychological problems; it can leave the subject feeling vulnerable and distressed. And then there is the nature of the exorcism ritual itself, in which the exorcist directly addresses the possessing demon and, using consecrated objects like crucifixes and holy water, commands the demon to leave the body and mind of the possessed. It's an antagonistic approach and can all too easily be felt as an aggressive, even violating experience.

The mainstream churches (Catholic, Anglican, Methodist, etc.) are well aware of these dangers, and in most cases are cautious about performing exorcisms. They have developed a graded approach to problems of suspected demon activity or possession: usually clergy will offer prayers for healing and cleansing and blessings before suggesting an exorcism, and permission for this must usually be given by a figure further up the hierarchy. But the Christian communion is huge and diverse, and there are many churches and faith communities who are much more eager to spot demons at work and to unleash their exorcism techniques on them, and on the poor 'possessed' member of the congregation.

This approach usually goes hand in hand with the belief that demons do not simply enter humans by chance but that the individual has to 'let them in' in some way. This does not have to involve occult practices, like summoning up a demon in an attempt to harness the powers of evil, or attempting to communicate directly with the devil. According to many Christian websites, a person leaves themselves open to demonic possession once they start reading horoscopes, practising transcendental meditation or going to yoga classes. By masturbating, reading Tarot cards or playing with Ouija boards they are practically laying down a red carpet for the demons to traipse up. And because these churches warn people about this, anyone who does get infected in this way has to accept an element of responsibility. As a result, there is often an underlying element of punishment in the exorcism rituals.

Often adding to this tendency is the strand of thinking that holds that the flesh itself is evil. God is lord of the heavens, the spirit world. Satan is lord of the earth, of matter, of flesh. By punishing the body of a victim of possession, you are in effect hurting matter and so hurting Satan. If, in the process, one human feels discomfort, doesn't that count as a justifiable casualty in the fight against evil?

No humans are comfortable with the idea of possession, but the monotheistic religions, Jewish, Christian, Muslim, are uniquely antagonistic. As well as the main classifications, the Internet has spawned a sort of obsession with demonic hygiene, as well as a conviction that demons are responsible for every embarrassing problem going, from bedwetting to masturbation. Martin Luther, the founder of the Protestant movement, believed that the devil was the cause of his chronic constipation; for him, every bowel movement was a victory for Christ. In many ways, we have not moved from there. A spoof website asks the question: Do You Have Demons in Your Colon? but the real joke is just how close this headline is to the truth.

Thus, in one online exorcism, a young man confesses to an exorcist that he masturbates, takes drugs, lusts after women and drinks alcohol – in other words, he exhibits every behavioural trait of a typical young man. 'You've got a bad case of it,' the exorcist replies, meaning that he is seriously infected with demonic powers, and cites the young man's yoga habit as being one of the causes of his possession.

This belief that demonic possession is the cause of so many run-of-the-mill behaviours can have profound social and personal ramifications. One website proposes that demons are interested in any sexual behaviour that takes place outside Christian marriage and, as all homosexual behaviour takes place outside Christian marriage, it must follow that homosexual behaviour is demonic.

This is by no means a fringe view. Father Jeremy Davies, from the same diocese as the Catholic archbishop of England and Wales, claims pornography, promiscuity and homosexuality leave the individual open to possession by demons. Even some Christian psychotherapists take a similar line, with the theory that homosexuality is a result of possession by a ghost of the opposite sex who steals the host's natural energy. This can result in anything from transvestism through homosexuality to gender reassignment. The cure? Hypnotherapy or 'releasement', a sort of New Age exorcism.

Obnoxious to homosexuals as this must be, such New Age treatments do at least have one thing to be said for them: they do not involve physical or spiritual violence. The problem with much religious exorcism is that the event itself is embellished with quasi-military formulations. Priests armour themselves against the armies of evil. The possessed, the person with the devil inside them, is perceived as battleground.

If there was no fallout, this would not be such a worrying trend, but there is. While it might be seen as bad enough that young people in America are being literally demonised for their sexual practices, in other parts of the world, people, especially children, are being tortured and killed, allegedly to save their souls.

In November 2003, a little girl was found barefoot on the steps of a block of flats in North London. When examined, it was found that she had forty-three wounds and scars on her emaciated body; after an investigation, she told the police that her aunt, whom she had been living with since she left her home in Angola, had been the one who had injured her. When her aunt was questioned, it was discovered that she was a member of a small, local fundamentalist church that warned all its members to be watchful all the time for the influence of witches. Witches were powerful, it argued; if they wanted to possess you, a piece of bread they had given you would be enough to put you under their spell. The woman believed her niece had been possessed and set about performing her own exorcism with three other friends: a woman and two men. First they starved the girl, then they performed a number of rituals that involved cutting her, hitting her, beating her with a belt, rubbing chilli peppers into her eyes and tying her into a sack before telling her that they were going to throw her away. They argued it was all in aid of ridding her of demons.

The girl was taken into care and her 'exorcists' were put in prison, but it is estimated that sixty such churches operate in the London. In Africa, where many of these fringe Christian cults originate, there are countless more.

So is there another way? Exorcism, in the Christian tradition, is about the personal interaction between the exorcist and the demon. At present, the tradition of violent exorcism seems to be in the ascendant – a sort of macho confrontation in which strength alone prevails. It is tempting to say that this results from a nervousness on the part of the exorcist, a symptom of a 'fight or flight' adrenalin reaction.

But how do other cultures and faiths tackle demonic possession? Islam, even though it is a monotheistic religion, takes a different view of the problem. For a start, possession is a rather more casual affair and can occur through simple carelessness: walking round the house naked is given as one reason, entering a toilet without first reciting a *du'a*, a protective prayer, is another. But if possession occurs easily, exorcisms in the majority of cases take a far more moderate path than in Christianity.

In a typical case, an illiterate manual labourer suddenly started reciting the Qur'an, although he had no knowledge of it. The exorcist worked out that he had relieved himself in a cave without fortifying himself by means of prayer beforehand. This had woken up a cave spirit, which, understandably enough, was annoyed, and possessed him in order to teach him a lesson. However, at some point during its lengthy existence, it had learned the Qur'an, and was now repeating it through him. In this case, in order for the spirit to leave, all the exorcist had to do was to tell it that it had been found out and it departed.

This relaxed attitude of the Muslims towards demons might make you blink. After all, sharia (Islamic law), as practised in Iran, Saudi Arabia and Sudan, is not exactly known for its tolerance, so it would seem logical for the more extreme groups to be at least as proactive on exorcisms as the right-wing Christians. The reason they are not is that in Islam demons are not seen as primarily interested in tempting people away from moral rectitude. They tend to affect people in physical ways, giving them tics or making them confused; underneath the symptoms, the possessed person will still be in charge of their own conscience and principles. So there isn't the same opening for exorcists to act as moral police.

The reason for this can be traced back to the origins of the djinns, the Islamic equivalent of demons. Known in the West as genies, they are perhaps best known to non-Muslims through the amusing spirit of the lamp in Walt Disney's *Aladdin.* People who have read the original version of the legend in the *Stories of the 1001 Arabian Nights*, will know that they are more dangerous creatures than the cartoon suggests. There is the story of the fisherman who picks up a bottle on the seashore and opens it to find himself engulfed in a dark and swirling cloud. This coalesces into a genie who, far from grateful, asks the fisherman how he wants to die. 'But I saved you,' the poor fisherman protests. The genie tells him that he was imprisoned so long that he has completely run out of patience and swore he would kill the person who let him out of the bottle. The fisherman pretends to submit to his fate, but cannily tells the genie that he cannot truly believe that so huge and powerful a figure could really fit into a tiny bottle. His vanity pricked, the genie pours himself back into the container and the fisherman promptly pops the cork back in. The story continues after that with bargains being struck, but the nature of the genie is clear: he is far more powerful than the fisherman but not as bright and, crucially, while he is dangerous, he is not evil.

This is plumb in line with mainstream Islamic tradition, which teaches that djinns were created by Allah out of smokeless fire, while humans were created out of earth. Less intelligent but physically stronger than humans, they possess free will and, as for humans, Muhammad is their prophet. However, they do not necessarily follow him and this is where djinns go bad. For although they are forbidden to harass or possess humans, not all can resist the temptation and some Muslims go as far as believing that each person has a djinn that is constantly trying to possess them and lead them astray.

The dangerous side of the djinns is revealed in this story from a young, Western college girl, which shows how closely they are woven into the lives of young Muslims. Just like Christians, they see no contradiction between these extraordinary supernatural creatures and the humdrum life of a twenty-first-century student.

In the relaxed, open atmosphere of her college, she makes friends with a young Arab man. In the course of one of their conversations, she sees another man staring at them. When she asks her friend if he knows the other man, his reaction is startling. He grips her arm, looks at her in the eyes and violently tells her that the other man is bad and she should have nothing to do with him.

The following week, she bumps into the student she has been warned off and discovers that, far from being a monster, he – we'll call him Abdul – is in fact a nice, open guy. They get on so well that she walks back with him in the direction of his digs. The only strange thing is when he asks her if she knows anything about the occult, a question she laughs off, claiming that she knows her birth sign and that is it.

She meets up with him a week later and they talk more. He is a lapsed Muslim, she discovers, which means little to her; then, out of the blue, he asks her if she knows about the djinns. She makes the connection with genies immediately and says she doesn't believe in fairy stories. He simply smiles and assures her that djinns are as real as the day, and he will prove it if she dares come home with him.

She agrees. He makes tea, then draws the curtains, lights candles, produces a black book and starts chanting in a foreign language. After a while the chant changes to a single word, Malikha, Malikha, Malikha, until the very air seems to vibrate. Then she hears a voice in front of her. It is not Abdul – he is still chanting – and the voice is angry, frightening. Next, the girl feels an awful heat on her face. Abdul is sweating, and a spark appears in the air, then seems to grow and swirl as if something is trying to take form. The girl cries out and runs from the room, with Abdul following her. All he says is: 'Do you believe now?'

Malikha, as the girl found out later, is the name of the Muslim angel who rules the underworld, and she assumed Abdul invoked him through the ceremony. While this is possible, she may have been jumping to conclusions. In the Christian mythos, the god of the underworld is Satan, the evil one. Muslims, however, do not accept that any of the angels can have fallen. All of them are subordinate to Allah and therefore controlled by him and Malikha is not considered evil. Further undermining her version of events is the fact that in everyday speech, Malikha means queen (the masculine form is Malik). Was Abdul summoning up a monstrous female djinn called Malikha, or was he luring a male djinn with promises of a queen?

In general, Muslims are more likely to accept djinns as part of their spiritual ecosystem than Christians, and only have to resort to exorcism when things go badly wrong. Even then, a Muslim exorcism is a more delicate business than the Christian equivalent. An imam describes how he called a beautiful female djinn out of a Pakistani girl. The first thing that strikes the reader of his account is that he had to be respectful of the djinn because it is one of Allah's creations so, instead of casting it into the pit, which would be the Christian response, he talked to her and found out that she was herself being controlled by black magic. The imam was able to free her and convert her to Islam, a surprise for the djinn as she had been a practising Hindu all her existence. The djinn also revealed that, when she went near heaven to look at the angels, they threw stones at her, breaking her arm, a revelation that caused the imam to break off his conversation and bless the angels for protecting heaven with meteor showers.

This tolerance of possessing spirits extends to other religions. Picture a remote village in the centre of Sri Lanka, where a sick person, diagnosed as possessed by a variety of demons, lies in a hut. By Western standards, we are in the middle of nowhere: the heart of darkness, perhaps. Alerted by the priests, the whole community attends. They come together around the hut, music starts, a frantic, jagged drumming and then . . . the party begins. A party? Boys and girls exchange glances, finally pluck up courage to talk. Old people chat and reminisce. A holy man is dancing, putting on different masks to represent different devils but, far from being frightened, the crowd is laughing. In fact, the whole atmosphere is like a festival, imbued with joy as demon after demon is laughed out of the body of the sick person.

On a Buddhist website, a man complains that his house is possessed and he wants to know if Buddhism has anything helpful to say on the subject. From the answers that come flooding in, the consensus is clear. Demons are sentient beings and, if it is causing him discomfort, the answer may lie in its state of mind. In other words, it may be causing him to suffer because it is suffering itself, and so, in the spirit of compassion, he should try and find out what is wrong.

Another story describes a woman whose house is possessed. She goes through the house, performing a ritual in each room in which she greets the spirit, introduces herself, speaks to it about the home they are both inhabiting and then asks it politely to look after her and her son. After that, whenever the spirit shows itself, she greets it as a friend and so finds a way of living quite comfortably with it. In other Buddhist traditions, the spirit is read a list of the problems it is causing, and then invited to tell the priest what caused it to invade its victim – what its problem was, in short. As a result, the spirit will apologise and leave.

In Japan, the sheer number of demons or spirits – call them what you will – seems to demand a form of tolerance; one simply could not get worked up about that many discarnate beings without getting a heart attack. The International Research Centre for Japanese Studies in Kyoto has compiled a database of 13,000 ghosts and ghost-sightings and adds up to 2,000 new ones each year. Spirit shrines can be found all over the country.

Yūrei closely resemble what people in the West call ghosts – that is spirits of the departed, often clothed in white. Like ghosts, they have unfinished business that often draws them back to the lands of the living.

Oni are grotesque gods whose terrifying images often grace temple entrances to scare evil-doers away.

Fushigi na dobutsu are mischievous animal spirits – often the troublesome fox who can shape-shift into human form or possess people.

Mononoke are the spirits that inhabit every physical object. When the spirit is disturbed and doors slam or stones scream, they can bear a passing resemblance to Western poltergeists.

A calm understanding of hidden forces can make exorcism, Japanese-style, a routine activity. Shinto priests often purify land before construction begins – the Nissan car factory in Sunderland, in the UK, was blessed in this way by a priest flown in for the occasion (it later went on to become one of the most productive car factories in the world and a jewel in the crown of Nissan's overseas operations). In Tokyo, workers at the Mitsui trading company refuse to sit with their backs to a ghost whose tomb is nearby. In the past, he has been responsible for a number of fatal accidents – not to mention the bankruptcy of the Long Term Credit Bank – around the site of his tomb when insufficient respect has been paid to him.

Exorcism can be a practical business in Japan, with the emphasis on business. In the small town of Tomika, a contractor discovered that a building he had put up was haunted. Residents saw curtains moving by themselves, heard children's running footsteps; ducked as plates flew through the air unaided, and watched rice steamers and other kitchen appliances rise up off counters. The cause was quickly established – the building was on the site of a bloody battlefield – and exorcists quickly came forward to offer their services.

The contractor turned down an offer to exorcise the building for around £80,000 and demanded his money back when an exorcist who charged only £200 failed to make a difference. (One exorcist, who had been contracted to purify a haunted hairdryer in the building, made off with it in lieu of payment but we do not know if he managed to exorcise it or not.) In the end, a woman mystic called Yoshiko Shimo brought in fifteen monks and managed to clear the building of evil spirits after three days of chanting. Interestingly, she didn't charge a penny.

And in Japan, human possession is more widespread than in the West, or, rather, the perceived need for exorcism is greater. Belief in possession by malevolent ghosts – as opposed to demons – springs from two core Japanese beliefs. One is a belief in reincarnation and the movement of spirits between bodies. The other comes from the belief that spirits needs assuaging or they will become angry. At the festival of O-bon, spirits of dead ancestors celebrate an underworld festival by visiting their living relatives.

So perhaps it's no wonder that since possession is so widespread and common, it is treated rather like a mild complaint – a cold, for example, or a slight sprain. One Japanese psychic/exorcist reckons an individual might be inhabited by as many as 4,000 spirits. In 2003, a man and his eight disciples were arrested for taking millions of yen (hundreds of thousands of pounds) for exorcisms. The man had developed psychic abilities when he nearly drowned as a schoolboy, and these were so finely tuned that he could see ghosts clinging to people as they walked down the street or boarded trains – a dead woman tied with string to someone's neck, a legless man hanging on to someone's waist. Exorcisms – incredibly expensive exorcisms, it has to be said – were performed in hotel rooms or at the group's special oratory in the mountain near Kanagawa and, although he was prosecuted for fraud, he always maintained that his powers were real and the exorcisms necessary. And many of his clients were quite satisfied with the services he offered.

One can find contemporary accounts of Japanese people visiting exorcism schools for treatment in which the exorcist, after performing simple hand gestures, simply talks to the spirit firmly and they leave – even the ghosts of samurai warriors. But the Japanese do not only experience possession by the ghosts of humans. Their rich and complex spiritual world is inhabited by animal spirits as well, and these can enter people and cause a variety of problems.

The most widespread and notorious Japanese animal spirit is the fox – the *kitsune*. Fox possession is known as *kitsunetsuki*, and there have been cases in which entire families or clans were ostracised because it was considered that they had unnaturally close relationships with foxes – *kitsune-mochi*, they were called. But even today, cases of fox possession are relatively common. When a fox spirit enters someone, they experience something like a splitting of their consciousness and are conscious of the fox's needs running alongside their own. They start to crave rice and sweet red beans, alternate between states of listlessness and restlessness, and are unable to look people in the eye. Exorcism, usually performed by a Shinto priest at a fox god shrine, involves a certain amount of arguing and discussion, but the fox will usually leave on the promise of gifts of its favourite cakes. Every year, in Totomi province, the fox-expelling ceremony takes place, with people following a monk up a hillside to a shrine where they bury wicker models of foxes.

Demonic possession and exorcism is common to almost every culture. What separates us is the way we deal with it. Once a year, every year, the little village of Malajpur in the Indian province of Madhya Pradesh becomes a scene of mass exorcism.

The moon is full, night is falling and tens of thousands of Indians from all over the subcontinent converge on the village's unspectacular temple. People are forcing their way through its doors so they can process around a simple raised platform, chanting as they go. Some wave their hands in front of them to hold off the demons that are attacking them; some run round and round as though there are devils at their heels; some shout and scream; others dance. Some just wait their turn to be exorcised. For the temple is a shrine to the guru Maharaj Deoji, an eighteenth-century holy man and miracle worker whose ability to exorcise victims of possession reaches from beyond the grave through a specially trained army of exorcists – descendants of his own followers. As the night falls properly, the victims are called to the tomb by the holy man who addresses the demon inside them. Some demons are reluctant to be helped out; others come out easily. All victims of possessions pay a fee to the priest, even if it is just a small amount of unrefined sugar.

Japan

The richness of Japanese ghost fauna is well attested. Unhappy ghosts of mistreated women float mournfully through concrete multistorey car parks, vengeful Samurai haunt shopping precincts and office blocks, propitiated by daily prayers from specially appointed civil servants. Outside the cities, the woods and valleys are inhabited by fox spirits and wood sprites, and then there are the other traditional ghosts or yūrei: onryō, ubume, goryō and funayūrei. There are rumours that a little boy, lost in the vast Hakkeijima Sea Paradise aquarium in Yokohama at closing time, was taken by a Kappa, a scaley, web-footed sea ghoul that delights in pulling its victims' intestines out of their mouths and anuses – although you can bribe them to keep away with cucumbers.

But it's the Japanese attitude to ghosts that is so fascinating, and nothing illustrates the difference between the West and East more vividly than the experiences of some Western language teachers and their pupils, staying in a hostel in the Yamagata Prefecture.

The group had just gone to bed, when loud screams were heard coming from a room that three girls were sleeping in. Their neighbours rushed into the corridor to find the girls huddled there, crying and insisting they had seen ghosts. Another door flew open and a teacher fled her room, her face white, and just managed to say that three people, bloodstained and broken, had just dragged themselves across the floor of her room and disappeared through the wall.

Alarmed, the group went to the front desk where the staff heard their story and nodded. They were quite used

to this: the figures were the ghosts of a family who had been killed in a car accident just outside the hotel and who spasmodically returned. They'd follow normal procedure and get the exorcist in the morning.

The exorcist, a Shinto priest, duly turned up the next day and calmly told people that the poor souls had come down to visit the nearest O-bon ceremony (held to honour the spirits of the dead). But no one should worry about them – they had just got lost and he put them on their way home.

In the whole pantheon of supernatural experiences, exorcism is unique. It brings humans more closely into contact with hidden forces than other experiences. It gives them an opportunity to interact with the spirits, to talk to them, to argue with them, to fight with them. If Christian exorcisms are more aggressive than those of other religions and cultures, the reason is that Christians see spirits and all representatives of the spirit world as threatening invaders – abominations – and are more predisposed to go in hard. At the other end of the scale, the Buddhists, for example, are far more likely to see demons as examples of a spiritual ecosystem that we must strive to live in harmony with.

But there is a category of exorcism, or a sub-category, that is common to almost all cultures, and can best be described as exorcisms gone bad. For, unfortunately, the case of Anneliese Michel is by no means unique, and there is evidence that the belief that demons can only be expelled through punishing the victim of possession is spreading.

A list of contemporary Christian exorcisms that have resulted in death covers almost every continent and makes for tragic reading: a child is held down by a pastor and his flock until he suffocates in the American state of Milwaukee; a woman is drowned in Wainuiomata, New Zealand; a girl is beaten to death in east London; a woman in Australia dies gasping for breath as her throat is punctured by a crucifix; a child is starved to death in Uganda . . . exorcists who cannot finish what they started without killing the subject of the possession – the list seems to go on and on.

In the town of Antwerp, in the Australian state of Victoria, a man belonging to a small Lutheran sect returned home to find his wife dancing and chanting in a wheat field close to his farm. A friend from the church diagnosed demonic possession, and the exorcism began, with congregation members reading passages of the Bible to the woman and ordering the demons to leave her. When this did not work, and the woman seemed to be growing more agitated, they pinned her to a mattress and continued.

The woman grew more agitated still. Her stomach swelled (believed by some to be a sign of demonic possession), and she started to bark like a dog, grunt like a pig, talk like a sheep-shearer and grew phenomenally strong, so that the congregation of exorcists could hardly keep her pinned down. Multiple possession was diagnosed, including the spirit of filth, the spirit of abuse, Jezebel, and two demons called Princess Joan and Princess Baby Joan, who entered the woman's womb when she was a child.

The case was getting more serious and an expert was brought in. He was a 22-year-old gardener from the local municipal golf course and he decided that more drastic action was needed. He ordered all the woman's possessions, including the plants she had grown, to be burned, and then began the final stage of the process. By dint of shouting, he got all the demons to leave, apart from Princess Joan and Princess Baby Joan, who refused to relinquish their hold on the woman's womb. The exorcist then ordered some of the congregation to hold the woman's eyes and mouth open while the rest of them pushed down on her belly. When she groaned and foamed at the mouth, it was taken as evidence that the demons were finally being expelled. The group redoubled their efforts and, four days after the initial diagnosis, the woman finally found peace, of a sort.

She died.

Was that the end? Not quite. Before leaving, the exorcist told the congregation that God intended to bring the woman back so, over the weekend, in sweltering, 40-degree heat, they prayed over the rapidly decomposing corpse, only giving up on the Monday, when they told the authorities and were arrested. Two (including the husband) were convicted of unlawful imprisonment, two of manslaughter.

But it is not just Christian exorcisms that go wrong. In an east London suburb, a woman called Farida Patel believed that she was possessed by djinns which threatened to cut out her tongue if she prayed or praised Allah. When she started to walk like an old woman and talk like a man, her family called in an exorcist, who brought along her friend, and the victim's sister and brother. While the Qur'an was read aloud, her brother set about beating her with a vacuum cleaner's flexible pipe for five hours. This was repeated the next day, followed by another attack by him when he jumped up and down on the victim, fracturing nine ribs and killing her.

In northern France, a possessed woman was killed by a cleric and the head of a local mosque. In an attempt to squeeze the demon out of her, the cleric tortured her for nine hours, forced her to drink gallons of salt water and beat the soles of her feet before strangling her. She suffocated.

In New Cross, London, a Nigerian woman strangled her son, whom she thought was possessed, believing that he would come back to life free of demons.

In Sukagawa, Japan, an exorcist was arrested after six decomposing bodies were found in her home. She had encouraged them to beat each other to death in order to expel demons.

A Thai woman was killed by an exorcist who beat her to death with the dried tail of a stingray.

Cases like this pose the unsettling question: can fear and hatred of evil actually help let evil in? Let's look at the evidence. On the one hand you have someone displaying odd, eccentric behaviour. On the other, you have a group of people who, by any standards, have lost their grip on reason and morality. You look at the effects: an innocent person tortured to death, others guilty of breaking the most sacred commandment common to all religions – not to kill. You think of the lives ruined, the waste, and eventually you have to ask – who is succumbing to evil when exorcisms go bad?

Borneo

The Dayak of Borneo accept that ghosts are all around them – even when they urinate, they warn any spirits that might be around so they have time to get out of the way. Traditional headhunters, they believed that the soul resided in the head, so by capturing a head, you not only

took possession of someone's life force, but also their status. But the spirits of Borneo are aggressive and demand respect from everyone. On a family outing to the beach, the children explored inland and found a wonderful lake that just seemed to invite them to plunge into it. But the following day, one of the children grew ill, started running a fever, and no doctor or hospital could work out the cause. Then the children confessed to their father that they had been swimming and he immediately realised that the sick child's soul had been captured by a spirit, angered that they had not first asked permission to go swimming.

A Chinese medium was summoned. She took the father back to the beach, where he made contact with the spirits and called the boy's soul back. At first nothing happened. Then the father heard the unmistakable sound of footsteps on dry leaves, which seemed to be coming from the hill above the beach – the same hill the children had climbed to reach the lake. The footsteps grew faster and faster and the hairs on the father's head stood up as the medium opened a bag and seemed to catch something in it.

'That's your son's soul,' he said. 'I've called it back.'

They drove straight home and the medium released the spirit from the bag. That very night, the boy's temperature came back down and he made a full recovery.

CHAPTER TEN

TOWARDS A WORLD MIND

The Darkest Modern Myth of All?

The date is 31 August, the time is 12.20 a.m., the place is the Ritz hotel in Paris, where the most famous woman in the world is leaving with her lover. They are ushered out through the back door and into a fast Mercedes S280, their driver swearing that he will be able to get them to their destination, Rue Arsène-Houssaye, avoiding the worst of the clattering shutters, flashing lights and harsh shouts of the waiting paparazzi.

They never get there. Princess Diana and her lover, Dodi Fayed, are killed when the Mercedes smashes into a pillar supporting the roof of the Pont de L'Alma road tunnel. In spite of their crashing into the 13th pillar and the numerous conspiracy theories surrounding the events, there is no mystery surrounding their actual deaths: the driver was drunk; the car hit the pillar at 65 m.p.h.; neither Diana nor Dodi were wearing seat belts.

At Diana's funeral service, her brother, the 9th Earl Spencer, commented on the paradox that a woman who shared her name with the goddess of hunting had in turn become the most hunted woman on earth. But the reaction to her death suggested that Diana did more than share her name with a goddess, as the world behaved as if genuine divinity had been killed. In an astonishing collective outpouring of grief, the demise of the first genuine icon of the Internet age was commemorated by complete strangers accessing wellsprings of emotion that normally they would have reserved for their nearest and dearest. The scale and depth of the grief took everyone by surprise, even in the UK where the people knew Diana best. Five days after her death, a journalist at one of the country's leading newspapers asked the editor how long 'this Diana nonsense' was going to keep everything else off the front page. 'We'll carry on for as long as it takes,' the editor replied. 'This is all the nonsense that anyone wants to read.'

If ever a scientist wanted to create conditions to measure something as vague as a collective global consciousness or to test a machine that could measure emotion, these were the ideal conditions. Interestingly enough, about ten years before these events, such a machine had been invented and it was now up and running.

Organised research into shared global consciousness dates back to the tail-end of the conscious-raising 1960s and the beginning of the more sceptical 1970s. Helmut Schmidt at the Boeing Laboratories started the ball rolling and it was picked up by Princeton University, where Robert Jahn established the Princeton Engineering Anomalies Research (PEAR) laboratory. He wanted to discover whether feelings or intentions could be measured, but in a radically new way. Up until that point, the main thrust of research had been to do with telepathy: two people communicating using their minds alone. But this was not about one person drawing a picture in one room and someone else trying to guess what it was. The subjects of the experiment would be the entire human race and we would not even be aware that our feelings were being measured. We just had to keep on going with our normal day-to-day life while the scientists saw if there was anything to measure. This was why an event such as the death of Princess Diana was so important, tragic though it was. For most of the time, everyone feels different things as we go about our daily lives. Events where millions have the same feelings at the same time are few and far between.

But the project was unique in two other respects. In most experiments, measurement of change is taken for granted and the researchers are more interested in the application of what they are seeing. In this experiment, all attention was focused on the measurement itself. If scientists could show that equipment registered changes in emotion, it would prove to sceptics firstly that mind could affect matter and secondly that there was such a thing as a global consciousness.

At the heart of the experiment is a specially designed piece of equipment called the Random Event Generator (REG). This is a programme loaded into a computer that generates an unending and regular stream of random figures. Another programme then analyses the results and any deviation from the norm can be timed and analysed. Experience suggests to scientists and statisticians that a certain proportion of randomness to apparent pattern can be predicted; if the results depart from this, the anomalies could be identified and matched to key events that might be said to affect mass consciousness. Research would also compare findings linked to important events with findings linked to no event at all, to establish whether or not there was a difference between them.

Early results were impressive and unexpected. In the USA, the jury verdict of the O. J. Simpson trial produced measurable readings – emotions ran high as the event prompted a full-scale national debate and much heart-searching – as did the Oscar ceremony, perhaps suggesting that humans are rather undiscriminating about what they expend their emotional energy on. An opportunity to broaden the experiment came in 1996, when the scientists met like-minded researchers at an international Gaia conference. During Princess Diana's funeral, data was sent in from twelve locations in Europe and the United States while the compelling funeral was being broadcast live from Westminster Abbey in London. The results were astounding. Significant anomalies were recorded during the process and in particular while the Lord's Prayer was being recited in the abbey. A week later, similar if less impressive results were recorded for the funeral of another international icon whose image and popularity crossed national and cultural boundaries: the funeral of Mother Teresa.

Both these events were linked with death and both with Christian ceremonies. This begged the question: was the project good for measuring any other form of emotion?

At the end of 1997, the project was ready to go international and become a genuine 'Global Consciousness Project'. The price of hardware was dropping so there were no cost barriers to supplying more and more Random Event Generators, while the Internet made it possible to link up the various locations. With enough nodes in place, researchers could not resist comparing the effect to putting electrodes on a human skull for an EEG recording. A new word was coined for the technology – an 'electrogaiagram', shortened to Egg. From now on, the recording nodes would be called 'Eggs', and as each Egg fed its data back to the headquarters in Princeton, the analytical software naturally went by the name of 'Basket'. Today, the Global Consciousness Project consists of between sixty and sixty-five Eggs, covering most continents and time zones.

So what is being measured? At this stage, no one is quite sure. Consciousness is hard enough to define in an individual and our understanding of it is still developing. A widely accepted definition of mass consciousness is therefore still some way off. Some people claim that just as we can talk about the biosphere, the sum total of all life on earth, so we need a term that describes the sum total of consciousness: the noosphere, derived from the ancient Greek work for mind. Any mass surge in emotion then creates a wave of energy and this in turn influences the readings from the nodes positioned all around the world. Thus an event like the New Year celebrations can be 'measured' as it creeps around the world, following the different time zones. Similarly traumatic events, such as the attack on the twin towers of the World Trade Center register too, because images of them are flashed around the world. Earthquakes show up, again because they are sudden and dramatic, so that news has a concentrated impact, which in turn affects the consciousness field.

Of course measuring the noosphere, or the sum total of global consciousness, does not mean that it has suddenly come into existence, and it is impossible to believe that such an effect would not have been noticed before. So what other theories or phenomena can we connect it with? In all likelihood, the noosphere is another term for *chi*, *ki* or *prana* – a life force that Asian doctors, philosophers and magicians have known about for thousands of years. But whereas in the past the emphasis was on looking at how this could affect the individual, in today's globalised world, the main focus of attention is broader – as broad as it could possibly be.

Research into it is also well advanced. In China and Japan, there has never been the strict demarcation drawn between science and religion. It is quite possible for scientists to talk seriously about *chi*, or *ki*, the life force that surrounds all living things, just as priests are happy to have their powers tested.

This is why you might find a priest sitting in a Faraday Cage to isolate him from electromagnetic waves, surrounded by cables that are picking up his energy and feeding it to an aerial a few feet away. The signals, translated into graph form, show a series of spikes and dips, indicating when the monk is emitting and radiating his life force.

Electrodes can measure the way *ki* passes around the body, and people who develop skills in directing it can achieve the most extraordinary feats of physical strength. Nishino Kozo, an octogenarian who can throw fully grown men across a room by applying his *ki*, believes that it is a form of communication – a spark that occurs deep within individuals' cells, connecting with the life force that surges through the world.

Quite independently, Russian scientists are also interested in this area (although we should ask what could be said to be truly independent if global consciousness really does exist). Their research into cellular chemistry is suggesting that DNA is an even more fascinating substance than we previously thought. Scientists set out to investigate the purpose of 'junk' DNA – that is the DNA that is not used for building proteins. Working from the hypothesis that life was not wasteful and therefore this type of DNA might have a purpose, they discovered that it had certain properties that suggested it might be used as a communication and data storage bank. The breakthrough came when they discovered that the components of DNA, the alkaline molecules, follow rules that can be directly compared to syntax, semantics and grammar as they build themselves into a double helix. Going one step further, they proposed that as DNA came before language, the structure of language is common to all human beings because it follows the same rules as the structure of DNA; because of this, it can be modulated using the same rules. Thus, while Western scientists concentrate on invasive, gene-splicing experiments, Russian scientists are learning how to change the structure of DNA using a combination of laser and sound technology.

This goes some way to explaining how some people have the knack of healing or influencing using sound through chanting, prayer or hypnotic talk. These people have the knack – or insight – to be able to tune into DNA frequencies of their patients and work on them remotely.

They are also working on the theory that DNA can receive information and pass it into our conscious minds. They call this hypercommunication and speculate that it has been lost as humans developed individuality. We can see a rough equivalent of this at work in the animal kingdom. Pack animals such as dogs have an awareness of each other quite independent of the five senses. They seem to operate within something called the morphic field (a term which some apply to global consciousness), which greatly extends the limits of awareness – for example, dogs can respond to members of their human family setting out on a journey home, even though this may be hundreds of miles away. Bee and ant colonies are known to merge into what are called superorganisms, whereby creatures of limited intelligence cooperate in such a way as to create structures far beyond the capability of the individual: the product of a mass consciousness, in short. Fascinatingly, however, they can only do so under the influence of a queen. When the queen is removed to a distance, they carry on with their work and the organisational structures remain in place; when the queen is killed, however, the whole social structure collapses. Superorganisms demonstrate two things: the ability of distributed intelligence to achieve extraordinary feats, and the possibility that behind them lies a single, controlling organisational force. Humans, the scientists speculate, lost this ability as a by-product of evolution although a few – magicians, telepaths and shamans – retain a vestigial power.

The occult means anything hidden and, at first sight, the Global Consciousness Project is opening doors and shining the bright light of rationality and science on a subject that has so far resisted definition and measurement. But the problem is this: it is easy to be dazzled by this. To put it another way, bright light produces deep shadow, and students of the occult must inevitably concern themselves with what can't be seen. Inevitably, therefore, we must think about those dimensions of the Global Consciousness Project that can't be seen and perhaps people would prefer not to talk about. In other words, apply a little bit of occult consciousness to it.

The first thing to do is try to unpick the name: Global Consciousness.

Consciousness implies some kind of will, and to date nothing in their research has shown any willed changes in the consciousness field. Indeed, the project would be better described as an unconsciousness project as, so far, the effects they are measuring are more like the twitches on a horse's skin when a gadfly lands on it. The skin reacts but in no way could it be called conscious. At present, then, the Global Consciousness Project measures what could be called the unconscious by-product of our conscious thoughts. No problem there, you might think, but within the project, some people talk about the development of a mass consciousness as the next evolutionary step, and this is where things become a little bit more disturbing.

Because suppose some people did evolve in such a way that they could influence the field: what would be the implications for them and for the rest of us? The purpose of an ant or a bee is really quite simple. It builds cells; it gathers food; it looks after the young; it defends the hive or nest. Human beings, on the other hand, have a moral – and by extension immoral – dimension and the development of powers that set them apart from their fellow humans would put them in a uniquely difficult situation.

Should they band together and pool their resources? Should they act to protect themselves? What would they do if their power was captured and harnessed? Would their extended consciousness and superior powers justify a sort of consciousness coup? And what about the rest of humanity? How would they feel if they knew that people with enhanced awareness were somehow tapping into their consciousness?

And then we must look at the global aspect of the project. If this evolutionary development was evenly shared out across the entire globe, how would people feel about being absorbed into a greater whole? For the rich and powerful, this might feel like a loss of control; for the weak and powerless, this might feel like they were giving up the only thing they had left: their individuality. Hypercommunication dovetails with the Global Consciousness Project but, without proper investigation into the negative potential of such developments, they must be regarded with concern. Talk of higher consciousness is all very well, but unless it is matched by a higher moral sense, the world may be facing a threat greater still than global warming: the development of an evil world mind.

The final implication is perhaps the most worrying of all, and this is the link between the project and Gaia-based philosophy. According to James Lovelock, the man who first coined the term, there is nothing benign to humans in Gaia.

Gaia refers not just to the earth's life force but its life instinct and, as such, it does not value any one form of life over another. If Gaia does exists as a force, and the Global Consciousness Project forms a bridge between it and the humans, Gaia's probably correct instinct would be to develop a mass consciousness in humans and then take immediate steps to wipe the species out. Humans are, as we keep on telling ourselves, the single greatest threat to life on the planet, responsible for a massive diminution of species diversity in this extraordinarily short period of global industrialisation.

The truth is that earth does not need us. For millions, if not billions of years, it was inhabited only by microbes and got on quite happily with them. You don't have to be particularly conscious to react to a threat – think of the horse and the gadfly. True global consciousness – when the earth itself wakes up – may well be the last thing we need.

AFTERWORD

THE SUPERNATURAL

The Last Free Space?

Humanity's relationship with the supernatural is constantly evolving. If we look at how humans react to anything that lies outside their immediate influence, we can see a cycle that moves from fear to propitiation to exploration and finally control.

I would argue that as a species we've moved past the fear stage, we're almost through the propitiation stage (sacrifices are definitely on the wane) and the age of exploration is just dawning.

Many different factors are driving this. One is technology. Far from pushing the supernatural to the margins of life, new technology is opening up channels for interaction, from direct contact, such as communication through digital devices, to indirect contact such as the extraordinary numbers of potions available on the Internet. Just recently, a householder in New Zealand captured spirits in holy water, bottled them and successfully sold them on eBay.

Another, curiously, is leisure. Foreign travel and the exponential rise in recreational Internet use are making foreign cultures more and more accessible. This can be negative: Islamic exorcisms seem to be learning how to be violent from sensationalist depictions of Christian ones, but in the main it is positive. The attitude to ghosts and spirits in most Asian countries is a world away from attitudes in the West: far more accepting, far more positive, far less judgemental. Whether this is bad or good remains to be seen, but the world has never suffered from having too many open minds. Television too is playing an important role in normalising paranormal events and supernatural intervention, with a proliferation of TV mediums and ghost hunters serving up a pretty routine menu of B-list celebrities receiving harmless shocks and scares.

Of course, there have always been men and women who sought both to explore and control the supernatural world but, in the past, such activity has been confined to elites or marginalised groups: wizards, witches, priests and shamans have made this their speciality. Today, the process has been democratised. Everyone is up for it and this shows, I believe, the largest relational shift between the natural and supernatural worlds. People are less afraid of ghosts than they used to be and more inclined to accept them as part of a 'natural' order of some sort.

This is bound to have an effect; the question is what?

In the first place, it makes the world a far more interesting place to be. Knowing we share it with owlmen, mothmen, sprites, spirits, ghosts and yes, demons is right in step with the impulse to embrace and learn from other cultures – not merely to try to colonise and exploit them. If fear drove a wedge between us and them in the past, that is certainly not the case now. Although there are exceptions, the supernatural world is no more dangerous than this. Such terror it does induce is likely to be generated by us.

The second effect of this increased traffic is to put us humans in our place. We are not alone and there is much to learn, and we do not have to go all the way into space to find it.

Thirdly, it should encourage the monotheistic religions to look with a bit more analytical insight into their own belief systems. Many people who profess a belief in God deny the existence of other supernatural forces or powers and label them mere superstition. Perhaps they are missing the point. There is nothing 'mere' about superstition and they would do well to bear in mind the evidence from Genesis, the first book of the Bible, that the God of Jews, Christians and Muslims is just one of many. He's described as jealous, not because he wants to stop followers worshipping gods that don't exist, but because he wants them to stop paying respect to gods that do. These gods – Moloch, Beelzebub et al. – were then recast as demons. Little wonder then if they feel a little hostile.

All this begs the question: what is the effect of the twenty-first century on the paranormal? It is hard to be definite but my hunch is that the more interaction, the more interesting things become. We have seen the negative side of this in exorcisms, where anything other than a firm request for a demon to leave generally creates an escalating cycle of violence. More positively, people who work in the field of EVP – Electronic Voice Phenomenon – discover that the longer they keep at it, the more responses they get, almost as if the spirits take a while to locate the device on the other side and then work out how to use it. Will any of this demystify the supernatural world? That is unlikely: the more glimpses we get, and the more curiously we look at it, the richer and more intricate it seems.

Ultimately, of course, we are just guessing and this is for the best. As the world becomes more crowded, as globalisation makes things more homogeneous, as science explains more and more, and business and legislation seem to intrude further and further into every area of our everyday lives, the supernatural is one space that the people have wrested away from the authorities. The church no longer has any real power over who worships what; governments – in Europe at any rate – no longer persecute witches. Once there was a dream that the Internet would provide total freedom for all. That proved impossible and cyberspace is now tagged and regulated. Perhaps the occult, the dark side, the supernatural is the last truly free space on earth – or somewhere close to it . . .

INDEX

DISCARD